THIS BOOK IS FOR

LINDA O. POLSBY

all by herself, and about time too.

PREFACE

The idea for this book grew out of two related problems that arose in connection with my courses in American government. I discovered, first of all, that the stock of ideas about American national government in general use among professional observers of politics had diverged sharply from notions readily available and in use among people whose main exposure to politics was through the mass media. Where professionals saw fallible men, fallibly pursuing comprehensible—though sometimes mistaken—policies, more distant observers of politics could see only contradiction, manipulation, and irrationality.

In a polity like ours, which demands periodic political decisions by large numbers of ordinary citizens, this is no trivial problem. And it was bound, I think, to seem especially acute to a teacher of politics. It was compounded, moreover, by a special characteristic of the population nearest to my own concerns: my students. So much of what older persons know of American politics is the distillate of experiences that students have not shared, a part of the memories of persons who have been aware of politics and who have lived through the last four or five decades as adults.

To understand these experiences unaided without having lived through them would take an exceptional leap of historical imagination and sympathy—both, qualities in notably short supply on college campuses these days. Yet there remains the problem of educating students—most of whom were born in the year of Dwight Eisenhower's first inauguration and were unconscious of politics until well into the sixties—about the real historical events that lie behind the responses of their elders to such abstractions as "cold war," "Great Depression," "New Deal," or "concentration camp." How many who lived through the thirties and forties will remind themselves that the youthful idealist—or young oaf—who makes facile analogies between contemporary injustices and Nazi atrocities has probably received his firmest conception of the latter from a Humphrey Bogart movie?

This book will not, of course, close the gap between generations that differences in experience have created. It can make a gesture in that direction, and this is part of its intention, dealing as it does with one very significant American political institution during a major period of its modernization. The treatment is not primarily historical or developmental, but rather analytical. The central purpose of the book is to lay before the reader some important themes of contemporary thinking about the Presidency within the context of their emergence in response to the administrations of the past six Presidents.

The task of any teaching book is somehow to bridge the distance between the relatively confused and indistinct worlds of the unconcerned, inexperienced, or ignorant and the somewhat more understandable and coherent landscape that generations of scholars have seized from the encroaching wilderness and tended ever since. That is what this book tries to do for the modern Presidency.

There is a powerful sense in which every book of readings is a tribute to Homer and Langley Collyer, late of 2078 Fifth Avenue, New York City. The Collyer brothers were extremely reclusive, as scholars who compile books of readings ought to be. Their demise at advanced ages, in March 1947, was the occasion for much comment in and around New York, owing to the extraordinary care they had taken to preserve everything that came into their possession. According to *The New York Times,* when the police went through the brothers' three-story brownstone, they found at the basement entrance:

. . . an old stove, several umbrellas, numerous packages of newspapers, a gas mask canister, an old stove pipe and a broken scooter. . . . The front hallway was completely blocked by . . . neat newspaper packages and half-empty cardboard crates tied by strings. . . . As far as could be seen, it was the same on the upper floors. Not only was the main entrance blocked, but through the window on the first floor the entire room was seen full of papers and other debris. . . . [Police] said the building was honeycombed with tunnel-like passageways through the piles of newspapers and debris.

The *Times* report on the following day continues:

All sorts of queer objects were removed from the building, including an intricate potato peeler, a nursery refrigerator, a beaded lampshade, a box of boy's tops, and a toy airplane. In the basement, the police found the chassis of an ancient car. . . . Most of the debris, however, consisted of old newspapers, magazines, and wood. These were loaded on a Department of Sanitation truck. . . . On its first trip, it carried 6,424 pounds; on the second, slightly less.

It is the spirit of conservation, which the Collyer brothers so handsomely embodied, that makes books of readings possible. To be sure, not everyone has this spirit in equal measure, and so I wish to thank Linda O. Polsby, whose tolerance of that spirit—not enthusiasm for it—made this particular book possible. She is confident that should we ever care to check the fine print on our marriage certificate it would be necessary only to burrow down to the late Eisenhower level in the midden of clippings, correspondence, papers, and odds and ends—some of it about the modern Presidency—that I have been collecting in the course of my life. What I am expressing gratitude for on this occasion is that she has never actually put the surmise to an empirical test. I wish also to thank, for their friendship and for providing a life style that makes books of readings such a good idea, Lisa Susan Polsby, whose birth certificate would probably be found at the early Kennedy level, and Emily Ann Polsby (early Johnson).

Some years ago Robert and Joan vom Eigen helped me put a very large file in shape, from which this collection is drawn. Barbara Hight Kelly provided important secretarial service later on. Barry Rossinoff and Jane Cullen of Random House made the production of the book happen smoothly. I am grateful to them and to the authors and original publishers of the material printed here. It is my hope that the coming together of all these diverse treatments through time on a singularly complex and powerful institution will give a new perspective upon the evolution, the limitations, and the promise of the modern Presidency.

N. W. P.

Berkeley, California
June 1972

CONTENTS

Preface — vii

Introduction — 3

1 Franklin D. Roosevelt — 7
Arthur M. Schlesinger, Jr., *The Evolution of the Presidency* — 9

2 Harry S. Truman — 37
Elmer Davis, *Harry S. Truman and the Verdict of History* — 39
Eric Sevareid, *The Man in the White House* — 49
Dean Acheson, *The President's Contribution* — 51
John Hersey, *Ten O'Clock Meeting* — 57
John Hersey, *Forty-eight Hours* — 69

3 Dwight D. Eisenhower — 87
Charles J. V. Murphy, *Eisenhower's White House* — 89
Chalmers M. Roberts, *The Day We Didn't Go to War* — 100
James Reston, *The Presidency: The Effect of Eisenhower's Illness on the Functioning of the Executive Branch* — 107
William V. Shannon, *Eisenhower as President: A Critical Appraisal of the Record* — 123

4 John F. Kennedy — 135
Douglass Cater, *A New Style, a New Tempo* — 137
Richard F. Fenno, Jr., *The Cabinet: Index to the Kennedy Way* — 141
Joseph Kraft, *Kennedy's Working Staff* — 146
Sidney Hyman, *How Mr. Kennedy Gets the Answers* — 157

5 Lyndon B. Johnson — 163

James Reston, *What's He Like? And How Will He Do?* — 165
Tom Wicker, *Johnson's Men: "Valuable Hunks of Humanity"* — 171
Ben H. Bagdikian, *The "Inner, Inner Circle" Around Johnson* — 178
William Chapman, *LBJs Way: Tears, Not Arm-Twists* — 185
Alan L. Otten, *By Courting Congress Assiduously, Johnson Furthers His Program* — 189
Alan L. Otten, *Criticism of President's Style, Methods Mounts Among Small but Important Group* — 193
Carroll Kilpatrick, *Often Moody, Defensive* — 197

6 Richard M. Nixon — 201

Robert B. Semple, Jr., *A Passion for Order and Privacy* — 202
John Pierson, *The Nixon Style: President Seeks Order in His Decision-Making, but Events Intrude* — 204
Don Oberdorfer, *The Presidency: Still Very Private After First Year* — 209
Robert B. Semple, Jr., *Nixon Staff Had Central Role in Missile Decision* — 215
John Pierson, *Presidential Isolation Is Part of the Job* — 221
Alan L. Otten, *The Scorecard: President's Cabinet Gets Mixed Reviews for Efforts to Date* — 224
U.S. News & World Report, *Nixon's Top Command: Expanding in Size and Power* — 231

THE MODERN PRESIDENCY

INTRODUCTION

In one sense, there is no modern Presidency; there are only modern Presidencies. What is arresting, meaningful, and of greatest ultimate consequence in the politics of the modern Presidency is not what Presidents share in the way of constraints and opportunities but the way each orchestrates his own set of these into a pattern of administrative and political activity. To draw this distinction is a little like asking whether it is the figure in the picture or the background against which the figure is set that contributes most to what is perceived as the line separating the two. But this is not to say that because there is no clear line there is no difference between what Presidents *share* and what they *contribute* to the modern Presidency.

If we consider the modern Presidency as an abstraction derived from the detailed understanding of modern Presidents, then good pedagogy would seem to require concrete familiarity with the circumstances and styles of modern Presidencies as a prerequisite to grasping the nature of the office in contemporary politics. Thus this book gathers together accounts of modern Presidents, showing from varying perspectives how they met the challenges of office, how they received and processed information, the kind of staff assistance they sought, the ways in which they solicited advice, the techniques they used to make decisions and to oversee the execution of decisions—and how well their jobs were done.

For each modern President, commentators have stressed certain themes that identified that Presidency for contemporaries. Many of these contemporary, and more recent, judgments are collected in these pages, but I have made no attempt conscientiously to balance the record so that knocks and boosts even out and each President is portrayed to be as successful as all the others. Our modern Presidents have not been equally ambitious, equally constrained, equally endowed with energy, intelligence, luck, common sense, good humor, or any of the other things that make for equality of results. And inequalities of result do stand in the record. But because these results were only partly under the control of the people against whose name they are written, the record is exceedingly difficult to read. Prudence—not merely compassion—suggests that we be slow and circumspect in praising or blaming.

Ultimately, neither of these global judgments will be as pertinent as the accumulation of understanding about the problems and possibilities of political leadership vested in our most powerful public office, so that we may better order our expectations and our requirements for future incumbents.

It seems gratuitous to say that knowing about the Presidency, how it is run and by whom, accounts for more consequences of more importance to more people throughout the world than knowledge of any other single political institution. Formulating a statement about the importance of the Presidency in this way avoids some awkward ambiguities. Within his system any petty dictator has more power than the President has in America. So, within his system, does the Prime Minister of the United Kingdom. But when viewed from a world-wide perspective, these are smaller, less resourceful, less consequential systems than the modern American polity. Thus one important element in giving the Presidency importance is the size and wealth of America.

Because there are obvious, conventional measures of size in which the United States is not first—area and population, for example—it is easy to forget how large and heterogeneous and resourceful an expanse is nevertheless governed under the Constitution of 1789. The United States is the fourth largest nation in area, stretching from side to side a little more than one-third the way around the globe. About 6 percent of the people of the world live in the United States; these 200 million of the more than 3 billion people on earth produce just a little under half of all the goods and services commercially available on markets of the world. They own over a third of the television receivers and slightly less than half of the radio receivers. They account for one-third of the world-wide production of commercially available energy and consume slightly more energy than they produce.

To list these American resources is not to say, of course, that the American President has control over them. They are mostly controlled directly by private (that is, nongovernmental) citizens, who in turn are influenced by other private citizens and by markets, by competitors, by suppliers, by subcontractors. Likewise they are influenced by laws, by regulations, by customs and practices and contracts enforceable by recourse to agencies of the state. Some of these agencies are directly under the formal jurisdiction of the President. The Attorney General, for example, can decide whether or not to prosecute a company for undertaking a merger that may have the effect of restraining trade. The Attorney General serves at the pleasure of the President and is appointed by the President. So there is a sense in which the economic resources of the nation are not wholly beyond the reach of the President for at least some purposes, although he does not himself invest or allocate them. By his control over the federal budget he can have a powerful influence upon the expenditure (or saving) of resources. By his powers to appoint officials and to supervise the activities of the government he can greatly influence the distribution of resources and the rate of their growth.

Economic resources are not the only resources within the reach of the President. He can confer prestige by attending to some persons, demands, programs, and activities, and ignoring others. He can influence the allocation of justice, of health, of education.

Because these things are well known, it is easy to forget them. The President, especially since the advent of television, has become so much the focus of the symbolic life of the American polity that the day-to-day consequences of his official acts for American citizens are lost from view. Instead we become preoccupied with the private lives of his children, the grooming of his wife, the tics of his rhetoric. And these, somehow, rather than the effects on the lives of people of the work he does, have become the Presidency.

But they are not the Presidency. This is not to say, however, that a President's presidential style is inconsequential. Of course style matters: it matters a little because some styles of presidential behavior lend themselves more easily than others to the rallying of popularity or to mobilizing the symbols of national honor. Style matters because it may be a meaningful clue to more significant characteristics of a President's pattern of work. The Presidency is, after all, in some ways a most delightful job, granting the incumbent great independence in all the small matters that serve to structure and harass the days of most of us. Thus a President's style will structure his work in ways that style cannot structure the work of most people. Most of us must be at a given place to do our jobs. The President can locate himself at will: helicopters, the Secret Service, diplomatic pouches, the signal corps, and so on follow along willy-nilly. Most of us have to make our telephone calls during business hours, get haircuts and go to movies when barber shops are open and the films we want to see are playing. None of these minor constraints exist for Presidents. President Eisenhower once sent an Air Force plane from Scotland to the United States to pick up his favorite partners for a round of golf at Saint Andrews. President Johnson's telephone calls at all hours of the day and night are legendary. Harry Truman's more regular habits, his acute and persistent consideration for those around him, were revelatory of the man precisely because each President invents his own rules for interacting with his staff and, within very broad limits, with everyone else as well.

Given that the ground rules are quite permissive and that the government—again within limits—pretty much runs itself on a day-to-day basis and is in any event much too vast to be within the direct or immediate supervision of the President, what the President does with the time and resources at his disposal is in some important ways truly a matter of choice. To discern a pattern in the choices a President makes and to unravel the strategy (or the characteristic rationalizations) that informs them is to analyze modern Presidencies.

1
FRANKLIN D. ROOSEVELT

1933–1945

When did the modern Presidency begin? By some standards with George Washington, who in his very person embodied the nation united. By others with Thomas Jefferson, who constructed and maneuvered the first presidential-congressional alliance. Other Presidents have legitimate claims: Andrew Jackson, standard-bearer for the first mass party; Rutherford B. Hayes or Chester A. Arthur, who neutralized the federal bureaucracies; or Grover Cleveland or Theodore Roosevelt, who consolidated the bureaucracies behind presidential priorities.

All these claims are just. It is certain that "modernization" is in no sense a monotonic unidirectional process. Each of the attributes I have named contributes to the modern Presidency, and the appearance of each therefore provides a legitimate point of departure for some purposes.

For the purpose of this volume, however, it will be sufficient to acquiesce in the conventional observation that a drastic and meaningful change did come over the Presidency when America became a permanent actor on the world stage. At about the same time, somewhere in Franklin Delano Roosevelt's second term, a number of administrative steps were taken to make available to the President a fairly sizeable professional staff. So by these criteria FDR became the first modern President. His administrative style has been much admired and copied. Arthur Schlesinger gives the canonical interpretation of it in the selections reprinted in this chapter.

The Evolution of the Presidency
ARTHUR M. SCHLESINGER, JR.

The White House routine had not altered much from 1933. The day still began for the President soon after 8 o'clock with breakfast on a tray in his bedroom. Beside the narrow white iron bedstead was a plain white table, covered with telephone, pencils, memoranda, ash trays, cigarettes, nose drops, and a glass of water. Ship prints and seascapes, old Roosevelt treasures, hung on the wall. Over the fireplace, on top of the marble mantelpiece with its grape carvings, was an assortment of family photographs, toy animals, and whatever other mementos had caught the President's fancy. Like every room in any Roosevelt house, the presidential bedroom was hopelessly Victorian—old-fashioned and indiscriminate in its furnishings, cluttered in its decor, ugly and comfortable.

While breakfasting, the President looked rapidly through half a dozen leading newspapers, half of them bitterly critical of his administration (the New York *Herald Tribune*, the Washington *Times-Herald*, and the Chicago *Tribune*). He usually wore a sweater or cape; a dressing gown was too much trouble for a crippled man. The breakfast conferences of the Hundred Days were now pretty well abandoned, except in moments of emergency. Even Eleanor Roosevelt, pausing to see her husband on her way out, usually said no more than good morning; "he liked no conversation at this hour." The newspaper scanning was the first phase in Roosevelt's unceasing effort to get the feel of the government and the nation.

Between 9 and 9:30 his secretaries—Steve Early and Marvin McIntyre, with Louis Howe, until he became ill, and then usually Colonel Edwin M. Watson, better known as Pa, the President's military aide—came in to discuss the day's schedule. In the next half-hour Roosevelt dressed and shaved. Often he combined this with business. Thus Harold Ickes:

When I got to his study, his valet ushered me into his bedroom, telling me that the President was shaving. He waved toward the bathroom and the President called out to me to come in. There he was, sitting before a mirror in front of the washstand, shaving. He invited me to sit on the toilet seat while we talked. When he was through shaving he was wheeled back to his room where he reclined on his bed while his valet proceeded to help him dress. . . . I was struck all over again with the unaffected simplicity and personal charm of the man. He was the President of the United States but he was also a plain human being, talking over with a friend matters of mutual interest while he shaved and dressed with the help of his valet. His disability didn't seem to concern him in the slightest degree or to disturb his urbanity.

Around 10:30 he was ordinarily pushed in his wheelchair along the newly constructed ramps to the executive office in the west wing of the White House. Here,

From "The Dynamics of Decision" and "The Control of Government," *The Coming of the New Deal* (Boston: Houghton Mifflin Company, 1959), pp. 511-532 and 533-552. Copyright © 1958 by Arthur Schlesinger, Jr. Reprinted by permission of Houghton Mifflin Company and William Heinemann, Ltd.

in the lovely oval room, he held his official appointments and spent most of his working day. The room had the usual Rooseveltian country-house informality. "You would think," said Emil Ludwig, "you were in the summer residence of the general manager of a steamship company, who has surrounded himself with mementoes of the days when he was captain." On the wall hung Hudson River prints by Currier and Ives; ship models stood on the mantel; a litter of memoranda, government reports, books, toy pigs, donkeys, and ship's rudders lay on his desk; on the floor, at the President's side, occasionally rising to be patted, were two fine Irish setters. The symbols of high office—the presidential flag, the Great Seal in the ceiling—were subdued and inconspicuous. Behind the President, light streamed softly in through great glass windows running down to the floor, and to the east, briefly glimpsed, were the quiet rose garden and the porticoes and the magnolia trees. In the commotion of Washington, this bright and open room had an astonishing serenity.

Most presidential appointments took place here in the two hours before lunch. The President aimed at seeing people at fifteen-minute intervals, but often fell behind, while visitors waited in the anteroom and McIntyre and Watson did their softspoken best to hurry things up. Lunch took place at his desk, with food served from a metal warming oven; it was often hash with a poached egg (when two eggs came, Roosevelt sometimes sent word to the housekeeper that this was a waste of food); lunch too was usually combined with business. In the afternoon there might be more appointments; then, about midafternoon, the President usually called in Grace Tully for an hour or two of dictation. About 5 o'clock during the first term, the office staff was briefly summoned for what he called "the children's hour," an interlude of relaxation and gossip. Soon after 5:30, the office day ended; and the President took twenty minutes in the White House swimming pool, installed as a result of money raised in a campaign sponsored by the New York *Daily News*. Refreshed by exercise, the President prepared for dinner, ordinarily preceded by a martini or an old-fashioned. After dinner, he often went to his private study, a genial oval room on the second floor next to his bedroom, and dictated some more or read papers or held further conversations. Usually in bed before midnight, he quickly threw off the concerns of the day and in five minutes was deep in sleep. Unlike other Presidents, Roosevelt never allowed the Secret Service to lock the doors of his room at night.

Roosevelt's immediate staff was loyal and efficient. The longest in point of service, of course, was Louis Howe, who had worked for Roosevelt nearly a quarter of a century. Howe was only in his early sixties, but, frail and wizened, he was older than his years. His devotion to the President was more proprietary than ever, and his waspishness toward everyone else more insistent. But both Franklin and Eleanor Roosevelt cherished him. On certain matters, especially politics and patronage, Roosevelt continued greatly to value Howe's counsel; and on most matters he welcomed his opinions. "I am going to talk this over with Louis," he would say. "He has forty ideas a day and sometimes a few good ones." While the President often dodged Howe's advice, if he had to bypass his old friend he did so with incomparable tact.

As for Howe, he did not allow his protege's eminence to constrain their relationship. Once McDuffie, the President's valet, brought him a message to which he replied snappishly, "Tell the President to go to hell." McDuffie, appalled, told his wife Lizzie, one of the White House maids, that he could not possibly deliver such a message to the President. Lizzie said she would fix it up; "Mr. President," she said, "Mr. Howe says that is a hell of a thing to do." The President laughed skeptically: "That isn't what Howe said, Lizzie. He told me to go to hell." Roosevelt's feeling toward Howe, as Richberg discerningly remarked, was that of a middle-aged son who still appreciated father's wisdom but was also impatient at father's efforts to keep him under parental guidance.

By the end of 1934, Howe's health, never good, grew steadily worse. He spent more and more of his time in his suite on the second floor of the White House. In February 1935 bronchial complications brought about a collapse. He was rushed to the Naval Hospital and put under an oxygen tent. Doctors despaired of him. "He seems to cling to life in the most astonishing manner," Eleanor Roosevelt wrote sadly to Molly Dewson, "but I am afraid it is the end." She underestimated his vitality. He rallied and, though he never left the hospital for long, he stayed alive another year. Much of this time he spent in bed, doubled up in an effort to reduce the pain; he let his beard grow into a straggling goatee which made his appearance more peculiar than ever. He continued to follow politics with sharp-eyed attention, sending out a flow of confusing directives to the National Committee and to cabinet members. The Roosevelts visited him regularly. But he knew in his heart that he had not long to live. One day a friend told him that everyone counted on him for the 1936 campaign. "No," the old man said. "No, they'll have to run this campaign without me." He paused for a moment; then said, "Franklin's on his own now." In mid-April 1936, Louis Howe died.

Eleanor Roosevelt always felt that Howe's death left an irreparable gap in Franklin's life. Howe was almost alone, she believed, in being ready to follow through an argument with her husband, forcing him by peevish persistence to see unpleasant sides of an issue: "After Louis' death," she wrote, "Franklin frequently made his decisions without canvassing all sides of a question." Harold Ickes said the same thing: "Howe was the only one who dared to talk to him frankly and fearlessly. He not only could tell him what he believed to be the truth, but he could hang on like a pup to a root until he got results." Moreover, Howe unscrupulously organized campaigns to press his views; at his instigation, Eleanor Roosevelt, Farley, Ed Flynn, and others would suddenly converge on the President and, as if by accident, make the same point. Eleanor Roosevelt felt in addition that her husband saw a better cross section of people and heard a greater variety of views when Howe was alive.

These things were probably true. Yet Howe's range was limited. "Louis knows nothing about economics," Roosevelt once said; in fact, he knew little of any aspect of public affairs, and was only vaguely aware what the New Deal was all about. Howe would have saved Roosevelt from mistakes in politics, but hardly from mistakes in policy. Still the subtraction of the most vehement nay-sayer from the entourage was certainly a misfortune.

Roosevelt had named Howe his Chief Secretary as a testimonial to his years of service. His other secretaries, Early and McIntyre, received the same salary as Howe and, as time went on, took over more and more of the day-to-day responsibility. Early, a tough, hard-driving, profane newspaperman just under fifty who had been for many years an ace for the Associated Press, had press relations as his main job. McIntyre, a gentle, agreeable man in his middle fifties, with a long and not especially distinguished background in newspaper work and public relations, was more or less in charge of political appointments (though, as in any Roosevelt operation, this seemed at times everybody's responsibility). Both Early and McIntyre were southerners, Early from Virginia, McIntyre from Kentucky. Both had worked for Roosevelt in the 1920 vice-presidential campaign. Both were aggressively non-ideological. Each preferred the political and business types with which they were familiar to the odd new breed of New Dealers; in McIntyre's case, an innocent fondness for the company of lobbyists was more than once a source of embarrassment to the White House. Both were loyal to Roosevelt rather than to his philosophy. But they kept out of policy questions and each strove to do as fair a job as possible.

Pa Watson, the military aide, who ran the general appointment schedule, was a more complex and subtle figure. An Alabaman in his early fifties who had been an aide to Wilson at Versailles, Watson was a man of winning personal charm. "I have never known anyone just like him," Ickes once said. ". . . He could be relied upon to keep us all in a mellow humor, and this without any effort on his part, but simply by being himself." People so adored the bubbling good nature that they sometimes missed the sophisticated awareness which lay beneath the quips and stories. Not a New Dealer, Watson had a greater understanding than Early and McIntyre of what the New Deal was about.

Of all the staff, Marguerite LeHand, the President's personal secretary, was undoubtedly closest to him and had most influence upon him. Missy was now in her late thirties, a tall, slender woman, prematurely gray, with a lovely face and attractive gray-blue eyes. She had worked for Roosevelt so long that she knew intimately his every expression and mood; his fondness for her was so great that he would listen to her as to few others on questions of appointments and even policy ("Mr. President, you really *must* do something about" so-and-so or such-and-such). She lived on the third floor of the White House, and, when Eleanor Roosevelt was away, acted as White House hostess, inviting people who she thought might divert the President. Eleanor Roosevelt, while respecting Missy's abilities and understanding her value to her husband, felt that "occasionally her social contacts got mixed with her work and made it hard for her and others." People like Bill Bullitt and Tom Corcoran, she suggested, "exploited Missy's friendship" for their own purposes. But "though occasionally someone fooled her for a time, I always waited for enlightenment to come, with confidence born of long experience." Missy was pretty and gay and liked lively company; there can be no question that she brought an essential femininity as well as a sympathetic common sense into Roosevelt's life, and there is no evidence that she ever abused the affection and trust he reposed in her. An attack of rheumatic fever in 1926 had strained Missy's heart; and more and more of the office work, as, for example, taking dictation, fell to Grace Tully, another pretty and lively girl, who had worked for Roosevelt since the 1928 campaign. Both girls were Catholics, Miss LeHand of French, Miss Tully of Irish descent. They both cared deeply about the objectives of the New Deal. Both were exceptionally able and devoted women.

One other key White House figure was the executive clerk, Rudolph Forster, who had been there since the McKinley administration. His responsibility was the channeling of state papers, and he did this with an austere and frightening efficiency. For him the job was an end in itself; Presidents came and went, but papers went on forever. "You would be terrified," he once said to a Roosevelt assistant, "if you knew how little I care." (Yet even Forster, in the end, succumbed. In the 1944 campaign, as Roosevelt was leaving the White House on a political tour, Forster, with what Robert E. Sherwood described as "the air of one who was willfully breaking all of the Ten Commandments but prepared to take the consequences," shook the President's hand and wished him luck. Roosevelt, astonished and moved, said as the car drove away, "That's practically the first time in all these years that Rudolph has ever stepped out of character and spoken to me as if I were a human being instead of just another President.")

The next concentric circle beyond the White House staff in the President's constellation was the cabinet. In the American system this had always been an ambiguous and unsatisfactory body. At the beginning of the republic, some conceived it as a sort of executive council. All grave and important matters, it was supposed, would be submitted to a cabinet vote in which, as Jefferson put it, "the President counts himself but one." But Presidents, even Jefferson, recoiled from such a conception; and Jackson, in his general process of revolutionizing the Presidency, decisively redefined the relationship between the President and his cabinet.

Jackson flatly declined, for example, to submit questions to vote. "I have accustomed myself to receive with respect the opinions of others," he said, "but always take the responsibility of deciding for myself." Lincoln, going even further, found cabinet meetings so useless that he often avoided them and at one time seemed on the verge of doing away with them altogether. As for voting: "Ayes one, noes seven. The ayes have it"—or so the old story went. "There is really very little of a government here at this time so far as most of the cabinet are concerned," complained Gideon Welles, Lincoln's Secretary of the Navy; "certainly but little consultation in this important period." Or again: "But little was before the Cabinet, which of late can hardly be called a council. Each Department conducts and manages its own affairs, informing the President to the extent it pleases." Theodore Roosevelt ignored his cabinet on important issues. Woodrow Wilson did not even bother to discuss the sinking of the *Lusitania* or the declaration of war with it. "For some weeks," wrote his Secretary of the Interior, Franklin Lane, "we have spent our time at Cabinet meetings largely telling stories."

Roosevelt remained generally faithful to this tradition, though he made rather more effort than Lincoln or Wilson to recognize the cabinet's existence. At first, he planned two cabinet meetings a week, on Tuesday and Friday afternoons. Effectively he had only one, however; the Tuesday meeting was first enlarged to include the heads of the emergency agencies and then dropped almost entirely. Sessions took place in an atmosphere of characteristic Roosevelt informality. The President ordinarily began with a recital of pleasantries, telling stories which tickled him or joshing cabinet members about their latest appearances in the newspapers. Then he might throw out a problem for a generally rambling and inconclusive decision. Or, turning to the Secretary of State, he might say without ceremony, "Well, Cordell, what's on your mind today?" Then he would continue around the table in order of precedence.

The men—and one woman—sitting around the table were of varying qualities and abilities. They had conspicuously one thing in common—a high degree of personal rectitude. "For integrity and honesty of purpose," wrote Raymond Clapper after twenty years of covering Washington, "I'll put this Cabinet against any that has been in Washington since the war. It is one thing that does truly distinguish this group. There is not a shady one in the lot." Beyond that, the people around the table represented a variety of viewpoints and temperaments, held together only by a loyalty to, or at least a dependence on, the President. There was Garner (whom the President, to his later regret, invited to attend cabinet meetings) with his complacent country sagacity; Hull, courteous and grave, always vigilant to defend his authority against real or fancied depredation; Henry Morgenthau, closest personally to the President, earnest, devoted, and demanding; the testy and aggressive Ickes; the preoccupied and thoughtful Wallace; Homer Cummings, bland, canny and unperturbed; Jesse Jones, wary and self-contained; the intelligent and articulate Miss Perkins (whose protracted discourses appeared to fascinate the President, but bored most of the others and at times enraged Ickes—"she talks in a perfect torrent, almost without pausing to take breath"); the amiable Farley, reacting only when politics came into the discussion—they were all forceful personalities, regarding each other with a show of conviviality which often only barely concealed depths of suspicion. For the most part, they chose problems of only middling—or else of highly general—significance to communicate to the group. This was partly because, in the inevitable jostling of bureaucracy, each felt that every man's hand was against him, and none wanted to expose vulnerabilities. It was also because the conviction grew that some members would "leak" tasty items—Garner to his cronies on the Hill, or Ickes to the columnist Drew Pearson. Questions that really troubled them they reserved for private discussion with the President afterward, a practice which Garner used to call "staying for prayer meeting." "Then you would stay behind," as Morgenthau described it, "and whisper in his ear and he would say yes or no."

The members of the Roosevelt cabinet, as usual, suffered frustration and, as usual, thought their experience unique. In private, they echoed the familiar laments of Gideon Welles and Franklin Lane. "Only the barest routine matters were discussed," burst out Ickes in his diary after a meeting in 1935. "All of which leads me to set down what has been running in my mind for a long time, and that is just what use the Cabinet is under this administration. The cold fact is that on important matters we are seldom called upon for advice. We never discuss exhaustively any policy of government or question of political strategy. The President makes all of his own decisions. . . . As a matter of fact, I never think of bringing up even a serious departmental issue at Cabinet meetings." "It seemed to me," wrote William Phillips, sitting in occasionally for Hull, "that a great deal of time was wasted at Cabinet meetings and much of the talk was without any particular import." "The important things were never discussed at Cabinet," said Morgenthau. "The President treats them like children," Tugwell wrote in his diary, "and almost nothing of any importance was discussed."

The meetings evidently retained some obscure usefulness for the President. The reaction he got from this miscellany of administrators perhaps gave him some idea of the range of public opinion. It also helped him measure the capacity of his subordinates. Grace Tully reports, for example, that he preferred Henry Wallace's willingness to speak out on a wide variety of problems "to the reticence or indifference of some Cabinet members." But, like all strong presidents, Roosevelt regarded his cabinet as a body of department heads, to be dealt with individually— or, sometimes, as a group of representative intelligent men, useful for a quick canvass of opinion—not as a council of constitutional advisers.

Beyond the cabinet there stretched the Executive Branch of the government—an endless thicket of vested usage and vested interest, apportioned among a number of traditional jurisdictions, dominated by a number of traditional methods and objectives. This was, in the popular understanding, the government of the United States—the people and departments and agencies whose office it was to carry out the national laws and fulfill the national policies. The President had few more basic responsibilities than his supervision and operation of the machinery of government. Little fascinated Franklin Roosevelt more than the tasks of presidential administration. And in few things was he more generally reckoned a failure.

This verdict against Roosevelt derived ultimately from a philosophy of public administration—a philosophy held for many years after by Civil Service professionals, expounded in departments of political science, and commending itself plausibly to common sense. This school's faith was in logical organization of government, founded on rigid definitions of job and function and maintained by the sanctity of channels. Its weapons were the job description and the organization chart. Its unspoken assumption was that the problems of administration never change; and its consuming fear was improvisation, freewheeling or unpredictability—which is nearly to say creativity—in the administrative process. From this point of view, it need hardly be said, the Roosevelt government was a textbook case of poor administration. At one time or another, Roosevelt must surely have violated every rule in the sacred texts of the Bureau of the Budget.

And this conventional verdict found apparent support in much of the literature written by men who worked for Roosevelt. Though these reports differed on many other things, one thing on which they very often agreed was in their complaint about Roosevelt as an administrator. They agreed on one other thing too—the perspective from which they were written. Nearly all exhibited the problems of the Presidency from below—from the viewpoint of the subordinate rather than from that of the President. The picture created by this mass of individual stories, while vivid and overwhelming, was inevitably distorted and too often querulous. For no subordinate ever got what he wanted or thought he needed. In later years, George C. Marshall would talk of "localitis"—the conviction ardently held by every theater commander that the war was being won or lost in his own zone of responsibility, and that the withholding of whatever was necessary for local success was evidence of blindness, if not of imbecility, in the high command. "Localitis" in one form or another was the occupational disease of all subordinate officials; and, in a sense, it had to be, for each of them ought to demand everything he needed to do the best job he can. But "localitis" offered no solid ground for judgment of superiors, whose role it must inevitably be to frustrate the dreams of subordinates. The President occupied the apex of the pyramid of frustration. The essence of his job was to enforce priorities—and thereby to exasperate everybody. And, in Roosevelt's case, there is little left in the literature to emphasize the view from the summit, where any President had to make his decisions. As Grace Tully (whose book does something to redress the balance) commented on other memoirists, "None of them could know that for each minute they spent with the President he spent a hundred minutes by himself and a thousand more with scores of other people—to reject, improvise, weigh and match this against that until a decision was reached on a public policy."

The question remains whether the true test of an administrator may be, not his ability to design and respect organization charts, not his ability to keep within channels, but his ability to concert and release the energies of men for the attainment of public objectives. It might be argued that the essence of successful administration is: first, to acquire the ideas and information necessary for wise decisions; second, to maintain control over the actual making of the decisions; and, third, to mobilize men and women who can make the first two things possible—that is, who can provide effective ideas and information, and who can reliably put decisions into effect. It is conceivable that these things may be more important than preserving the chastity of administrative organization—that, indeed, an excessive insistence on the sacredness of channels and charts is likely to end in the stifling of imagination, the choking of vitality, and the deadening of creativity.

Franklin Roosevelt, at any rate, had some such philosophy of administration. The first task of an executive, as he evidently saw it, was to guarantee himself an effective flow of information and ideas. And Roosevelt's first insight—or, at least, his profound conviction—was that, for this purpose, the ordained channels, no matter how simply or how intricately designed, could never be enough. An executive relying on a single information system became inevitably the prisoner of that system. Roosevelt's persistent effort therefore was to check and balance information acquired through official channels by information acquired through a myriad of private, informal, and unorthodox channels and espionage networks. At times, he seemed almost to pit his personal sources against his public sources. From the viewpoint of subordinates, this method was distracting when not positively demoralizing. But Roosevelt, with his voracity for facts and for ideas, required this approach to cross-check the official system and keep it alert as well as to assure himself the balanced and various product without which he could not comfortably reach decisions.

The official structure, of course, maintained a steady flow of intelligence. Roosevelt was, for a President, extraordinarily accessible. Almost a hundred persons could get through to him by telephone without stating their business to a secretary; and government officials with anything serious on their minds had little difficulty in getting appointments. In addition, he read an enormous number of official memoranda, State Department cables, and government reports, and always tried to glance at the *Congressional Record*. The flow was overwhelming, and he sought continually to make it manageable. "I learned a trick from Wilson," he remarked to Louis Brownlow. "He once told me: 'If you want your memoranda read, put it on one page.' So I, when I came here, issued a similar decree, if you want to call it that. But even at that I am now forced to handle, so the oldsters around tell me, approximately a hundred times as many papers as any of my predecessors." Certainly his subordinates paid little attention to the one-page rule.

What gave Roosevelt's administrative practice its distinctive quality was his systematic effort to augment the official intelligence. The clutter of newspapers on his bed each morning marked only the first stage in his battle for supplementary information. In this effort, reading was a useful but auxiliary weapon. Beyond government documents and newspapers, he read little. So far as current magazines were concerned, the President, according to Early, "sketches the field," whatever that meant. As for books, Roosevelt evidently read them only on holiday, and then not too seriously. When Frances Perkins sent him the Brookings study *America's Capacity to Produce*, he replied, "Many thanks. . . . I am taking it on the trip and will guarantee to browse through it but not of necessity to read every word!" On the whole, he preferred to acquire both information and ideas through conversation.

Many visitors, it is true, left Roosevelt with the impression that he had done all the talking. This was markedly less true, in his first term, however, than it would be later. Indeed, Henry Pringle, reporting the Washington view in 1934, wrote, "He is a little too willing to listen." And the complaint against Roosevelt's overtalking meant in some cases only that a visitor had run into a deliberate filibuster (thus William Randolph Hearst's baffled lament after a session with Roosevelt in 1933, "The President didn't give me a chance to make suggestions. He did all the talking"). "Words are a good enough barrage if you know how to use them," Roosevelt told one visitor. Like many talkers, moreover, Roosevelt absorbed attitudes and ideas by a mysterious osmosis on occasions when the visitor complained he hadn't got a word in edgewise.

Conversation gave him an indispensable means both of feeling out opinion and of clarifying his own ideas. He talked to everybody and about everything. His habits of conversation out of channels were sometimes disconcerting. He had little hesitation, if he heard of a bright man somewhere down the line in a department, about summoning him to the White House. Ickes complained bitterly in his diary about "what he does so frequently, namely, calling in members of my staff for consultation on Department matters, without consulting me or advising with me." And often he bewildered visitors by asking their views on matters outside their jurisdiction. "He had a great habit," said Jesse Jones, "of talking to one caller about the subject matter of his immediately preceding interview." "I would go to see the President about something," wrote James P. Warburg, "and the fellow who was there before me talking about cotton would be told by the President, 'Well, why don't you stay.' Before we were through the guy who was there talking about cotton was telling him what to do about gold." All this, irritating as it was to tidy minds, enlarged the variety of reactions available to him in areas where no one was infallible and any intelligent person might make a contribution.

Moreover, at this time, at least, conversation around him was unusually free and candid. Always sensitive to public criticism, Roosevelt could take a large measure of private disagreement. Moley describes him as "patient, amenable to advice, moderate and smilingly indifferent to criticism." "In those days," wrote Richberg, "he enjoyed the frankness and lack of deference with which the original 'brain trusters' and I discussed problems." When people disagreed, they said so plainly and at length. "I had numerous quarrels with him," wrote Ed Flynn, who once (in 1940) hung up on him in the midst of a phone conversation. "However, as with sincere friends, the quarrels never impaired our friendship."

In seeking information, Roosevelt took care not to confuse the capital with the nation. "Pay no attention to what people are saying in Washington," he once told Molly Dewson. "They are the last persons in the country to listen to." He loved going out to the country himself and got infinite stimulus from faces in crowds, from towns quietly glimpsed out of the windows of slow-moving trains, from chance conversations with ordinary people along the way. But polio and the Presidency limited his mobility. Instead, he had to urge others to get out of Washington. "Go and see what's happening," he told Tugwell. "See the end product of what we are doing. Talk to people; get the wind in your nose."

His first reliance was on his wife. From the first days after his disability, he trained her to do his looking for him. "That I became, as the years went by, a better and better reporter and a better and better observer," she later wrote, "was largely owing to the fact that Franklin's questions covered such a wide range. I found myself obliged to notice everything." While he sometimes doubted her judgment on policy and especially on timing, he had implicit faith in her observations. He would say at cabinet, "My Missus says that they have typhoid fever in that district," or "My Missus says that people are working for wages way below the minimum set by NRA in the town she visited last week." "It was not unusual," said Grace Tully, "to hear him predicate an entire line of reasoning upon a statement that 'my Missus told me so and so.' " In addition, he liked detailed reports of the kind Lorena Hickok and Martha Gellhorn rendered on the situation of people on relief. And he listened with interest to any reasonably succinct account of human conditions anywhere.

Another great source of information was the mail. Five to eight thousand letters a day came normally to the White House; in times of anxiety, of course, many more. The mail was regularly analyzed in order to gauge fluctuations in public sentiment. From time to time, the President himself called for a random selection of letters in order to renew his sense of contact with raw opinion. As the White House mail clerk later wrote, "Mr. Roosevelt always showed a keen interest in the mail and kept close watch on its trend."

In all these ways, Roosevelt amassed an astonishing quantity of miscellaneous information and ideas about the government and the country. "No President," wrote Alben Barkley, "has ever surpassed him in personal knowledge of the details of every department"; and he could have added that probably no President surpassed him in specific knowledge of the geography, topography, and people of the nation. Roosevelt took inordinate pride in this mastery of detail and often displayed it at length when those around him wished to get down to business. But, at the same time, the information—and the pride in it—signified the extraordinary receptivity which was one of his primary characteristics.

This receptivity produced the complex of information systems by which he protected himself from White House insulation. It oriented the administrative machinery away from routine and toward innovation. It made possible the intellectual excitement of the New Deal; it helped provoke a tempest of competing ideas within government because everyone felt that ideas stood and fell at the White House on their merit, not on whether they arrived through the proper channels. Good ideas might pop up from anywhere. "You sometimes find something pretty good in the lunatic fringe," Roosevelt once told his press conference: after all, America today was remade by "a whole lot of things which in my boyhood were considered lunatic fringe." Anyone with new theories had a sense that they were worth developing because, if good, they would find their way to the center. Sometimes this caused problems: Roosevelt was occasionally sold on harebrained ideas which more orderly procedures would have screened out and which taxed responsible officials before he could be unsold. But, on balance, benefits far outweighed disadvantages. H. G. Wells, who saw in Roosevelt's union of openness of mind and resolution of will the realization of his old dream of the Open Conspiracy, wrote with admiration in 1934, "He is, as it were, a ganglion for reception, expression, transmission, combination and realization, which I take it, is exactly what a modern government ought to be."

If information was the first responsibility of the executive, the second was decision. American Presidents fall into two types: those who like to make decisions, and those who don't. One type designs an administrative system which brings decisions to him; the other, a system which keeps decisions away from him. The second technique, under its more mellifluous designation of "delegation of authority," is regarded with favor in the conventional theory of public administration. Yet, pressed very far, "delegation of authority" obviously strikes at the roots of the Presidency. One can delegate routine, but one cannot delegate any part of the serious presidential responsibility. The whole theory of the Constitution makes the Chief Executive, in the words of Andrew Jackson, "accountable at the bar of public opinion for every act of his Administration," and thus presumably accountable in his own conscience for its every large decision.

Roosevelt, in any case, was pre-eminently of the first type. He evidently felt that both the dignity of his office and the coherence of his administration required that the key decisions be made by him, and not by others before him. He took great pride, for example, in a calculation of Rudolph Forster's that he made at least thirty-five decisions to each one made by Calvin Coolidge. Given this conception of the Presidency, he deliberately organized—or disorganized—his system of command to insure that important decisions were passed on to the top. His favorite technique was to keep grants of authority incomplete, jurisdictions uncertain, charters overlapping. The result of this competitive theory of administration was often confusion and exasperation on the operating level; but no other method could so reliably insure that in a large bureaucracy filled with ambitious men eager for power the decisions, and the power to make them, would remain with the President. This was in part on Roosevelt's side an instinct for self-preservation; in part, too, the temperamental expression of a restless, curious, and untidy personality. Co-existence with disorder was almost the pattern of his life. From the day of his marriage, he had lived in a household of unresolved jurisdictions, and it had never occurred to him to try to settle lines finally as between mother and wife. As Assistant Secretary of the Navy, he had indulged happily in the kind of administrative freewheeling which he was not much concerned to penalize in others now. As his doctor once said, Roosevelt "loved to know everything that was going on and delighted to have a finger in every pie."

Once the opportunity for decision came safely into his orbit, the actual process of deciding was involved and inscrutable. As Tugwell once put it, "Franklin allowed no one to discover the governing principle." He evidently felt that clear-cut administrative decisions would work only if they expressed equally clear-cut realities of administrative competence and vigor. If they did not, if the balance of administrative power would not sustain the decision, then decision would only compound confusion and discredit government. And the actualities of administrative power were to be discovered, not by writing—or by reading—Executive orders, but by apprehending through intuition a vast constellation of political forces. His complex administrative sensibility, infinitely subtle and sensitive, was forever weighing questions of personal force, of political timing, of congressional concern, of partisan benefit, of public interest. Situations had to be permitted to develop, to crystallize, to clarify; the competing forces had to vindicate themselves in the actual pull and tug of conflict; public opinion had to face the question, consider it, pronounce upon it— only then, at the long, frazzled end, would the President's intuitions consolidate and precipitate a result.

Though he enjoyed giving the impression of snap decisions, Roosevelt actually made few. The more serious complaint against him was his weakness for postponement. This protraction of decision often appeared a technique of evasion. And sometimes it was. But sometimes dilemmas did not seem so urgent from above as they seemed below—a proposition evidently proved when they evaporated after the passage of time. And Roosevelt, in any case, justified, or rationalized, delay in terms of his own sense of timing. He knew from hard experience that a person could not regain health in a day or year; and he had no reason to suppose that a nation would mend any more quickly. "He could watch with enormous patience as a situation developed," wrote his wife, "and would wait for exactly the right moment to act." When people pressed proposals on him, he often answered (as he did to Frank

Walker in 1936), "You are absolutely right. . . . It is simply a question of time." The tragedy of the Presidency in his view was the impotence of the President. Abraham Lincoln, Roosevelt said, "was a sad man because he couldn't get it all at once. And nobody can." He was responding informally to an important young questioner. "Maybe you would make a much better President than I have. Maybe you will, some day. If you ever sit here, you will learn that you cannot, just by shouting from the housetops, get what you want all the time."

Yet his caution was always within an assumption of constant advance. "We must keep the sheer momentum from slacking up too much," he told Colonel House in 1934, "and I have no intention of relinquishing the offensive." Woodrow Wilson had given him a cyclical conception of social change in America. Roosevelt told Robert H. Jackson that he had once suggested that Wilson withhold part of his reform program for his second term. Wilson replied in substance: We do not know that there will be a second term, and, if there is, it will be less progressive and constructive than the first. American history shows that a reform administration comes to office only once in every twenty years, and that its forward impulse does not outlast one term. Even if the same party and persons remain in power, they become complacent in a second term. "What we do not accomplish in the first term is not likely to be accomplished at all." (When Roosevelt told this story to his press conference in the first year of his second term, he lengthened the period of possible accomplishment from four to eight years.)

This technique of protraction was often wildly irritating to his subordinates, enlisted passionately on one side or another of an argument and perceiving with invincible clarity the logic of one or another course. It was equally irritating to his opponents, who enjoyed the advantages of oversimplification which come from observation without responsibility. But the President's dilatory tactics were, in a sense, the means by which he absorbed country-wide conflict of pressures, of fears, of hopes. His intelligence was not analytical. He did not systematically assess pros and cons in his own mind. What for others might be an interior dialogue had to be externalized for Roosevelt; and it was externalized most conveniently by hearing strong exponents of divergent viewpoints. Listening amiably to all sides, watching the opposing views undergo the test of practice, digesting the evidence, he gradually felt his way toward a conclusion. And even this would not often be clear-cut. "He hated to make sharp decisions between conflicting claims for power among his subordinates," noted Francis Biddle, "and decided them, almost always, in a spirit of arbitration: each side should have part of the morsel." Quite often, he ordered the contestants to work out their own compromise, as in NRA and on farm policy. In this connection he liked to cite Al Smith: "He said if you can get the parties into one room with a big table and make them take their coats off and put their feet up on the table, and give each one of them a good cigar, you can always make them agree."

With the conclusion, however reached, a new phase began. When Garner once tried to argue after Roosevelt had made up his mind, the President said, "You tend to your office and I'll tend to mine." ("I didn't take offense at that," said Garner, "because he was right.") "You could fight with Roosevelt and argue with him up to a certain point," said Morgenthau, "—but at no time during his waking hours was he anything else but a ruler." Wayne Coy, who was a Roosevelt assistant for some years, observed that one could say exactly what one thought to Roosevelt, so long as he was saying only "in my judgment" or "I think." When he said "The President thinks," the time for discussion was over. To another assistant, James Rowe, who insisted that he should do something in a particular way, Roosevelt said, "I do not have to do it your way and I will tell you the reason why. The reason is that, although they may have made a mistake, the people of the United States elected me President, not you."

Often he announced his decisions with bravado. He liked to tell advisers, "I'm going to spring a bombshell," and then startle them with novel proposals—or rather with proposals novel to them, not perhaps to another set of advisers. "He delights in surprises—clever, cunning and quick," said Hugh Johnson. "He likes to shock friends as well as enemies with something they never expected." But he seems rarely to have supposed that any particular decision was in a final sense correct, or even terribly important. "I have no expectation of making a hit every time I come to bat. What I seek is the highest possible batting average." He remembered Theodore Roosevelt's saying to him, "If I can be right 75 per cent of the time I shall come up to the fullest measure of my hopes." "You'll have to learn that public life takes a lot of sweat," he told Tugwell, "but it doesn't need to worry you. You won't always be right, but you mustn't suffer from being wrong. That's what kills people like us." After all, Roosevelt said, suppose a truck driver were doing your job; 50 per cent of his decisions would be right on average. "You aren't a truck driver. You've had some preparation. Your percentage is bound to be higher." And he knew that the refusal to decide was itself a form of decision. "This is very bad," he said to Frances Perkins, "but one thing is sure. We have to do something. We have to do the best we know how to do at the moment." Then, after a pause: "If it doesn't turn out right, we can modify it as we go along."

This dislike of firm commitments, this belief in alternatives, further reduced the significance of any single decision. As Miss Perkins observed, "He rarely got himself sewed tight to a program from which there was no turning back." The very ambiguity of his scheme of organization—the overlapping jurisdictions and duplicated responsibilities—made flexibility easy. If things started to go bad, he could reshuffle people and functions with speed which would have been impossible in a government of clear-cut assignments and rigid chains of command. Under the competitive theory, he always retained room for administrative maneuver.

Only a man of limitless energy and resource could hold such a system together. Even Roosevelt at times was hard put to keep it from flying apart. But he did succeed, as no modern President has done, in concentrating the power of executive decision where the Constitution intended it should be. "I've never known any President," said W. M. Kiplinger, "who was as omnipresent as this Roosevelt." "Most people acting for Roosevelt were messenger boys," said Ed Flynn. "He really made his own decisions."

As a President's conquest of the problem of information makes decision possible, so his conquest of the problem of decision leads on to the third responsibility of administration: execution. Success in administration obviously stands or falls on skill in execution. Execution means, above all, the right people—it means having men and women capable of providing the information and carrying out the decision. Nothing is more important for a President than to command the necessary abundance of understanding, loyalty, and ardor on the part of able and imaginative subordinates.

Different Presidents want different things from their subordinates. Some want fidelity, some diligence, some flattery, some no more than the undemanding competence which will take things off their own back. Roosevelt no doubt wanted all of these at various times. What he evidently wanted most was liveliness, vitality, vision. He sought out men who had ideas and drive; and he designed the kind of administrative system which would bring him the men he wanted. Again, as in the case of information, the competitive approach to administration best served his purposes. The men around Roosevelt were not easily contented or contained. They were always fanning out, in ideas and in power. A government well organized in the conventional sense would have given them claustrophobia. The looseness of the New Deal gave them the feeling of scope and outlet which made public service for them tolerable and amusing.

To guarantee the scope, Roosevelt had to revamp the structure of government. By orthodox administrative theory, the antidepression activities should have been brought in under the appropriate old-line departments—Agriculture, Commerce, Labor, the Treasury. But Roosevelt felt that the old departments, even with new chiefs, simply could not generate the energy and daring the crisis required. "We have new and complex problems. We don't really know what they are. Why not establish a new agency to take over the new duty rather than saddle it on an old institution?" Hence the resort from the start to the emergency agency, an essential instrument in the Rooseveltian technique of administrative improvisation. If the obvious channel of action was blocked and it was not worth the political trouble of dynamiting it open, then the emergency agency supplied the means of getting the job done nevertheless. And the new agencies simplified the problem of reversing direction and correcting error. "We have to be prepared to abandon bad practices that grow out of ignorance. It seems to me it is easier to use a new agency which is not a permanent part of the structure of government. If it is not permanent, we don't get bad precedents."

The New Dealers, particularly those of the Brandeis-Frankfurter school, talked a good deal about the importance of a first-class Civil Service on the British model. Roosevelt accepted this as an aspiration. "Public service," he said proudly in 1934, "offers better rewards in the opportunity for service than ever before in our history." But in practice the professional Civil Service often seemed an arsenal of obfuscation. It had become, said Tugwell, "a way of choosing and keeping 'the best of the worst,' of making certain that, barring revolution, war or economic disaster, the chosen dullards could have a long, uneventful, thoroughly secure working life." More than that, the Civil Service register for upper-grade positions reflected the generally Republican character of the professional and business classes. Mathematics thus indicated that staffing the New Deal through the Civil Service would fill key positions with anti-New Dealers. In consequence, the new agencies did their best to bypass the Civil Service. By 1936 the proportion of employees under the "merit system" had materially declined.

The new agencies were plainly indispensable. They tended to have an administrative dash and *élan* which the old departments, sunk in the lethargy of routine, could not match. Yet the theory could be pushed too far. At times Roosevelt acted as if a new agency were almost a new solution. His addiction to new organizations became a kind of nervous tic which disturbed even avid New Dealers. By 1936 we find Tugwell pleading with him not to set up new organizations. "My experience— and Harry's—is that it takes almost a year to perfect a country-wide administrative organization and that while it is being done there is political turmoil over the jobs, criticisms of procedure from the field, jealousy on the part of old organizations which fancy their prerogatives are threatened and other sources of irritation."

Each new agency had its own distinct mission. But in many cases jurisdictions overlapped each other and even spilled into cabinet departments. This was sloppy and caused much trouble. Yet this very looseness around the joints, this sense of give and possibility which Henry Stimson once called the "inherently disorderly nature" of Roosevelt's administration, made public service attractive to men of a certain boldness and imagination. It also spurred them on to better achievement. Roosevelt liked the competitive approach to administration, not just because it reserved the big decisions for the President, but perhaps even more because it enabled him to test and develop the abilities of his subordinates. How to tell which man, which approach was better? One answer was to let them fight it out. This solution might cause waste but would guarantee against stagnation. "There is something to be said," Roosevelt once observed, ". . . for having a little conflict between agencies. A little rivalry is stimulating, you know. It keeps everybody going to prove that he is a better fellow than the next man. It keeps them honest too. An awful lot of money is being handled. The fact that there is somebody else in the field who knows what you are doing is a strong incentive to strict honesty." One can see, for example, in the diaries of Harold Ickes how the overhanging presence of Hopkins and Morgenthau caused Ickes to spend hours and days in intrigue and invective. One can also see how the feuding stimulated him and them to more effective accomplishment and kept every part of the relief and public works effort forever on its toes.

Sometimes the competitive theory could meet political needs too. Roosevelt, as the leader of a coalition, had to keep a variety of interests satisfied, or at least hopeful. What better way than to give each representation where decisions were made? Some agencies seemed to be staffed on the ancient Persian theory of placing men who did not trust each other side by side, their swords on the table. Everywhere there was the need to balance the right and the left—let Cohen and Corcoran write the act establishing the Securities and Exchange Commission, but let Joe Kennedy administer it, but flank him with Jim Landis and Ferdinand Pecora. Rather than sitting on creative vitality anywhere, give each faction something of a head and try to cope with the results. "He had an instinct," wrote Frances Perkins with insight, "for loose, self-directed activity on the part of many groups."

Competition in government, inadequately controlled, would mean anarchy. Adequately controlled, it could mean exceptional creativity. One consequence under the New Deal was a darkling plain of administrative confusion, where bureaucrats clashed by night. Another was a constant infusion of vitality and ideas. In a quieter time, when problems were routine, there would have been every reason to demand tight and tidy administration. But a time of crisis placed a premium on initiative and innovation—and on an organization of government which gave these qualities leeway and reward.

Getting bold and imaginative subordinates, however, by itself hardly solves the problems of execution. The worst error a President can make is to assume the automatic implementation of his own decisions. In certain respects, having able subordinates aggravates that problem, since strong personalities tend to have strong ideas of their own. Civil government operates by consent, not by command; the President's task, even within his own branch of government, is not to order but to lead. Students of public administration have never taken sufficient account of the capacity of lower levels of government to sabotage or defy even a masterful President. Somehow, through charm, cajolery, and the communication of ideals, as well as through pressure, discipline, and coercion, the President must make the Executive Branch *want* to carry out his policies.

The competitive approach to administration gave Roosevelt great advantages. It brought him an effective flow of information; it kept the reins of decision in his own hands; it made for administrative flexibility and stimulated subordinates to effective performance.

At the same time it exacted a price in morale. It placed those close to him under incessant strain. Even for men who could have operated in no other way, it was at best nerve-wracking and often positively demoralizing. Yet this too Roosevelt turned to his own purposes of control. Their insecurity gave him new opportunities for manipulation, which he exploited with cruel skill, while looking blandly in the opposite direction. He pretended not to know what was going on around him; but, said Tugwell, "those who knew his weakness for not grasping really nasty nettles knew from small signs that he was peeking through his fingers." In a way he liked the agony below: "he gave" said Cordell Hull a bit dolefully, "the impression almost of being a spectator looking on and enjoying the drama." "If he seemed to ignore the heaving bosoms presented to him," said Tugwell, "it did not mean that he did not know all about the agitation, or . . . did not enjoy it."

"You know," Harry Hopkins once said, "he is a little puckish." Puckish at times must have seemed an inadequate description. What Roosevelt could regard with equanimity from his place at the summit was often unbearable for those beneath. And it was not just that he seemed oblivious or entertained; at times he appeared to take a light and capricious pleasure in intensifying anxieties. His sometimes unfeeling ribbing of his associates expressed a thin streak of sadism of which he was intermittently aware and for which he was intermittently remorseful. "However genial his teasing," said Francis Biddle, "it was often . . . pointed with a prick of cruelty, because it went to the essence of a man, hit him between the ribs into the heart of his weakness, which might often be his unreasonable affection for his chief." Others shared Biddle's apprehension "that if we came too close I might suffer from his capacity to wound those who loved him."

No one came closer than Henry Morgenthau, and no one suffered more. Selfless devotion, as Biddle observed, sometimes became a bore; "one had to dissipate the irritation—the mild irritation—by stroking Henry against the grain in public now and then. One could not tease a man in private." Roosevelt himself once confessed to Morgenthau, "I was so tired that I would have enjoyed seeing you cry or would have gotten pleasure out of sticking pins into people and hurting them." As almost a member of the family, Morgenthau bore more than his share of Roosevelt's excess irritability. But the President had his way of tormenting everybody. Against others, indeed, the very closeness to Morgenthau was itself a weapon. The intimacy demonstrated in their weekly Monday luncheons created heartburning and indignation among other top officials who saw (or affected to see) nothing of talent or interest in the underrated Secretary of the Treasury. As Richberg said, "This relationship between the President and Secretary Morgenthau caused a great many jealousies." "For one thing," said Tugwell, "everyone else by contrast felt himself neglected; for another, no one could understand it."

And so the President went around the cabinet table. He played Ickes like an expert fisherman, giving him plenty of line, watching him fight and flap with fury and occasionally hauling him in. To each Attorney General he would at some point outline an objective and say: "If you are a good Attorney General tell me how I can do it." "They always give him a silly laugh," said Morgenthau, "and go out and tell him how to do it." He bypassed Hull, limited his relations to Farley, kept Wallace at arm's length, and blew hot and cold on a dozen others. "He watched his subordinates at their games," said Tugwell, "checked them when necessary, contributed to their build-up when it was convenient, reprimanded them effectively by non-recognition, rewarded them by intimacies."

No one ever could be sure where he stood. Ickes once burst out at him: "You are a wonderful person but you are one of the most difficult men to work with that I have ever known." Roosevelt said, "Because I get too hard at times?" "No," Ickes replied, "you never get too hard but you won't talk frankly even with people who are loyal to you and of whose loyalty you are fully convinced. You keep your cards close up against your belly. You never put them on the table." (Roosevelt, Ickes added, "took all of this frank talk in a perfectly friendly manner.")

As Roosevelt saw the Presidency, no President could ever afford to lay his cards on the table. His way of playing the game frightened his subordinates. He had a genius for being indirect with people. Nearly all around him had the chilling fear, generally shoved to the back of their minds, that he regarded them as expendable. As Frances Perkins said, "He reserved the right not to go out and rescue you if you got into trouble." "It was your battle," said Tugwell, "and you were expected to fight it. If you ran to the President with your troubles, he was affable and even, sometimes, vaguely encouraging, but he never said a public word in support." In a bitter moment, Jerome Frank proposed a principle of liberal politics: "A liberal leader can always count on the active support of certain persons, because of their belief in his major policies, regardless of how badly he treats them. (Item: Some of them are masochists who apparently work harder when they are ill-treated.) Therefore rewards should not be wastefully bestowed upon them but should be saved for potential enemies."

The more self-centered among Roosevelt's subordinates furiously resented this attitude and took it out on the President when their time came. The more philosophical regarded it as inevitable. "If this made you indignant," said Tugwell, "and it practically always did, there was nothing you could do and, when you thought it over, nothing of any use that you could say. The President was not a person; he was an institution. When he took political chances, he jeopardized not himself but the whole New Deal. And the New Deal could not afford to be responsible for practitioners who threatened its life—that is, who might lose it votes." It was up to the President to judge what endangered his essential objectives, and he made the judgment "in the recesses of his own considering apparatus which no one ever penetrated." Morgenthau, looking back, observed with insight, "He never let anybody around him have complete assurance that he would have the job tomorrow." Morgenthau added, "The thing that Roosevelt prided himself the most about was, 'I have to have a happy ship.' But he never had a happy ship."

Yet, as Morgenthau in other moods would freely admit, it was not altogether an unhappy ship either; for, if the manipulation of insecurity was part of Roosevelt's method, the provision of charm and consolation was an equally indispensable part. Probably no President was ever more skilled in the art of persuasion. He used every trick in the book, and most of them with the relish of a virtuoso. He had, as Biddle said, an intuitive grasp of people's weaknesses; and he employed this with stunning effect, not only to make them sad or scared, but to make them happy as well. As William Phillips put it, "He had a rare capacity for healing the wounded feelings which he had inadvertently caused." Roosevelt called this process "hand-holding." To it he devoted considerable energy and talent. "The maintenance of peace in his official family," Grace Tully reports, "took up hours and days of Roosevelt's time."

Hand-holding emerged as naturally from his complex personality as did the instinct to tease. His concern for people was perfectly spontaneous and genuine—and immensely disarming. After telling Morgenthau that he had been so tired he would have enjoyed seeing him cry, he added, "We both must take regular vacations . . . and never permit ourselves to get so tired again." Such messages were addressed again and again to all his associates. "When he detected signs of nerves or overwork," said Grace Tully, "he was quick to propose rest trips to Warm Springs or irregular vacations. More than once, he picked up substantial doctors' bills for members of his personal staff." Thus in January 1934 we find him urging Ickes and Wallace to go away. "He was quite insistent about it," Ickes reported. "He told me that it was beginning to worry him just to look at me and that if I didn't go away he would get mad." In May he ordered Wallace and Ickes to go to Santa Fe for a few days' rest ("This continued concern for my well-being," said Ickes, "really touched me"). In June, he ordered Hopkins on a trip abroad for his health. In December he wrote Richberg, "I am terribly sorry that you are still feeling so wretchedly and all I can do is to give you a definite order from old family Doctor Roosevelt. . . . Don't think about my 'problems' until you have a chance to come and talk them over with me." (Richberg commented, "The calming influence of such a communication as this can be imagined.")

He could not bear to fire anybody—perhaps his best noted and most conspicuous administrative failing. He shrank from disagreeable personal interviews and pronounced himself "a complete softy" in face-to-face relations. In 1936 he described as "probably much the hardest decision I have had to make since coming to Washington," not any great issue of domestic or foreign policy, but his failure to reappoint his old friends Adolph Miller and Charles Hamlin to the reconstituted Federal Reserve Board. In addition, he could hardly bear to have people resign. Harold Ickes, who resigned often, came fuming away from one conference with Roosevelt, "The reason I wanted to send in my resignation right away was because I was afraid the President would do just what he did do. He side-tracked me. It is almost impossible to come to grips with him." Richberg, another chronic resigner, once was defeated when Roosevelt said gently to him, "You aren't going to let the old man down, are you, Don?"; and was equally defeated another time when Roosevelt, who thought his grievance trivial, said satirically, "I have just had some bad news, Don. Secretary Hull is threatening to resign. He is very angry because I don't agree with him that we ought to remove the Ambassador to Kamchatka and make him third secretary to the Embassy at Svodia." ("I felt thoroughly chastened after this conversation," said Richberg, "and very grateful that the President had betrayed only friendly amusement instead of the stern displeasure which a Chief Executive with a poorer understanding of human nature or less of a sense of humor might well have shown.")

The President spent a good deal of time dealing with what he called his "prima donnas"—the people who felt neglected and kept demanding attention and sympathy. Ickes and Morgenthau, of course, were pre-eminent in the cabinet. The Secretary of the Interior, whom Roosevelt used to refer to privately as "Donald Duck," at times made himself so unbearable with his self-righteous insistence that Roosevelt for long periods avoided seeing him; at other times, the President soothed his hurt feelings with flattery. As for Morgenthau, if the Secretary of the Treasury took more punishment than most, he also received more balm. Once when Roosevelt was telling his staff how he wanted his naval prints in his office, Marvin McIntyre said, "You are right, Mr. President, you ought to have them hung to suit yourself. After all, you are in this office more than anyone else except Henry Morgenthau."

There were always minor personal squabbles requiring attention. Once Morgenthau denounced Ickes in cabinet for some jurisdictional transgression. Roosevelt scribbled on a piece of paper, "You must not talk in such a tone of voice to another cabinet officer," showed it to Morgenthau and tore it up. But the argument continued, Roosevelt finally saying, "Don't you understand, Henry, that Harold said he knows nothing about it and that ends the matter." Morgenthau replied, "I am afraid that I am very dull, Mr. President, I do not understand." Roosevelt answered coldly, "You must be very dull." That evening Roosevelt called Morgenthau and was, as Morgenthau put it in his diary, "most sympathetic and kind." He finished by saying, "Stop worrying, Henry, go to bed and get a good night's rest." He made a similarly tranquilizing call the same evening to Ickes, deprecated Morgenthau's attitude and hoped Ickes hadn't minded; "he was plainly," Ickes noted in *his* diary, "trying to apologize for Morgenthau." By such efforts, Roosevelt kept the peace.

There were other prima donnas. Roosevelt complained particularly about Joe Kennedy ("the trouble with Kennedy is you always have to hold his hand . . . he calls up and says he is hurt because I have not seen him") and Moley ("he usually gets upset once a month"); about Johnson and Richberg. Still, for all the irritation and drain, Roosevelt obviously enjoyed the role of assuming people's burdens and keeping them happy. John Gunther has perceptively noted that he liked to refer to himself as "Papa." After a speech or a press conference, he would say, "How did Papa do?"; or, to administrators, "If you do get into trouble, come back to Papa." Grace Tully heard him say more than once to subordinates, "All right, send it over to me. My shoulders are broad. I can carry the load." His doctor used to protest in vain that too many people ran to him with their problems. "Instead of giving these 'leaners' the boot," McIntyre later wrote, "the President encouraged them in the habit." "Instead of being vexed by appointees returning for advice and consultation," said George Creel, "he *loved* it."

At times he certainly did love it. At other times, as was often the case with this bewildering personality, he loved the opposite. Once, discoursing on the problem of prima donnas, Roosevelt held up Tugwell as an example to the contrary. No one, the President said, had been subjected to such criticism. "Yet Rex has never whimpered or asked for sympathy or run to anyone for help. He has taken it on the chin like a man." (Ickes, to whom this lesson was addressed, listened solemnly and wrote it all down later without supposing any application to himself.) Roosevelt liked Hopkins for the same reason.

And, indeed, for all his insistence on controlling big decisions and for all his fascination with detail, Roosevelt's intervention into the administrative affairs of his subordinates was rarely petty or nagging. He did, of course, constantly pass along ideas that struck his fancy, scribbling laconic chits on White House memo pads. But, in the main, he gave his appointees wide discretion—even to the point of overlooking their disregard of presidential directives—so long as they seemed on top of their responsibilities. (As one presidential assistant, Jonathan Daniels, commented, "Half of a President's suggestions, which theoretically carry the weight of orders, can be safely forgotten by a Cabinet member.") "He would give you a job to do," testified General Philip Fleming, who did a succession of jobs for him, "and leave you free to do it by yourself. He never told you how to do it." "He never meddled in Selective Service matters," said Lewis B. Hershey. "He gave me a job to do and he let me do it without ever breathing down my neck." "If he asked me to do something which in my opinion we could not or should not do—and that happened only a few times—" said Jesse Jones, "we just did not do it." As Frances Perkins put it, "He administered by the technique of friendship, encouragement and trust. The method of not giving direct and specific orders to his subordinates released the creative energy of many men." "He gives them a *blank check,*" said Frederic A. Delano, "and even when they nearly *ruin* him, he shows no outward evidence of anger. . . . On the whole his method has developed lots of men who otherwise would never have been heard from."

One way or another, he managed people. He was prepared to pay the price in time and temper to hold the loyalty of men of drive and ideas. Everyone who worked for him went through periods of disillusion and despair, questioned his integrity, contemplated bitter letters of resignation; in the end the President talked most of them around. "Never in my experience," said Colonel House, "have I known a man who could handle men as well as Roosevelt."

Yet it would be a great error to regard Roosevelt's success with people as essentially a triumph of technique. He was unquestionably a great operator; but he did not finally succeed because he was an operator. His greatest resource lay not in charm of manner or skill at persuasion. It lay in his ability to stir idealism in people's souls. "His capacity to inspire and encourage those who had to do tough, confused, and practically impossible jobs,' wrote Frances Perkins, "was beyond dispute. I, and everyone else, came away from an interview with the President feeling better." And his tendency to make himself personally felt on all levels of government, however destructive to orthodox theories of chain of command, had a wonderful effect in permeating the administration with his hopes and ideals. The President, instead of being a shrouded and remote figure at the peak of an unintelligible bureaucracy, was a leader whose personality and ethos touched and galvanized most officials of government.

Roosevelt had decided early that he wanted an inventive government rather than an orderly government. It was as if, given the need to arrive quickly at a destination, he chose, not a team of reliable work horses, but a miscellany of high-spirited and sensitive thoroughbreds. One sees him trying to ride herd over this rearing, tossing, jostling collection. His horses are overflowing with temperament, and he spends an unconscionable amount of time combing their manes, stroking their brows, and feeding them lumps of sugar. More tractable horses would not have pulled so far or run so fast. The proof of his control was the way, once the reins fell from his hand, the horses plunged wildly in all directions.

Yet the supervision of a government could not be altogether a personal matter. Roosevelt went as far as he could in trying to make it so. The fact remained that he was not driving a team of horses. He was attempting to run a great and multifarious country. The size and variety of the problems crowding in on him were bound to defeat him. There had to be some means beyond the personality of the President to bring coherence into the formulation of policy and coordination into its execution.

From an early point in his administration he played around with one after another person or structure hopefully designed to improve coordination among the departments and agencies. Indeed, the word coordinator had fallen into such disrepute as early as September 1933 that Louis Howe could sourly reassure Morgenthau, "Henry, when you have been in the Government service as long as I have, you will recognize that coordinators come and coordinators go, and that furthermore sometimes it is good business to place so much work on a man that he cannot handle any of it." The theoretical instrument of coordination during the first six months was a body known as the Executive Council, established on July 11, 1933, and composed of the heads of departments and agencies. Its executive secretary was Frank Walker, a Montana lawyer of exceptional evenness of temper and fairness of mind, deeply devoted to Roosevelt and always in demand as an arbiter in New Deal disputes. "Everyone trusted and liked him," Tugwell said. "He was one character in the New Deal cast without taint of self-interest, of ambition, or of vindictiveness." But what Walker possessed in sweetness he more than made up for by absence of force; and the Executive Council, though its weekly meetings superseded the Tuesday cabinet meeting, was largely ignored by the demonic administrators of the day, especially Johnson and Peek. Lacking both an agenda and aggressive leadership, it came to life only when the President attended it himself. As Johnson summed up its impact, "It left the situation about where it was before."

In November 1933, Roosevelt tried again, this time creating the National Emergency Council, a less inclusive body designed to coordinate the recovery agencies. Frank Walker was also its director. The National Emergency Council absorbed the Special Industrial Recovery Board and eventually (in October 1934) the Executive Council itself. At its first meeting, on December 19, 1933, Roosevelt explained that, when Congress was in session, he had "probably on the average of between three or four hours a day of conferences with congressional leaders" and consequently could not devote enough time to the administrative end of government. On the whole, he thought the recovery program was going along well; "it is quite remarkable to me that we have not had more overlapping and clashes"; but the time had come "when I have got to have somebody to act as sort of *alter ego* for me during the congressional session, going around and acting as my legs and ears and eyes and making certain—what might be called suggestions . . . working out these things in such a way that they will not come up to me during the session of Congress."

The National Emergency Council did at least have an agenda. But its membership—it rapidly grew from ten to thirty-three persons—was far too large for effective discussion; and its meetings consisted largely of the reading of mimeographed reports already rendered by the various agencies to the executive director. "I never saw a real question of major importance arise until the end of each of these meetings," wrote Johnson later, "when the President came in. . . . From the moment, things would begin to happen." This was certainly true. The minutes of the National Emergency Council remain, next to the press conferences, the most spectacular exhibit of Roosevelt's range and mastery in face of problems of governmental administration.

In the middle of 1934, Walker had to retire to look after his private affairs. Roosevelt, seeking to put new energy into his mechanisms of coordination, handed both of Walker's jobs on to Donald Richberg. Richberg, nervous and ambitious, was far more vigorous than Walker. At one time, according to Richberg, Roosevelt even contemplated appointing him to a new office, that of Assistant to the President. On

October 29, 1934, the Executive Council and the National Emergency Council were finally consolidated, with Richberg the apparent beneficiary in terms of power. *The New York Times* headline was typical of the reaction: RICHBERG PUT OVER CABINET IN NEW EMERGENCY COUNCIL . . . NOW NO. 1 MAN. Newspaper stories spoke of Richberg as Assistant President. Roosevelt was always jealous of the presidential prerogative; and his reaction was prompt and explosive. "Get hold of Krock," he said to Steve Early, "and tell him . . . that this kind of thing is not only a lie but that it is a deception and a fraud on the public. It is merely a continuation of previous lies such as the headlines that Moley was running the government; next that Baruch was Acting President; next that Johnson was the man in power; next that Frankfurter had been put over the Cabinet and now that Richberg has been put over the Cabinet. . . . This whole story is made out of whole cloth and illustrates why the public is believing less and less the alleged news columns of the newspapers." To the cabinet, which thoroughly shared Roosevelt's dismay, the President explained that Richberg was, in Ickes's rendition, no more than "an exalted messenger boy."

The National Emergency Council gradually built up a formidable administrative apparatus of its own. Each state had its own NEC director, and the Council soon developed a set of divisions to service its field operations. But in its formal operations the Council was dependent on the accuracy of the reports made to it. More and more, these became public relations blurbs rather than candid accounts of problems and difficulties. Furthermore, as the NEC grew in size, it became too unwieldy for frank exchange. "In the end," Roosevelt said, "I couldn't take it any more because I found myself making stump speeches to the council instead of listening to its members."

Still, certain tangible gains were made toward coordination. The President found the weekly meetings useful in amplifying his "feel" of things in government. "The whole NEC," he once said, "was a wonderful essay in democracy. It was exactly like a New England town meeting. It gave everybody a chance to blow off. I learned many things there—many things that those who were reporting never suspected that I learned and some that they wouldn't have liked me to know anything about. They also learned a lot about each other."

In a more specific sense, the NEC enabled the President to begin to gain control of the administration's legislative program by providing for central clearance of all legislative proposals coming out of the Executive Branch. All requests for appropriations, he said, should go through the Bureau of the Budget, all requests for new legislation through the NEC. During the previous session, he explained in 1934, he had been "quite horrified—not once but half a dozen times—by reading in the paper that some department or agency was after this, that, or the other without my knowledge." "If you are going to ask for any legislative action," he continued, "it has got to come through Donald Richberg and up to me if necessary."

Roosevelt was perfectly frank about his purposes. Legislative proposals, as he explained to a later meeting of the Council, fell from his point of view into three categories: those which he could not possibly support; those which the department or agency might press for but could not be adopted as major administration bills; and the so-called *must* legislation, to which "I have to confine myself." "If I make every bill that the Government is interested in *must* legislation, it is going to complicate things. . . . Where I clear legislation with a notation that says 'no objection,' that means you are at perfect liberty to try to get the thing through, but I am not going to send a special message. It is all your trouble, not mine." Centralized clearance through the Council and the Budget, in other words, was an essential means by which the President preserved his initiative and defended his authority.

The new system was by no means an immediate success. The President, indeed, was in practice one of its main saboteurs. Thus few major bills in the 74th Congress passed through the new machinery. The President even on occasion thwarted the Budget's attempt to bring order into the allocation of funds already voted. Morgenthau describes, without too much exaggeration, an incident early in 1935: "He assured me and Harry Hopkins that he would not allot any more money until we had another meeting. I understand a couple of weeks ago he allotted Hopkins $125,000,000 secretly. Next Tugwell appeals to him directly and he gives him what he wants. The result is that everybody is angry and frothing at the mouth. Then when I draw his attention to it, instead of doing the straightforward thing and cancelling Tugwell's authorization which could not have yet reached him, he doublecrosses Tugwell by telling me to tell Bell [the Director of the Budget] that Tugwell cannot have one cent until the Budget passes on it. This makes a complete circle and everybody will be sore." Morgenthau added, "This is so typical of the President."

Nevertheless, the National Emergency Council established certain principles; and these principles, in time, created precedents which in a few years, as the Bureau of the Budget increased its power, were converted into practices. Though the Council itself, especially after Richberg's departure from government in 1935, withered away, it left its imprint on the Roosevelt administration in the shape of a new desire for the unification of policy.

Still, the first experiments in structural coordination failed. Lacking a mechanism, or, to put it more precisely, disliking a mechanism, Roosevelt fell back on people as the means of coordination. From time to time, he would talk about the existence of an "inner Cabinet." In late 1934 he defined it to Ickes as Morgenthau, Cummings, Ickes, Miss Perkins, Wallace, Hopkins, Chester Davis, and the man who would head NRA. But even this was too cumbersome a group for his purposes. As a lone operator, Roosevelt could best find the extension of his personality—the long sought *alter ego*—in an individual. And, as a lonely man, Roosevelt could best find the intimacy of exchange he occasionally needed not in a council but in a person.

Howe, of course, had been that *alter ego* for many years. But age, ill health, and new issues outmoded him by the time Roosevelt reached the White House. The President thereafter looked endlessly for a substitute. As Eleanor Roosevelt commented, "For one reason or another, no one quite filled the void which unconsciously he was seeking to fill; and each one in turn disappeared from the scene, occasionally with a bitterness which I understood but always regretted."

Moley was the first to come and the first to go. Even after he left the government to become editor of *Today*, he continued throughout 1934 and 1935 to visit the

White House and to work on speeches. Yet he began increasingly to doubt the new directions of the New Deal; and he regarded himself—and Roosevelt regarded him—less and less as a confidant on policy. "I was summoned, in such cases," Moley later wrote, "as a technician at speech construction, just as I'd be called in if I were a plumber and a pipe needed fixing." He came in time to take a perverse pride in giving forceful expression to ideas with which he disagreed.

In 1934 Tugwell began to take Moley's place as policy confidant. Tugwell lacked Moley's skill as a middleman of ideas and as an organizer of talent. However, his brow rarely needed to be stroked, and his loyalty was invincible. By Tugwell's theory of discipline, he must follow Roosevelt whether or not he agreed; "nothing could be done at all unless we hung together under a leader . . . we had no real right to make [independent] judgments." Tugwell had, in addition, a glowing enthusiasm for the forests and the land and for America as a great estate, to be nurtured and cherished; this passion was, of course, deep in the President, and it was something he shared with few of his urbanized associates. Above all, at precisely this moment, before the horizons of possibility had really begun to close in, Roosevelt was probably drawn by the challenging, questioning bent of Tugwell's mind, forever stimulating the presidential imagination to new visions of things to be done. "There was nothing we could not discuss with him," said Tugwell in retrospect of 1933 and 1944, "and the opportunities were sufficient for the purpose."

Tugwell was perhaps the least pliant of the Roosevelt intimates. He conceived his role, not to try and find out what the President wanted, but to tell him what he ought to want—to serve as a sort of conscience, representing to Roosevelt his "more consistent self." Standing for coordination in economic policy, he tried always to use the logic of coordination as the measure of the New Deal. Looking back, Tugwell felt that he must sometimes have seemed insistent and stubborn. "He must have had many impatient hours with me. [Yet] he seldom showed any irritation." In 1935, however, the philosophy of coordination began to recede. Tugwell, moreover, had none of Moley's facility as a speech technician to keep him useful beyond his time. His new assignment as head of the Resettlement Administration occupied him more; and, with a mutually delicate appreciation of the changed situation, he and the President talked less, though their friendship remained undiminished.

For the present, Roosevelt himself, as the essential ganglion for reception, transmission, and realization, had to serve as the substitute for a structure of coordination. He did it with zest and energy. His instinct for the basic general issue, his flypaper mastery of detail, his capacity to carry a large variety of problems in his mind, his ability to shift with speed from one problem to another, his appetite for long hours of plain hard work, his "vast and gracious tolerance" (in a phrase of Adolf Berle's) for a whole series of forces and people, from the noble to the self-seeking and from the decent to the corrupt—all this enabled him to stay more or less ahead of crisis. Perhaps he could have done it in no other manner. "He, more than any man," wrote Hugh Johnson, "is almost utterly incapable of acting organizationally or any other way than individually." He succeeded, said Johnson, "not as a master of planning or knowledge, but as a master of dexterity."

An account of his Presidency which deals topically with the problems Roosevelt confronted . . . does scant justice to his skill as an executive. To visualize Roosevelt in action, one must conceive these things happening all at once, in chaos and urgency, from NRA, AAA, relief, conservation, and monetary policy to disarmament, the Good Neighbor policy, Manchuria, Ethiopia, and Hitler, an incessant series of explosions, minor and major, at the presidential desk, with the President nearly always in touch, generally in command, and never disturbed. His patience, his personal solicitude, his fantastic grasp of detail, his instinct for timing, his jocose and evasive humor, his lightheartedness, his disingenuousness, his reserve, his serenity, his occasional and formidable severity, his sense of his office, his sense of history— these were the means by which he ordered and dominated the crises of his administration. One understands why most who worked for him had to burst out from time to time against him. But one understands too why most of them submerged indignation in a larger sense of admiration. In the end, one doubts whether the Presidency can ever be effectively bureaucratized. Its essence is an independence, initiative, and creativity which requires and relies on its own lines of communication to the world outside. Vigorous government under the American system would seem almost impossible without something like the Rooseveltian sleight-of-hand at the center.

Harold Smith, who became the Director of the Budget in 1939 and shared his Bureau's prejudices in favor of order and symmetry in government, once reflected on Roosevelt's concept of administration. Nothing had seemed more maddening at the time, but in retrospect Smith wondered whether Roosevelt's apparently erratic methods did not produce exceptional results. "I think I'd say," Smith concluded, "that Roosevelt must have been one of the greatest geniuses as an administrator that ever lived. What we couldn't appreciate at the time was the fact that he was a real *artist* in government."

2
HARRY S. TRUMAN

1945-1952

Harry S. Truman and all those around him were acutely conscious of the fact that the Roosevelt Presidency was a difficult act to follow. It was certainly not until Truman's stunning upset victory in the election of 1948 that serious commentators in Washington began to pay closer attention to the distinctive features of his own administrative style, of which the most remarkable was orderliness (which his predecessor did not value) harnessed to an appetite for decision (which his successor did not share). By this historical coincidence, the Truman Presidency spanned the Roosevelt and Eisenhower years, inheriting a Presidency that was at the center of things and handing on a rationalized structure that could be used to protect as well as engage a President.

It is fashionable in these days to attack the Truman Presidency from the left, because Truman was President during the height of the cold war. In Truman's time, Stalin was still the ruler of the USSR. The urge among Americans swiftly to demobilize the armies they had raised to fight World War II was overwhelming. We withdrew from a Europe that nearly a decade of hostilities had devastated, leaving behind shaky economies, divided polities, and the Red Army.

This is not the place to argue the ultimate merits of such significant policy innovations as postwar aid to Greece and

Turkey, the Marshall Plan, or other manifestations of what is now looked upon dismissively in some quarters as "cold-war diplomacy." Americans have often thought themselves the only force in world history. In Truman's time this was expressed in ardent right-wing attacks on the President and his Secretary of State for "losing" China. The illuminations of our present day insist that America caused the cold war in international affairs, and at home McCarthyism was not caused by McCarthy and his friends, but rather by two of those McCarthy sought for his victims, namely, Harry Truman and his Secretary of State, Dean Acheson.

Students should be alert to the existence of this latter-day view, lest they be taken in by the remarkable affection Truman inspired in those who were close to his administration, sentiments such as are expressed in the three selections printed herewith. Truman's strengths and his weaknesses as a President and as a person were not hard for his contemporaries to spot, especially as compared with his complex, charming, cynical, play-acting predecessor. As Roosevelt drew advantages from his complexity, Truman drew strength from his simplicity. In office he became the embodiment of an authentic American type: straightforward, tough, and dutiful. This, at least, is what two brilliant and learned contemporary Washington journalists, Eric Sevareid and Elmer Davis, saw in him, and this image can also be found in Dean Acheson's moving recollection. The final selections, by writer John Hersey, are an elaborate circumstantial account of the routines of the Presidency under Truman, an account that illustrates in some detail the qualities in Truman as President that the other writers discuss.

Harry S. Truman and the Verdict of History
ELMER DAVIS

As Harry S. Truman goes out of office on January 20, the editorial pages of the eighty per cent of American newspapers that opposed him will probably be filled with anticipations of the Golden Age about to dawn. But they will doubtless devote some attention also to the protagonist who is leaving the stage. Most of them will probably say they are glad he is going, in language ranging from decorous gratification to obscene howls of joy. Some may attempt to estimate his achievement, or the lack of it; but the judicious may well leave such assessment as he himself hopes it will be left—to the verdict of history.

What history? Whose? And when? If Hitler had won the late war, Dr. Goebbels would have supervised the writing of the histories, and nobody would ever have known what happened. If Stalin should win another one (which I do not expect), Ilya Ehrenburg or somebody of the sort would be entrusted with rearranging the sequence and motivation of events in a manner of which the late trials in Prague have given us an example.

But in the countries where thought is still free it usually, and properly, manifests that freedom in disagreement. After two thousand years, historians are by no means unanimous as to the merits of Julius Caesar; was he plus or minus, net? (I think plus, if anybody cares.) At the moment there is pretty general agreement that Caesar Augustus was distinctly plus; but a hundred or two hundred years ago most people regarded him as a tyrant who had abolished liberty—failing to realize that the only liberties he had even constricted were those of the Roman equivalent of the once-famous American Liberty League.

In our own history, the verdict of the jury seems unanimous on Washington and Lincoln—for the moment. Yet within the last few years a book was published which endeavored to show that Washington was never interested in public affairs except when his own pocketbook was affected; and I have no doubt that somewhere there lurk unpublished manuscripts which maintain that Lincoln was just another snollygoster. With even a minor turn in public opinion, they might get into print.

HISTORIANS WORKING; DON'T DISTURB

Which is to say that history is written by members of the human race, who have their share of the emotional predilections of all humanity—modified, it may be hoped, by their training in evaluating evidence, but seldom entirely expunged. Our Federalists, when they could no longer make history, got their revenge by turning to the writing of history, and they dominated American historiography through most of

From *The Reporter* (February 3, 1953), pp. 17-22. Copyright 1953 by Fortnightly Publishing Company, Inc. Reprinted by permission.

the nineteenth century; the Jacksonians were too busy making history to notice them, and by the time people did notice them, the climate of dominant opinion was again Federalistically inclined. We have the greatest difficulty in finding out what happened in Rome in the third century A.D. because the surviving histories were written in the fourth century by hangers-on of a Senate which by that time was no more than a disregarded Fronde; the Emperors, facing an increasingly impossible job, were too busy making history to worry about their reputations in future centuries.

Eduard Meyer wrote the history of Athens and Sparta in terms of Prussia and Austria, with Themistocles as a Bismarck *manque;* as a work of art it is magnificent, but one cannot help wondering what really happened. The great Dr. Toynbee has predicted that three thousand years from now, what will mainly interest historians in our age is its religious sentiments. If that is so they won't have much to write about; but nobody can now prove that Toynbee is wrong.

And underlying all these variations in historiography due to personal inclinations or to the intellectual and emotional climate of an age is the one great constant that will be with us so long as thought is free: the necessity that confronts each successive generation of historians of making its reputation by proving that its predecessors were wrong. That impelling need has been responsible for many advances in human knowledge, also for a considerable number of wanderings on wrong tracks.

So the verdict of history on Harry Truman in 1953 is about as likely to be right—provided it is an attempt at history and not a partisan editorial—as the verdict of 1983, or 2353, for that matter. It is true that in the course of decades more documentation will come to light, but unless it is documentation from the Kremlin it will be of minor importance. It is possible that Stalin does not keep notes and memoranda—the imprudence of the Nazis in setting down all their skulduggery on paper should have been a warning; and it is doubtful if any other member of the Politburo could trust his secretary, his valet, or even his wife enough to keep them. Anyway, if notes are kept, they are unlikely to survive the eventual collapse of the Kremlin organization, whether from external or internal causes. (And if, contrary to expectation, we and not they collapse, none of this will matter.)

As for yet-unpublished material in American government archives, it is hard to imagine what there is left to say. In the MacArthur hearings a year ago last spring, the Secretary of State, the Joint Chiefs of Staff, and everybody else of importance (except the President) in the executive branch of the government lay down on the couch of the Senatorial psychoanalysts and said everything that came to mind in free association. If any detail of American diplomatic and military thinking, or the reasons therefor, was omitted, it was only because no Senator thought to ask about it. Our recent history could be summarized in that sentence with which the Victorian novelist used to commence his final chapter—"Little remains to be told."

"THE TWO TRUMANS"

The reasonably objective attempts to estimate Harry Truman, as of 1953, are so similar that they express themselves in paradoxes that have become cliches. There are two Trumans—the White House Truman and the courthouse Truman. He does the big things right, and the little things wrong. He has a high conception of the dignity and prestige of the Presidential office, yet he lowers it by his occasional outbursts at news conferences and by those famous letters.

I would not question the general validity of these estimates. Still, the estimates seem to me to require modification and adjustment.

Take the last item first—the letters. I am told on good authority that he wrote them (by hand) before breakfast, when no man is at his most judicious, and slipped them into the mailbox himself before anybody had a chance to say, "Wait—are you sure you really want to say that?"

Yet some of those letters, which nobody has rushed into print, are of a very different sort—letters such as perhaps no President since Lincoln would have thought of writing. Add them all up and you have a man who, in becoming President, did not cease to be a member of the human race; if you cut him he bled, and if you cut him too deep he was likely to slash back, whether it was wise to do so or not. But he retained more amiable human sentiments too.

One of Mr. Truman's chief advisers has told me that perhaps his greatest accomplishment has been that he "institutionalized" the Presidency. He could not institutionalize responsibility; but he could do, and he has done, a great deal to see that the President has thorough information and competent advice before he exercises that responsibility. It is to some extent true that many of these institutions merely take the place of Harry Hopkins, who did most of their work for Roosevelt; but you are not going to get a Hopkins very often, and it only makes sense to try to provide that any President shall have the best possible substitutes.

Not all of these institutions work as well as they should. The National Security Resources Board should be important, and apparently was intended to be; but it had hardly got started before it was overlaid by the Office of Defense Mobilization, and it has hardly been able to get its breath ever since.

The Council of Economic Advisers was an excellent idea, but any President is likely to pick advisers with whose economics he agrees beforehand. If not, the advisers may give up and quit, as did Dr. Edwin Nourse.

Potentially the most important of all is the National Security Council. In emergencies it can work fast, as it did in the Korean crisis, but normally the flow of policy decisions through its channels is viscous indeed. Most of its members are heads of departments; usually being busy running their departments, they have to delegate their duties on the Council; often the delegates subdelegate, and so on. So General Eisenhower was (or seemed to have been during the campaign) converted to a proposal that had several times been advanced by private citizens—that the

National Security Council should be enlarged by the appointment of two or three more members who would have nothing to do but sit and think about the most basically important national problems. But the results of their thinking, when translated into policy, would have to be carried out by the operating heads of departments; and suppose these men do not agree with the policies evolved by the thinkers? Anyone who has ever worked in government knows how much foot-dragging there can be before an overworked President has time to notice it.

A similar reform has been proposed for the Joint Chiefs of Staff by Dr. Vannevar Bush, who knows as much as anybody about the way our government actually works. At present three of the four Joint Chiefs are the operating heads of the armed services, with a chairman who has great prestige but no vote and—at least as spelled out by statute—no power. Actually the present chairman, General Omar N. Bradley, seems to have been principally useful by informally performing the functions of a no longer existent post, Chief of Staff to the Commander in Chief, which was held by his wartime predecessor Admiral William D. Leahy. Dr. Bush truly observes that the heads of the Army, the Navy, and the Air Force have full-time jobs running their services; let them be replaced on the Joint Chiefs by senior officers about to retire who can sit and think. But suppose the results of their thinking do not commend themselves to the operating chiefs who would have to carry them out; suppose the things the operating chiefs feel they must do serve to create a policy that has not been digested and approved by the thinkers?

This is the old hiatus between policy and operations that has probably been a problem of government ever since the days of Cheops and Lugalzaggisi. Unless our descendants are wiser than we are, it may still be a problem of government when Dr. Toynbee's fiftieth-century scholars are turning to the lighter task of recording and analyzing the religious sentiments of our times. All that can be said is that Mr. Truman has created a good deal of machinery which ought to make it easier for any President to reach sound and well-informed decisions. His successor may thank him for it, unless Sherman Adams should turn out to be another Hopkins.

WHITE HOUSE AND COURTHOUSE

Now for the Great Antithesis—the White House Truman and the courthouse Truman—the Kansas City politician who worked his way up in an unsavory machine, remaining personally untarnished but acquiring an acute reluctance to admit that his associates could do anything wrong; and who, after some years of service in the Senate, suddenly found himself the Chief of State and chief of government of the most powerful nation in the free world, not long before it became evident that the modus vivendi between the free and the non-free worlds was breaking down. And who, as he faced these stupefying responsibilities, brought into his immediate entourage some of his associates of his courthouse days; who in turn, whatever their faults or virtues, retained the limitations of the courthouse.

Nobody could have predicted seven years ago that the White House Truman would succeed in pulling the world together when it was in grave danger of coming apart, while the courthouse Truman would be unsuccessful, even by courthouse standards. He did indeed get himself re-elected, and he did so by a very able display of the higher type of politics. With that faith in the people which is one of his most profound and genuine emotions, he took his argument to the people; he had a good story to tell—the record of the Eightieth Congress—and he told it effectively.

But four years later the formula no longer worked. Maybe it could not have worked, against the glamour of a great military hero who promised everything, and under the increasing burden of a party too long in power. But that burden had become heavier in four years than the mere lapse of time would justify; the Democratic Administration had grown tired and lax—in some spots shabby, and in some spots worse than that.

There will always be some corruption in government, and there has been much less than was alleged in the past four years. But there was too much, more than usual; and it was concentrated in the departments which above all others should be free from it, the money agencies and the administration of justice. There would have been less if Harry Truman had not had in unusual degree the normal human reluctance to believe ill of his friends, or even of their friends.

When Senator Fulbright found evidence of grave misdoing in the Reconstruction Finance Corporation, he took it to the White House to give the President a chance to clean it up. The President refused to believe that a clean-up was needed, and when the Fulbright Report was published he called it asinine. Eventually he had to clean it up; he put in Stuart Symington, who handled the situation promptly and effectively, took away a reproach, and got no thanks for it. For when Symington went after the Democratic nomination for Senator from Missouri, Truman supported his opponent— an old friend and associate whom he may have felt he had to support, but he might at least have said something kind about Symington's public services. Symington was nominated and elected, and the net result was a serious blow to the President's prestige in his home state. Not good, even by courthouse standards. Nor did the President remove those men around him whose behavior, though not criminal, had made them obvious political liabilities. (Congress, of course, did nothing about its members who were touched by the various scandals; but nobody ever expected Congress to do anything.)

ALL OR NOTHING

All in all, in domestic affairs Mr. Truman has been an unsuccessful President. The first great setback, the Congressional election of 1946, could not perhaps have been avoided in a nation then hell-bent for "normalcy." That calamity Mr. Truman succeeded in retrieving two years later (with considerable help from the Congress elected in 1946); and he presented to the new Congress a liberal program which was coherent and logical as the New Deal had never been. Congress, not being liberal, refused to take it; yet every year he persisted in offering it all to them again, and they still wouldn't take it. Lincoln, in such a situation, would have astutely judged how much of his program he could get with smart management and would have played off one group against another so as to get some of it at least. Truman kept asking for all of it and getting none of it.

His enemies, of course, maintained and perhaps believed that he wanted to keep it in dispute, as a winning platform for the next election. I doubt that, but I am not privy to his motives. Whatever the motive may have been, his behavior didn't look to me like smart politics. If it seems so to any generation of future historians, they will be judging by standards incommensurable with ours.

But as time went on, domestic issues were increasingly overshadowed by foreign affairs; and there the White House Truman shone ever more brightly.

We had seen that Truman earlier, on a different issue. When in 1946 the Republicans regained control of both houses of Congress, it was generally taken as a forecast of what would happen in the next Presidential election. After a year and a half of Truman the nation had had enough of him; let him resign, as would a British Prime Minister after a similar vote of want of confidence, and turn the Administration over to the Republicans. So argued, among others, Senator Fulbright (which may explain why Truman was disinclined to listen to him later, when Fulbright happened to be right).

For a mere politician this would have offered an opportunity to throw the Opposition into utter confusion. As the law then stood, the Secretary of State was next in the line of Presidential succession, there being no Vice-President; all the President had to do was persuade Secretary Byrnes to resign, which he did a few weeks later anyway, and offer to appoint in his place any man whom the Republicans might choose as the successor to the Presidency. Party machinery offers no method of making such a selection, except the quadrennial national convention; there would have been a dogfight among half a dozen competitors, which might well have ended with the President announcing that he must reluctantly retain the office, since the Opposition was not harmonious enough to select a man to take his place.

But he said he would not resign; nor did he accept the innocent though no doubt well-meant suggestion of the Washington *Post* that he appoint a Republican Cabinet and content himself with signing its decrees, with no more power than a President of the French Republic theoretically enjoys, and considerably less influence than President Auriol has actually been able to exercise.

Mr. Truman knows American history; he knows how the Constitution was made and why; and he chose to stick by the Constitution rather than amend it by his own action under the pressure of the Republicans' civic ardor. (Such a resignation might easily have set a precedent; the Canadian Constitution says nothing about the Prime Minister's being dependent on a majority of the House of Commons, but he is.) Our form of government might have been completely changed, and without going through the deliberate process which the Constitution prescribes for such changes, except for the fact that Harry Truman could not be pushed around.

FIRST-RATE AND THIRD-BEST

Mr. Truman's loyalty to his friends has been responsible for much of his trouble, but it has its good side. He not only stood by Donald Dawson and Merl Young and Harry Vaughan; he stood by Dean Acheson, against such a storm of abuse as no Secretary of State since Seward has had to face. (Seward, so copiously damned in his time, is by the current verdict of history the second-best Secretary of State we ever had; my guess is that Acheson will be recorded as third-best, by at least some generations of future historians.) Mr. Truman, replacing Stettinius in the State Department, made a bad choice to start with in Jimmy Byrnes; but he followed him with Marshall, and Marshall with Acheson, and it is hard to see how he could have done better. Except, of course, in the opinion of those who hold that anything he did was wrong. That view, widely advocated last fall, may be modified now that the election is over and the Crusaders, so often disappointed, have at last surmounted the walls of Jerusalem.

The modus vivendi with Russia which Mr. Roosevelt hoped he had established—though that hope had begun to fade just before his death—fell apart during the first year of Mr. Truman's Presidency; but what that implied did not become apparent till the end of February, 1947, when the British suddenly declared that they couldn't carry Greece and Turkey any longer, and somebody else would have to pick them up if they were to be carried at all. This was such a decision as the United States had never had to face in peacetime, and Harry Truman stood up to it.

I do not know who was responsible for his generalizing that decision into its logical conclusion—that "it must be the policy of the United States to support free peoples who are resisting attempted subjugation by armed minorities or by outside pressures"; but it *was* the logical conclusion, even though we were then by no means prepared to live up to such a spacious commitment.

We did live up to the immediate commitment to Greece and Turkey—ultimately with complete success, though we owed that in large measure to a break of luck, the excommunication of Tito. Later it was argued that this principle required us to give all-out aid to Chiang Kai-shek; the argument had logic behind it, but it conveniently ignored the fact that China is fifty times as big as Greece.

After the Truman Doctrine, the Marshall Plan. During the late campaign the Republicans sometimes pointed out that after all it was adopted by the Eightieth Congress; so it was, and the credit belongs in about equal measure to Arthur Vandenberg and to Joe Stalin, who seized Czechoslovakia at just the right moment to make most of even the most myopic Congressmen realize that something had better be done.

Also, however, it was denounced in the late campaign as a giveaway program, as buying friends; but this seemed halfhearted. It had too obviously pulled western Europe out of a ditch into which it was rapidly slipping; all they could say against it was that it proved not to be enough and had to be supplemented by NATO; and not much could be said against NATO, in view of General Eisenhower's immense contribution to its success. Attacks on foreign policy had to be mostly centered on Asia, where, visibly, we had not been successful. We had lost China—or sold China, depending on the conscience of the man who was doing the talking; and few people ever bothered to ask how China had come to be ours to lose or to keep.

For that matter, few members of Congress who damned our Far Eastern policy ever said whether or not they would have voted for the extensive recommendations of the Wedemeyer Report if it had not been withheld from publication for two years out of consideration for Chiang Kai-shek's feelings; still less whether they would have voted for whatever else might have been necessary to "save China" if the Wedemeyer recommendations had not been enough.

STOPPING THE MARCH

However, China had not been saved, by us or by the Chinese; meanwhile there was "Truman's war" in Korea to talk about. . . . It is hard to remember back, now, to June 25, 1950. Here the familiar parade was starting again—Ethiopia, the Rhineland, Austria, the Sudetenland, Czechoslovakia. Then, it could have been stopped in time; did anybody remember that in 1950? Some men did; including the man who had to make the decision.

While I do not know, I doubt that on that June night either Mr. Truman, Acheson, Louis Johnson, General Bradley, or even the infallible Douglas MacArthur knew how much of a war we were getting into. The original idea of mere sea and air support to Republic of Korea troops looks not so much like adherence to a strategic doctrine which Taft and Hoover adopted after its fallacy had been proved (as it had not been then) as like a conviction that this demonstration of American power would be enough to cow the lesser breeds without the law.

Unfortunately it was not enough. And if they had realized that they were getting into a war which would absorb a third of American ground and air power and would still be undecided after two and a half years—a war whose inconclusiveness would win an election for the Republicans—would they have gone in anyway?

I think they would. For they all knew what it would have meant if Communist conquest of another nation had gone unresisted. Every nation on the borders of the Communist world would have wondered, "Are we next?"—and they would have had no hope that anybody would help them.

Also they all knew—even MacArthur—what it would have meant to have Communism on the Straits of Tsushima, ten minutes by jet plane from a Japan which would have felt that it stood not only defenseless but alone. Even Eisenhower, in the late campaign, said that the decision to fight in Korea was right, though he felt it necessary to bow in the House of Rimmon by talking about the disastrous policy blunders that made the Korean War possible.

The greatest moment in Eisenhower's life, it would seem, was when he made the command decision to go ahead with the once-postponed Normandy landings in the justified hope that the more optimistic weather reports were right. The greatest moment in Truman's life—greater even than the moment of decision to support Greece and Turkey—was the moment when he decided: If we don't stop this thing now, we may never be able to stop it.

This, it seems safe to say, will be the verdict of history—some history, at some time in the future; but the next generation of Ph.D.s will overturn it, with conclusions which themselves will in due course be proved erroneous.

JACKSON? POLK?

One estimate made by some of Mr. Truman's admirers can be discounted now. Among his predecessors the one he seems most to admire is Andrew Jackson; and it has been said that if he is not a Jackson, he is at least a Polk. Well—he could ask little better, for James K. Polk was one of the most dazzlingly successful Presidents we ever had, though the vagaries of historiography have kept most people from realizing it. He got the principal measures of his domestic program enacted into law; he fought and won a war, and honorably avoided another war that he might not have won; and he extended our frontier to the Pacific, adding several hundred thousand square miles to the territory of the United States. Truman can record no such successes as that.

Polk had Truman's firmness; he also had a lot of luck. Once or twice, when the percentage favored a finesse, he banged down his ace and caught the lone king. He was at the head of a still fairly well united party; it began to go to pieces in his day, but it lasted long enough for him to get his domestic measures through. He won the Mexican War pretty much by main strength and awkwardness. (Truman would have been utterly incapable of an idea Polk once considered, of appointing a Democratic Senator with next to no military experience as commander of the Army simply because the generals who were winning battles belonged to the Opposition party.)

Polk showed at his best, perhaps, in the negotiations with England over Oregon. He bluffed hard, convinced that the English were bluffing too; eventually they quit raising him and then he compromised on the present boundary, which previous Administrations had been willing to accept. Such a settlement today would be denounced as appeasement and was denounced then as its equivalent in the idiom of the time. But we were just getting into another war, and even most of the war hawks had sense enough to realize that we couldn't manage two at once.

But the England of 1846 was no such antagonist as the Russia of 1950—if for no other reason than because there were still major powers on the continent of Europe; and English involvement in a large-scale war in North America would have weakened England's influence in European affairs gravely. Also England was a power which by definition and ideology could compromise; as no Communist power can, except as a matter of temporary tactics.

A CENTURY LATER

Truman confronted the only other strong power in the world at a time when not only the American people but every other people in the world that had anything to say about what was going to happen was war-weary; most of them were willing to do almost anything to avoid another conflict. At the end of seven years, somebody had "lost" China—maybe we did it, maybe the people who had China to lose. But nobody had lost Greece, or Turkey, or France, or Italy; and it is extremely probable that they would have been lost but for Mr. Truman's interventions. Nobody had lost the part of Korea that was free when he came in; and nobody had lost Japan, which would pretty surely have gone if the Communists had conquered Korea.

JOHN FOSTER JOSHUA

He was telling the simple truth when he told the Alumni Association of the Industrial College for the Armed Forces, in December, that thanks to the policies of his Administration hundreds of millions of people are living in freedom instead of in slavery. The Republican platform, however, denounced this as "the cowardly and futile policy of containment," and one understands that all this is now to be changed. The man who damned containment as cowardly and futile is to become Secretary of State; he has promised us a new policy which will be affirmative, dynamic, and at the same time absolutely safe; and it won't cost us a nickel.

All we need is a sense of mission and purpose; then moral and spiritual forces will penetrate into the minds and souls of those under the ruthless control of the Soviet Communist structure, and the edifice of despotism will surely crumble. Just a few toots on the trumpet, and the walls of the Kremlin will come tumbling down.

Amen; let us all hope Mr. Dulles is right, for if he is we shall all share in the benefits. A world in which there was no tyranny and no danger of war would be a far happier as well as a far less expensive world; I shall be out there leading the cheering when the stonework of the edifice of despotism crumbles to dust, leaving the free peoples of the world to build them more stately mansions in its place.

But somebody had to lay the foundations on which those more stately mansions will be erected, even if he gets no credit for the architecture of the completed structure. In my judgment, it will be the verdict of a good many generations of future historians that the man who laid the foundations was Harry S. Truman; even though each of those generations will be succeeded by another whose duty it will be to earn its reputation by proving that its immediate predecessors were all wrong.

The Man in the White House
ERIC SEVAREID

Like any headquarters away from the lines, this capital city deals in abstractions, with what men think, write, and say—not in visible realities that they touch and see. And so it is a place constantly agitated by intellectual contagions; gossip and speculation blow this way, then that, depending upon the events of the moment that set the breezes in motion. Right now the talk in semiofficial circles—or what my friend Elmer Davis, in a fit of boredom, once called official semicircles—the talk centers on the President. Because of his sojourn at Key West, it centers on the President's personal condition. Because of the new 22nd Amendment, on the President's future prospects.

Harry Truman has held the office, now, almost an even six years, a confused period of great successes as President, and considerable failures; the period of the great disillusionment with the world peace he had expected to preside over in tranquillity; a confused, baffling period that has been neither peace nor war, a period unlike any that a previous President has had to manage through; a time in which any one of a dozen policies might be the right one, and yet a time in which any basic misstep could produce fruits of evil such as mankind has never suffered; a time in which the quality of any given ally has been extremely difficult to figure, and the real intentions of the one potential enemy quite impossible to calculate for sure. Six years of constant maneuvering on the world stage, with the whole future at stake but—in the nature of things—with very few immediate results to show, that people can see and feel.

But what about the President himself, after this extraordinary experience of hopes and fears and ceaseless pressures? In the bedrock of his nature, it seems to this observer, Harry Truman remains the man he was. Essentially a happy man, a positive personality, with a gift for friendship, clinging to the concept that was never even questioned in the time of his youth—the idea that there is progress in human affairs, the concept that in the end life "turns out" to be something, something good, better than anything known before. This is his strength, which enables him to go on, and were it lost he could serve no further purpose; for it is only men whose prime mover is the intellect who can function from a base of pessimism, and Harry Truman is moved primarily by faith.

He remains an essentially modest man, but he never was the humble man he appeared to be when he first took the office; his prayerful demeanor then we took for humility, but what it really was, was fear. A fear he has long since surmounted. One side of his nature enjoys the office and the honor, another side resents the pressures, and hankers for relief. With most private callers he is buoyant and energetic, yet with the same breaths repeatedly seeks their sympathy by half-veiled references to the heavy burdens upon his shoulders. At first, in his uncertainty, he listened carefully, a little anxiously, to all that his callers and advisers had to tell him.

From *In One Ear* by Eric Sevareid (pp. 209-213). Copyright 1952 by Eric Sevareid. Reprinted by permission of Alfred A. Knopf, Inc.

Now he closes his mind to much of it, for much is trivial, much he already knows, and he must have relief from the constant hammering upon him. Every President develops his own little techniques to find relief. Roosevelt, in his later years, did it by monopolizing the conversation so that the caller had but a few moments left to present his case. Lincoln did it by saying: "That reminds me of a story," then launching into one of his back-country anecdotes, often to the annoyance of his more pompous visitors.

Truman finds relief in physical activity, more so than any President since Theodore Roosevelt. He sometimes complains of the little trips, the back-garden ceremonies, and the rest of it, but he enjoys them for the relief they give him. His recent, famous letters provide part of this pattern of relief. If columnists and other proper people are offended, he knows by instinct and by his constant reading of American history that the people in general are not upset. He knows what was said and written about Andrew Jackson. He has read the "informed comment," so-called, about Lincoln when Lincoln approached his second term—the grave statesman who wrote: "It is only just to say that the reports from Washington . . . did impute a frivolity of language and demeanor in President [Lincoln] which could not but offend many earnest men." But the people were not offended. Lincoln never insulted anyone. Jackson could insult and never forgive. Truman can insult a man and then, by the nature of his apology, captivate the victim and win a lifelong friend.

But Harry Truman has changed in these six hard years; and it is evident in his increasing need for relief. And in the manner of it. He can no longer drop instantly to sleep, or empty his mind and relax while doing nothing. Now, his rest takes the form of changing his scene and his activities, which is what most overburdened men come to when their nerves become even a little frayed. This change in Truman probably dates from two events that occurred close together—the violent attempt on his life, and the Chinese invasion of Korea. He is conscious of the change within him, and that is one reason why more and more friends of his are becoming convinced that, even if next summer coincides with one of his high peaks of popularity, he will not run again. World tension shows no convincing signs of relenting between now and then, and Truman would be in his seventies at the close of another term.

And another event this week will make it harder for him to run, easier for him to step gracefully out, no matter what the pleadings of his party machine may be. The new amendment to the Constitution legally exempts Mr. Truman from its rule that no man may be elected more than twice, but if he runs, his opponents will ceaselessly claim that he runs in moral defiance of the Constitution and the thirty-six states that ratified the amendment. If Truman is popular next year, such argument may cut no great amount of ice with the American people. Lincoln's opponents tried to stop his renomination on the grounds that no President in thirty years had held *two* terms and that Lincoln was defying the *one*-term tradition. Not that Truman next year, under any combination of circumstance now visible, will enjoy the popularity Lincoln did then, and a Constitutional amendment is a firmer reality than a tradition. But whether his prestige is high or low next year, the amendment offers him a perfect excuse for stepping out, with honor and party ties intact, as many of his friends now believe he expects to do.

That of course is one result the Republicans who pushed the amendment had in mind. But it's just possible the amendment may boomerang against them. If the Democrats should come up next year with a very powerful successor in nomination—an Eisenhower or a reasonable facsimile thereof—the Republicans may deeply repent having made it so easy for Harry Truman to smile and politely bow himself out the door.

Of all familiar political sayings, the most familiar is Lord Acton's, "power corrupts." Power too long enjoyed gradually corrupts, in complacency, in stubbornness, in a dangerous sense of infallibility; and those who favored the new amendment can surely make all these charges against this Administration. But there is another side to the coin, which political thinkers forget. If one group is in power too long, the opposition group is *out* of power too long, and freedom from responsibility, in the end produces its own corruption. Opposition leaders, despairing of power themselves, tend to oppose for the mere sake of opposing: any switch to beat those in power comes handy to their groping fingers. A long lack of responsibility can lead to irresponsibility. Men without power can come to the point of proposing courses of action—even where the national security is involved—that they must know in their hearts they could not pursue if they did achieve power.

A leading oppositionist in Congress is fond of quoting the political saying, "The duty of the opposition is to oppose," forgetting that its original meaning was: ". . . to oppose with an alternative."

The President's Contribution
DEAN ACHESON

It is usually a waste of time to discuss whether any of our contemporaries should be called great. The word means too many different things to different people. To some it carries implications of immense impact upon one's times or future development, as in the case of Alexander, Augustus, Charlemagne, Galileo, or Einstein; to others, it is a moral or spiritual leader, as was Confucius, Buddha, or Jesus; to some, a political leader with spiritual overtones like Lincoln, or an artistic genius like Raphael, Leonardo da Vinci, or Beethoven. Always the term involves some larger dimension than is possessed by even outstanding mortals. For my purposes it is enough to say of Mr. Truman, as was remarked at the beginning of the startled reappraisal of him

Reprinted from *Present at the Creation, My Years in the State Department*, by Dean Acheson. By permission of W. W. Norton & Company, Inc. Copyright © 1969 by Dean Acheson.

that came soon after the political hubbub he loved to create had quieted down, that if he was not a great man, he was the greatest little man the author of the statement knew anything about.

Among the thirty-five men who have held the presidential office, Mr. Truman will stand with the few who in the midst of great difficulties managed their offices with eminent benefit to the public interest. On assuming responsibility in 1945, he followed the second most controversial President in a century, who was, when living, perhaps also the most popular in our history. The world outside of the United States had just gone through greater disruptive change than at any time during the life of our nation. As suggested in the Apologia, the President's task was reminiscent of that in the first chapter of Genesis—to help the free world emerge from chaos without blowing the whole world apart in the process. To this task, Mr. Truman brought unusual qualities.

The first of these was one for which he can claim no credit. Some remote ancestor, like the undistinguished squire-ancestor of the Villiers family in England, bequeathed him the priceless gift of vitality, the lifeforce itself that within certain strains bubbles up through the generations, endowing selected persons with tireless energy. Mr. Truman could work, reading and absorbing endless papers, and at times play, until well past midnight and be up at six o'clock walking deserted streets with hardy Secret Service men and reporters. He slept, so he told us, as soon as his head touched the pillow, never worrying, because he could not stay awake long enough to do so.

Energy brought bounce and cheerfulness. Not long after we left office, one of our colleagues revisited the White House offices. Seeing a well-known and more genial than informed character heading for the President's office, he cocked an inquiring eyebrow. "Oh," he was told, "he's going in to cheer up the President."

"That's funny," said my friend, "in our day the President used to cheer us up." A namesake gave the same cheer the night before Agincourt:

> . . . every wretch, pining and pale before,
> Beholding him, plucks comfort from his looks. . . .
> His liberal eye doth give to every one . . .
> A little touch of Harry in the night.

The "little touch of Harry," which kept all of us going, came from an inexhaustible supply of vitality and good spirits. He could, and did, outwork us all, with no need for papers predigested into one-page pellets of pablum. When things went wrong, he took the blame. One "little touch of Harry" appeared in a motto framed on his desk— "The buck stops here." When things went wrong, he took the blame; when things went right, he followed his hero, "Marse Robert," General Robert E. Lee, by giving one of his lieutenants the credit. None of his aides had a trouble in his public or private life that the President was not quick to know and quick to ease.

These are qualities of a leader who builds esprit de corps. He expected, and received, the loyalty he gave. As only those close to him knew, Harry S. Truman was two men. One was the public figure—peppery, sometimes belligerent, often didactic, the "give-'em-hell" Harry. The other was the patient, modest, considerate, and appreciative boss, helpful and understanding in all official matters, affectionate and sympathetic in any private worry or sorrow. This was the "Mr. President" we knew and loved.

Today no one can come to the Presidency of the United States really qualified for it. But he can do his best to become so. Mr. Truman was always doing his level best. He aspired to the epitaph reputed to be on an Arizona tombstone—"Here lies Bill Jones. He done his damnedest." His judgment developed with the exercise of it. At first it was inclined to be hasty as though pushed out by the pressure of responsibility, and—perhaps also—by concern that deliberateness might seem indecisiveness. But he learned fast and soon would ask, "How long have we got to work this out?" He would take what time was available for study and then decide. General Marshall has called this capacity the rarest gift given to man and often said that President Truman had it to a high degree.

No one can decide and act who is beset by second thoughts, self-doubt, and that most enfeebling of emotions, regret. With the President a decision made was done with and he went on to another. He learned from mistakes (though he seldom admitted them), and did not waste time bemoaning them. That is, he learned from all mistakes but one—the fast answer in that nightmare of Presidents, the press conference. We kept on hand, as a sort of first-aid kit, a boxful of "clarifications" for these events.

The capacity for decision, however, does not produce, of itself, wise decisions. For that a President needs a better eye and more intuition and coordination than the best batters in the major leagues. If his score is not far better than theirs, he will be rated a failure. But the metaphor is inadequate; it leaves out the necessary creativity. A President is not merely coping with the deliveries of others. He is called upon to influence and move to some degree his own country and the world around it to a purpose that he envisions. The metaphor I have often used and find most enlightening is that of the gardener who must use the forces of life, growth and nature, to his purpose—suppressing some, selecting, encouraging, developing others. The central role of directing so great an effort of imagination, planning, and action cannot come, as some seem to imagine, from such spontaneous intuition among the hired hands as guides a flock of shorebirds in flight. It must come from the head gardener. If he tries to do it all himself—to "be his own Secretary of State" or Defense, as the phrase goes—he will soon become too exhausted and immersed in manure and weed-killer to direct anything wisely.

When the Truman government found its footing in foreign affairs, its policies showed a sweep, a breadth of conception and boldness of action both new in this country's history and obviously centrally planned and directed. We had seen it in the early domestic policies of the New Deal and in our vast military effort in the 1941-45 war, but not before in foreign policy. The 1947 assumption of responsibility in the eastern Mediterranean, the 1948 grandeur of the Marshall Plan, the response to the blockade of Berlin, the NATO defense of Europe in 1949, and the intervention in Korea in 1950—all those constituted expanding action in truly heroic mold. All of them were dangerous. All of them required rare capacity to decide and act. All of them were decided rightly, and vigorously followed through.

Furthermore, to have restored the health and strength of our allies and sought their help in this effort would have been novel enough in American history, if one remembers the aftermath of the First World War. But the new conception went beyond that, persevering, over considerable opposition from our allies, in restoring and enlisting the help of our former enemies as well. Earlier enticing mistakes were put aside in favor of a peace of reconciliation and a policy of transforming liabilities into assets, enemies into allies. As in the case of Castlereagh and Metternich, a distinction was made between a nation and its leaders. As France was restored to an honored and responsible place in the earlier period, the same was done with Germany and Japan in the later one.

What sort of mind and methods had the man who directed American leadership in this constructive period? To answer this question, we must go beyond the nature of the individual and of his relations with fellow workers to some idea of his postulates and his habits in decision and action. These are easier to describe than to explain. No one was more attached to the democratic bases of American life and institutions than Mr. Truman and no one was less bemused by the prophets of the Enlightenment about how these came about and what moved peoples. He did not overestimate, as they did, the influence of wisdom, virtue, and understanding of experience and even "enlightened self-interest." Deeply trained in the moral values of Graeco-Judaic-English thought, he was also aware of the power of suspicion and fear when aroused against domestic opponents or against foreigners by a Hitler, a Peron, a Nasser, a Sukarno, or a McCarthy.

Similarly, he did not share the indiscriminate condemnation of power in politics, domestic or foreign, that American liberals had learned from Lord Acton. Military power he had experienced in use. He knew its nature, its importance, and its limitations. He knew that its primary effectiveness was in overcoming opposing military power or deterring another's use of it, or in overawing an opponent and gaining acceptance of one's own will. He knew that its limitations in administering subject or conquered peoples sprang from the cultures of both its potential users and victims. Only utterly ruthless possessors of power could use it to crush resistance in those not wholly under the restraint of caution or fear of physical suffering. The less ruthless were soon reduced to the process of persuasion in gaining consent, even to the extent of giving up dominion, whether in Ireland, India, North Africa, or occupied Germany and Japan.

He learned also, and learned quickly, the limits of international organization and agreement as means of decision and security in a deeply divided world. Released from acceptance of a dogma that builders and wreckers of a new world order could and should work happily and successfully together, he was free to combine our power and coordinate our action with those who did have a common purpose.

These postulates were held by a truly hospitable and generous mind, that is, a mind warm and welcoming in its reception of other people's ideas. Not in any sense self-deprecating, his approach was sturdy and confident, but without any trace of pretentiousness. He held his own ideas in abeyance until he had heard and weighed the ideas of others, alert and eager to gain additional knowledge and new insights. He was not afraid of the competition of others' ideas; he welcomed it. Free of the greatest vice in a leader, his ego never came between him and his job. He saw his job and its needs without distortion from that astigmatism.

Mr. Truman brought another major asset to decision. He had a passion for orderly procedure and a deep, if simple, idea of how to attain it. Although many Presidents had been lawyers, none of them—notably his immediate predecessor—utilized in administration the law's most fundamental procedure. For centuries courts have required all parties in interest to be present before the court at the same time with the right to be heard and to hear one another. President Truman introduced this procedure into executive administration. To it he added an equally ancient, and in administration equally novel, practice of law: the decision was immediately reduced to writing.

The vehicle for these innovations was the National Security Council. This was created in the Truman years and reached its highest usefulness during them. It was kept small; aides and brief-carriers were excluded, a practice—unfortunately not continued—that made free and frank debate possible. Those present came prepared to present their views themselves, and had previously filed memoranda. Matters brought before the council were of importance worthy of the personal attention of the highest officers and decision by the President. In succeeding administrations practice deteriorated in two ways. The first was toward a desire by the President for "agreed recommendations." This was a deathblow. Agreement can always be reached by increasing the generality of the conclusion. When this is done, the form is preserved but only the illusion of policy is created. The President gives his hierarchical blessing to platitudes. To perform his real duty must involve the anguish of decision, and to decide one must know the real issues. These have to be found and flushed like birds from a field. The adversary process is the best bird dog.

Another way in which a President's role can become diluted and weakened is through yielding to the temptation to take over and run all operations. This not only wastes a vast amount of time and effort by a committee system for executing every important task and making all minor decisions, but limits, by narrowing, the President's attention to a few subjects that he allows to absorb him. The administrative tasks of the great departments of government are beyond the capacity of even the President's large personal staff to assume. To attempt to do so impairs both the broad direction of national affairs and the specific administration of particular parts of the whole. President Truman's strength lay not only in knowing that he was the President and that the buck stopped with him, but that neither he nor the White House staff was the Secretary of State, or Defense, or Treasury, or any other. To him the heads of departments were secretaries of state and members of his staff, as Lord Burghley was to the first Elizabeth. He made the ultimate decisions upon full and detailed knowledge, leaving to lieutenants the execution. This conception of the supreme role runs the risk that a lieutenant may fail as Longstreet did at Gettysburg or MacArthur in North Korea. The other conception runs the greater and more hazardous risk that the chief will fail in his infinitely more important role. It was such a failure, I fear, that blighted the high promise of President Johnson's administration.

The decision made in writing was also an innovation of the Truman administration in this country, though Mr. Truman was not the first head of government to employ it. On July 19, 1940, Prime Minister Churchill sent a note to the Secretary of the Cabinet: "Let it be very clearly understood that all directions emanating from me are made in writing, or should be immediately afterwards confirmed in writing, and that I do not accept any responsibility for matters relating to national defence on which I am alleged to have given decisions, unless they are recorded in writing." His Military Assistant Secretary, Sir Ian Jacob, adds his comment: "Much of the conduct of the war was determined by the personal habits of the Prime Minister. Everything had to be done in writing, and he made it clear at the outset that nobody who said that the Prime Minister had ordered this or that was to be heeded unless the Prime Minister had written so in black on white."

In Washington the Secretary of the National Security Council, first Admiral Souers and later James S. Lay, Jr., issued the President's orders to all members.

Justice Holmes has said that "legal progress is often secreted in the interstices of legal procedure." No small part of Mr. Truman's distinction in the presidential role derives from the fact that he instituted procedures that contributed to the statesmanship of his decisions and the quality of their execution. They insured that a flow of ideas would be encouraged, that his colleagues in the Administration would be welded together in loyalty to one another and to him by considerate, fair, and orderly consultation, and that decisions should be precise and known to all on equal terms. President Roosevelt has been praised for a supposedly deliberate secrecy in consultation and vagueness in decision that left policy fluid, relationships uncertain, and great freedom of maneuver for the President. In the currently fashionable phrase, his constant purpose was "to keep his options open." Flexibility in maneuver may be highly desirable in certain circumstances, but when it leaves one's own and friendly forces and commanders uncertain of the nature and purpose of the operation or of who has responsibility for what, it can be a handicap. Machiavelli was writing advice for weak princes.

In the last analysis Mr. Truman's methods reflected the basic integrity of his own character. He could have said of them what Mr. Lincoln said of his: "I desire to so conduct the affairs of this administration that if, at the end . . . I have lost every other friend on earth, I shall have at least one friend left, and that friend shall be down inside of me."

Ten O'Clock Meeting
JOHN HERSEY

At ten o'clock on Tuesday morning, November 28, 1950, President Truman, who has evidently never learned to ring summoning buzzers, appeared at the door between his office, in the West Wing of the White House, and its anteroom to call his staff in to their daily conference with him. Eleven members of the staff were waiting in the outer room for his summons: his Appointments, Press, and Correspondence Secretaries; his Assistant; his Special Counsel; three Administrative Assistants; his Military and Air Force Aides (his Naval Aide, Rear Admiral Robert Lee Dennison, was sick at the time); and his Executive Clerk. "Now, gentlemen," the President said, "I'm ready for you if you're ready for me." He put his hands on his hips, in an attitude of mock impatience he often adopts, but the exuberant, defiant mien he would normally wear under such circumstances was absent; he was grinning, but the grin was faint and formal.

The staff straggled into the President's office, and each man took his customary seat. The President sat in a swivel chair at his massive desk, within the southern arc of the oval office. Behind him, between the slats of a Venetian blind in a high French window, bars of cheery, haze-softened sunlight were stacked up, as if on glorious, tiny shelves. Facing him, on the curving north wall about thirty feet away, portraits of three American liberators—Simon Bolivar, George Washington, and Jose de San Martin—glistened in the pleasant light. On a hearth beneath the trio of portraits stood a terrestrial globe, nearly a yard in diameter, which Eisenhower used at SHAEF and later gave to his Commander-in-Chief, and which the President occasionally pats just before he shows a visitor out, saying, "We won the war on this old globe; I hope we can win the peace on it, too." From where he was sitting, Truman could cast his eye at any one of eight timepieces: three ship's clocks on the mantel and walls, four clocks on his desk, and on his wrist a chronometer that Winston Churchill gave him, accurate not only as to second and hour but also as to phase of the moon and year under the sun. Furthermore, the President was surrounded by mementos that could tell him where he stood in his century and in history: on one end of the mantel, in a small case, stood, as a reminder of the hazards and the continuity of his station and nation, a piece of wood that had been built into the original White House, in 1793, and had been licked at by flames the redcoats touched off in 1814; on a pedestal, off to his left, reared a small equestrian statue of Andrew Jackson, Truman's favorite President and his political lodestar; all across a console table behind his desk were ranged photographs of his family, holding his every act under their vigilant stares; on the wall, to his right, to make him feel the weight of the mantle on his shoulders, was a portrait of Roosevelt, caped for the sea and storm-blown; while before him on his desk, as a hedge against lapses in the wisdom of his own viziers, were various magic charms—a tiny totem pole, some monkeys shunning evil, a model of a French seventy-five, and a miniature electrotype plate of the *Chicago Tribune's* jubilant banner headline: DEWEY DEFEATS TRUMAN. Four of the staff took chairs grouped

Reprinted by permission; © 1951 John Hersey. Originally in *The New Yorker* (April 14, 1951), pp. 38-50.

close around the executive desk. The seven others sat against the wall, flanking Truman—three in chairs beside a television set, to his left, and the rest on a leather sofa and, nearer him, in a chair against the opposite curve, under the portrait of FDR.

When the members of the staff were all settled, the President, without calling for order, began handing out papers from a huge folder on his desk to various men. He murmured a sentence or two in a low voice as he passed each document out: "John, here's some stuff for you that has accumulated. . . . Look this over, will you, Murphy. . . . This is much too long, Elsey. Boil it down to a page. . . . Do you know what we did with that thing the Attorney General gave me, Matt?"

Then suddenly the President turned to Charles G. Ross, his Press Secretary (who died at his desk of a coronary thrombosis not many days after this meeting), and said, "What've you got, Charlie?"

Ross was sitting close to the desk, at the President's left. Eighteen months younger than the President, Ross was born and brought up in Truman's home town, Independence, Missouri. They were both in the Independence High School class of 1901. Ross was the valedictorian and all-round big man of that class, and from high school he went on, as Truman was unable to do, to college. (Truman passed examinations for West Point but was rejected because of poor eyesight.) After graduating from the University of Missouri, Ross taught journalism there for ten years; then he practiced it for twenty-eight on the St. Louis *Post-Dispatch*. Truman took him on as his Press Secretary in May, 1945. Ross was a tall, slender man with a long and weary face, so thin that instead of circles or puffs under his eyes, he had curious little purses perched on his cheekbones; these made him look sadder than he ever was. Besides handling the President's press relations, Ross, a gentle and quiet man who had long suffered from arthritis and heart trouble, considered it his duty—and he had the ability—to make his friend feel comfortable, to ease the tautness of office. He always carried into staff meetings, together with his regular business, two or three trivial, entertaining items that he might or might not bring up, depending on how the President was feeling. This morning, apparently mindful of the wan grin with which Truman had greeted the staff, Ross shuffled his papers, picked out a clipping from the Washington *Post,* and said, "Mr. President, did you see this item this morning? It's the column called 'Town Topics,' and it has one delightful bloomer in it that I thought you might enjoy. It describes a cocktail party given yesterday by Mr. and Mrs. Morris Cafritz, and it says here, 'It was good to see Secretary of the Treasury John W. Snyder and Mrs. Snyder in silver-blue mink.'"

The staff all laughed. So did the President, but without much heart. It almost seemed as if he were trying to please Charlie Ross, who was trying to please him. "That's a good one, Charlie," the President said.

Now Ross got down to work. "Is there anything that can be said about the appointment of an Ambassador to Spain?" he asked. "Smitty [Merriman Smith, the White House correspondent of the United Press] was questioning me about it yesterday, and I promised to check up."

"We're going to appoint Stanton Griffs on January 15th," the President said, "but we don't want to announce it just now."

"Then there is no information on that subject?" Ross said.

"Not a word," the President said.

Truman seemed preoccupied. In staff conferences, he usually speaks in a low, patient, easy voice, and not with the brisk, belligerent stridence of his press-conference utterances or with the earnest, primer-reading care of his radio speeches; this morning he was speaking quietly and with his customary grave politeness, but he was obviously thinking about something else. Ross came up, therefore, with another playful triviality. "Did you see, in the column of Roosevelt's letters the *Post* is running," he asked, "that one complaining to Sumner Welles about leaks in the State Department and telling him to tighten up over there?"

At this, the President brightened a little. "Did it cure the situation permanently?" he asked with faint irony.

"Oh, but did you see the next one?" said William D. Hassett, the President's erudite Correspondence Secretary, who is seventy years old. Hassett was sitting by the television set, and the President swung slightly to the left in his swivel chair to face him. Hassett, the only holdover from Roosevelt's staff among the men in this meeting, has under Truman—as he also had under FDR—two important functions: he nourishes and delights the President's aesthetic side, and tries, manfully and humorously, to persuade the President to let his Correspondence Secretary do all his corresponding for him. "The next letter," he said, in his granitic Vermont accent, "concerned a matter of some import that FDR sent over to Sumner with *instructions to leak it.*"

"In other words," the President said, smiling, "it was one of those two-way streets that don't really lead both ways—was that it, Bill?" Then Truman turned back to Ross. "Go on, Charlie," he said.

Ross picked up a document and began, "I have this memorandum—"

"Yes," the President said, interrupting; he had looked at the papers in Ross's hand and had evidently seen what they were—a list of legislative recommendations for the lame-duck session of the Eighty-first Congress, which had just convened. "I'd like to put that out. That's the memo for the leaders in Congress on things we want to have done. They're the matters I discussed yesterday with the Big Four [the Vice-President, the Speaker of the House, and the Majority Leaders of the Senate and the House, with whom the President confers on Congressional strategy once each week]. I think we ought to let the public know what we're trying to do. Those things are listed in the order in which we want to see them done. Yes, I'd like to make all that available."

The President swung around to his right, toward Charles S. Murphy, his Special Counsel, who was sitting on the chair beside the sofa. "Murph," Truman said, "can you see any reason why we shouldn't put that out?"

Murphy, who is, in effect, the President's lawyer, is charged mainly with helping to prepare plans and recommendations for legislation—an assignment to which he brings the benefit of twelve years' experience in the office of the Legislative Counsel of the Senate. He has, however, like every member of the President's staff, other duties by the dozen; they include, most importantly, the supervision of speech- and message-drafting. A forty-one-year-old North Carolinian, Murphy is husky, nearly bald, stolid, cautious, unhurried, and systematic, and he talks jurisprudential language slowly, with a mild Southern accent. "Sir," he now said, "there are two categories of legislation on that list—matters of considerable urgency and others that are less pressing. The only trouble I can see in releasing the list might come in the second category. That matter of education benefits for disabled veterans, so far as I know, hasn't been made public in any way."

"We could leave that item out," the President said. "Anything else?"

"I wouldn't like to be too definite about it in an offhand way," Murphy said. "That's a long list."

"I can get together with Murphy," Ross suggested, "and go over it with him."

The President said, "You do that—but let out everything you can on that list."

Ross shuffled his papers again. "We have a long draft of a proposed statement on the naming of a Point Four Committee—"

"It's terrible!" the President said. "I read it last night and I wanted to tell you to redraft it. You can cut out every other paragraph without losing anything."

George McK. Elsey, one of the President's Administrative Assistants, an alert Jack-of-all-trades who, at thirty-two, is the youngest man on the staff, sitting now on the sofa, to Murphy's right, said, "Mr. President, I ran across that draft, saw it was unsuitable for you, and briefed it into a more concise statement for you to work on." He handed up two typewritten pages.

"That's much better," the President said after glancing at Elsey's draft. "I'll go over this. All we need to say about Point Four is that I've been for it, I'm still for it, and I'm going to stay for it."

"That's all I have," Ross said.

The President turned to Dr. John R. Steelman, his Assistant, who had pulled his chair right up to the desk and spread out a folder and a number of papers on its outer edge. Steelman, who was born in Arkansas, was a professor at Alabama College before he entered the United States Conciliation Service, in 1934. He helped Truman out in the lacklustre days of late 1945 and early 1946 as a special assistant on labor matters, and in December, 1946, was given the title The Assistant to the President; he still keeps his "The," though W. Averell Harriman has since been made "Special" Assistant to the President. Steelman serves mainly as the President's liaison man with Cabinet members, but his many other functions make him the closest thing to an alter ego that Truman has. Although Steelman is fifty, he maintains an eager, hypercheerful, undergraduate look. He now handed a document of several pages across the desk to the President and said, "Here's something to look at when you get a chance."

The President, glancing at the document, saw that it was a digest of the opinions of labor leaders as to why the Democratic Party had suffered such reverses in the Congressional elections earlier in the month. "I'll be glad to read this," he said. "Say! Did you fellows see the ad on the back of the *Post* this morning? That gives one answer to why we lost in some places."

This was an instance of the inconvenience to his staff of the President's industrious use of the early-morning hours. Most of the staff members had to go out after the conference and look for the ad the President spoke of: it was a full page paid for by the pro-Taft Toledo *Blade,* warning Senator Taft not to take his victory in

Ohio as a sign that he was now the undisputed leader of his party—or even that he was particularly popular in his home state. His victory, said the *Blade*, was due largely to the circumstance that the Democrats had put up such a pitiful hack against him.

Steelman began his next point: "On that price-increase matter—" (He was referring to the fact, previously discussed in a staff meeting, that the big steel companies had asked authorization to raise their prices, in anticipation of future wage raises. At the time of the present staff meeting, wage and price controls had not been decided on. The companies had alleged that general wage increases, when they came, would have many immediate, costly secondary effects—increased prices of materials, for instance—but that their own price increases would not recompense them for the labor costs for a long time, since they habitually operate on future orders and would not make collections on orders at the new prices for several months.)

The President broke in quickly. "Stu [W. Stuart Symington, Chairman of the National Security Resources Board] started to talk with me about that, and I expressed such a violent opinion"—Truman smiled—"that I don't think he dared go any further with the thing."

Steelman, seeing that the President's mind was made up, dropped the matter. He then said, "Senator Kilgore [of West Virginia] is very worried about the big snow-and-ice storm these last few days in the Alleghenies. He says if we get a sudden thaw there'll be a dreadful flood—the worst we've known."

Elsey spoke up. He said, "Does he propose that we turn off the sun?"

The President laughed and said, "I think maybe the Senator places too much confidence in the powers of the Chief Executive. Anyway, that's one power the Congress hasn't ceded me." Truman, who worked closely with Harley M. Kilgore on the Truman Committee and is intensely loyal to him, broke off the levity. "But the Senator has a point there," he said. "Will you see that we take whatever precautionary steps we can, John?"

"That's all," Steelman said, squaring off and putting away in a folder several memoranda on other points he might have raised but now had apparently decided to hold for some other day.

"Matt?" The President had turned to Matthew J. Connelly, his Appointments Secretary, who was seated at the right end of the desk.

Connelly, a Massachusetts man, spent several years working as an investigator for the WPA and then for a number of Congressional committees; it was when he was an investigator for the Truman Committee that he caught Truman's eye. He has been secretary to the Boss, as he and the other staff members call Truman, since 1945. He is slender, dark, quick, neat, gay, and shrewd. His job is to arrange the President's schedule and make sure it's adhered to. He sees more of Truman, face to face, than anyone else, and, as Ross was, he is sensitive to the President's moods. Seeing that the President was oppressed this morning, and knowing that friendly ribbing is one of the President's principal amusements and that Hassett is a good-humoredly cantankerous goat for pranks, Connelly now said, "Mr. President, Bill Hassett has got you in for a full-blown production on this Wilson deal." The

"Wilson deal" was that Truman was soon to receive the Woodrow Wilson Foundation Award for efforts to achieve a lasting world peace, which had been given in previous years to Lord Robert Cecil, Elihu Root, Cordell Hull, Thomas Masaryk, Henry L. Stimson, Jan Smuts, and Bernard M. Baruch; the award to Truman, the first President to receive it, was to be, in the tentative words of the citation, "in recognition of his wisdom, courage, and leadership, by his action of June 25, 1950, in strengthening the United Nations as an effective instrument of world law." "Thanks to Mr. Hassett," Connelly went on, his eyes twinkling with malice, "they're all set for an evening broadcast, with a reception for some two hundred people, and now they have come in with a proposal for a big dinner."

Hassett snorted. "I wish to be heard," he said, "and I will express myself in language as restrained as I can command. When this whole business first came up, I let loose the opinion upon Louis Brownlow that it might be possible to set up a dignified ceremonial of some nature here on these premises. 'Who shall be present,' I then said, 'shall be mutually decided between your group and Mr. Matthew Connelly.' Next, Arthur Sweetser came to me with a more ambitious plan. Assuming that you share my detestation of banquets—"

"I do! I do!" the President said. Now he seemed to be enjoying himself a little.

"—I told Sweetser that we'd better start all over again, for it was one thing to honor a private citizen with a public spread; such formalities for a busy President, even considering the exceptional honor of this award, would be unbecoming in these times. I urged him to consider a simple ceremonial in this room—something that wouldn't require the use of a flying trapeze."

"In daylight hours," Connelly put in.

"In daylight hours," the President agreed, already serious again. "That'll be all right."

"I'm very glad I happened to be here to defend myself this morning," Hassett said.

Connelly then said, "A—— says you have made him a commitment to see B——."

"I made no such commitment," the President said.

"That's good," Connelly said. Then he handed across a letter from a friend of the President's in Missouri, and said, "This will interest you."

Truman looked at the signature, said "What's biting C——?" and tucked the letter into his folder for later reading.

"You won't forget," Connelly said, "that you're to make a speech on December 5th, at ten in the morning, to the Mid-Century White House Conference on Children and Youth."

"Oh, yes," Ross said. "I've been asked whether radio facilities would be available, and I've made tentative arrangements. I assume that is your wish."

"That'll be all right," the President said.

"I suppose that it will be a prepared speech," Ross said.

"Yes," Truman said, "it will have to be a prepared speech. I think we'll have a chance then to discuss public morals a little bit. I think we could say something on that subject, and it certainly is needed. I was talking to Scott [Senator Scott W. Lucas, of Illinois, then Majority Leader of the Senate, who had been defeated in the November election] the other day, and he was telling me what a dirty, rotten, lying campaign the D— — E— — [an organization] and F— — [a man] put on against him out there in Illinois. It was a vicious, libellous campaign. It seems that candidates for public office and their followers in this country won't stop at saying anything. I tell you, it's pretty bad. Look at what happened to Tydings, with that scurrilous, fraudulent composite photograph his opponents put out that made it seem as if he'd been talking as a friend to Earl Browder. And look at the lies and hints and all that they used on Graham and Myers and Elbert Thomas and the others. I tell you, we're liable to run into a situation where we'll repeat the mistakes our people made, beginning with the eighteen-thirties, in the anti-Masonic campaign and all the Know-Nothing business that led to the line of weak Presidents we had up until the Civil War. It's exactly the same kind of thing. We ought to learn by our mistakes. We've repeated this sort of hysteria over and over in our history—in 1692, 1798, 1832, 1855, 1866, and again in 1920 to '22. Those were waves of ignorance and prejudice and anti-religion." (The dates referred to the Salem witch hunts, the Alien and Sedition Acts, the year the Anti-Masonic Party ran a Presidential candidate, the height of the anti-Catholic Know-Nothing movement, the organization of the Ku Klux Klan, and the Red scare and reappearance of the Klan after the First World War.)

Hassett, like the President a lover of the past, chimed in, "The reign of D. C. Stephenson all over again!"

"That's right," the President said. "With Stephenson you had the revival of the Klan. I think we ought to try to put some of that into a speech, and try to help people keep level heads. We have to recognize subversion for what it is, and stamp it out when it appears, but that doesn't mean we should turn on each other with a lot of hatred and lies. I tell you, we've got to stop this name-calling. It weakens us here in this country. What we've got to do is persuade people to lay off personalities and talk about issues. Anything else, Matt?"

"That's all," Connelly said.

The President swung to the right again and asked, "What do you say, Murphy?"

"Well, Mr. President," Murphy said, "in mapping the legislative program for the next Congress, it seems evident that we're going to have to reexamine the existing legislation on manpower. It's a matter that will need considerable groundwork and talking around and coordination between the various departments and agencies of the government. John [Steelman] and Dave [David H. Stowe, an Administrative Assistant] and I have talked the question over, and we agreed that Dave would be admirably qualified to receive your appointment as informal coordinator on manpower problems."

"Yes," said the ebullient Dr. Steelman. "We three settled on Dave. It was unanimous, by two to one."

"That's all right," the President said, not laughing. "I guess Dave can handle that."

"Now, as to the present Congress, Mr. President," Murphy went on, "I'd like to ask how you feel about the advisability of meeting the principal members of both parties in Congress, especially the foreign-relations people, in the near future. It would give those gentlemen an opportunity to blow off some steam before we go at them with our proposals for this session. It appears that next Monday morning might be a suitable time to have a meeting. That's when you'll be seeing the Big Four; then you could take the Big Four in and talk with the others. Both Mr. Harriman and Senator McMahon have called to say that it would be helpful to convene such a meeting as soon as possible."

"The main value of having them in here," the President said, embodying assent in his comment, "is to have people from both parties come down to the White House, so they'll feel we all belong to one country, after all." A shadow crossed his face, and he added, "But I want to say something more about that a little later on. Hold your horses on that."

"That's all I have," Murphy said.

"Dave?" the President said, turning to Stowe, who was sitting at the far end of the sofa.

Stowe, a native of Connecticut who was for some time a college professor, and then a civil servant in North Carolina, went to work in Washington, in the Federal Bureau of the Budget, in 1941, and eventually became Chief Budget Examiner. Truman, who keeps as close and anxious a watch on the federal budget from month to month as most men do on their own domestic accounts, liked Stowe's work. Steelman took Stowe into his office, and in 1949, the President made Stowe an Administrative Assistant. Stowe, who is forty, has a talent for detail work, and the President gives him, for the most part, complicated operational assignments—like the coordinating of manpower problems, which had landed in his lap just a few minutes before.

"We have a problem in civil defense," Stowe said. Because of Murphy's slow speech, Stowe seemed to have the loquacity of a flock of starlings; his sentences and facts were run tightly together in a rapid murmuration. "You may be aware that we've had a barrage of adverse editorials coming down on us, making invidious comparisons between what we've done in civil defense and what they've done in Great Britain, but don't forget that the British were making plans from 1927 onward, and then they had the breathing spell of the phony war, from 1939 forward, and then they had several years of unpleasant laboratory experience, with the blitz and all, while we're building on mere plans and theories, and have only recently had our first realization that this isn't just fancy dancing. Up to now, our main troubles have been vagueness and generalization. Symington and Lawton [Frederick J. Lawton, director of the Bureau of the Budget] and I met at nine this morning to put some specificity into the setup." And Stowe went on to outline, at some length, details the three had agreed upon. The most important decisions had to do with the division of cost between federal and local governments on such things as stockpiles of medical supplies.

"That's all right, Dave," the President said when Stowe had finished. Truman had hardly seemed to be listening. Members of the staff told me later, however, that the President, who has trained himself to listen carefully, very likely had absorbed ninety per cent of this swift lecture, and that they confidently expected him to purl out most of Stowe's facts on some occasion when they would be needed—at a meeting of the Cabinet, or of the National Security Council, two or three months later.

"What do you say, Elsey?" Truman then asked.

Elsey said, "The letter to Congress on the appropriation for assistance to Yugoslavia will be ready this afternoon. The over-all requests for supplemental appropriations won't be ready until tomorrow morning. The supplemental-appropriations message is a cat-and-dog message that doesn't include defense requirements; the Yugoslav appropriation will be the most important part of these requests. Should the letter go up ahead of the message?"

"No," the President said. "The supplemental message ought to go up at the same time the letter does. Hold the letter until morning."

"That's all," Elsey said.

The President turned next to Donald S. Dawson, another Administrative Assistant, who is charged with screening and liaison work on Truman's governmental appointments. Before the President put him into his present delicate job, Dawson worked for fourteen years on the administration of government loans; for some time he was Director of Personnel of the lately controversial Reconstruction Finance Corporation. Dawson, who was sitting on the sofa with Stowe and Elsey, had returned the day before from a week in Florida, and his tanned face, framed in silver sideburns and split by a habitual, handsome grin, made him look like a prosperous banker among a number of pale, workaday, cage-dwelling tellers and clerks. He began to discuss some intricate maneuvers on important appointments. An implication of the conversation between Dawson and the President that followed was that it had proved hard to persuade prominent men to go to work for the government, even in crucial times—partly, it seemed, because so many important men were Republicans, and partly because so many were distinguished liberals who, whichever their party, were jealous of their reputations and their privacy and were unwilling to subject themselves to the humiliations of the Congressional investigation preceding confirmation. At one point, the President, speaking of his own current efforts to get one extremely famous American, who happened to be a Republican, to take a very big job, said, "I tried to get him on the phone for two days, but he was always out, so last night, at one o'clock in the morning, I sat down and wrote him a longhand letter and mailed it right away, special delivery. He ought to have it on his desk today. I expect I'll hear from him tomorrow." At another point, speaking of a far lesser, bureaucratic post, the President said, "I think I'll reappoint G——. He's always been right." Then he smiled, and added, "He's always been on our side."

Next, the President called on Hassett.

"I hold in my two hands," Hassett said, lifting a bundle of papers from his lap, "some material from the H—— I—— [an organization]. It contains recommendations on how to dispose of the Communists. I have no idea how this matter reached my lowly desk, unless it was by White House belt conveyor. I would like to take this occasion to pass it along, as it was passed to me, to the Messrs. Murphy, Steelman, Ross, Elsey, and others. As far as I'm concerned, they can forward it to each other for the rest of their born days."

The President and the staff laughed. Evidently thinking back to the way Murphy and Steelman had unloaded manpower onto Stowe, the President said, "Well! There seems to be a fair amount of buck-passing going on here this morning."

"Seriously, though, Mr. President," Hassett said, "I've studied this material, and it's not for you. I have also one thing to pass on to you. Yesterday, you handed me this book, offering to endorse it over to me as a Christmas gift." Hassett laid on the television set beside him a huge, boxed volume—"The Mystery of Hamlet, King of Denmark," by Percy MacKaye, four Neo-Elizabethan plays written in the twentieth century in Shakespearean blank verse, set in Elsinore, Denmark, and concerned with events preceding those of "Hamlet." "I have perused, though sketchily, the eight hundred pages of this work," Hassett said, "and I'd like to turn it in for a new model."

"All right," the President said. "I have something else for you. I brought it in specially for you this morning." He picked up and handed to Hassett a copy of "Kon-Tiki," by Thor Heyerdahl.

Hassett opened the front cover and smiled when he saw, on the end paper, in the President's hand, this inscription:

HARRY S. TRUMAN
Bought and Paid For.

"It's not going to be easy for you to endorse *this* over to me, I see," Hassett said.

"You seem to have the idea that everything I own has been given to me," the President said. "But you're wrong. Every once in a while, the Madam and I will order a book that we've read about in the Saturday Review of Literature or in one of the Sunday book sections, if it looks interesting. I think you'll like that one, Bill."

"I thank you," Hassett said.

"Anything this morning, Harry?" The President addressed this question to Major General Harry H. Vaughan, his Military Aide and old friend, who was sitting next to Hassett. Vaughan made Truman's acquaintance during the First World War, in which Vaughan ultimately commanded a battery of the 130th Field Artillery Regiment, while Truman had a battery in the 129th Regiment. They became close friends as fellow reserve officers, along with John Snyder, now Secretary of the Treasury, in summer training camps in the twenties and thirties. As Military Aide, Vaughan's function is mainly social; he is really a kind of court jester. He seldom speaks at staff meetings except to crack jokes. This morning, responding in his own way to the President's serious mood, he was subdued and matter-of-fact as he said, "Frank Pace [Secretary of the Army] tells me they announced the decision on that Gilbert case yesterday."

"I know," the President said. "That's the colored officer in Korea who ran away in the face of the enemy. First they were going to shoot him. Then they were going to give him life. Then they were going to give him thirty years. What did they finally decide to do?"

"They've reduced the sentence to twenty years," Vaughan said. "Here are the final orders for you to sign." He put some papers before the President.

"I know one thing—" Truman said. Then he broke off and stared into space for a moment. (He might have been thinking—since the parallel was so close—of the first important test of his own courage, the episode that in reunions of his Battery D is now known as the Battle of Who Run. On the night of August 29, 1918, on a mountain called Herrenberg, in the Vosges, some near misses by German artillery caused Captain Truman's battery to panic and flee for cover under the screaming leadership of a terrified sergeant. Only Truman's rare virtuosity in Missouri cursing drove the men back to the guns. Afterward, Truman refused to court-martial, but tried instead to salvage the disgraced sergeant as a private.) "I know one thing," he resumed. "If this had happened in the other war, and if I'd been this fellow's commanding officer, we wouldn't have needed any trial at all; we would have handled it in our own way. That's a serious thing, to run away in the face of your country's enemy." The President hesitated, then quickly took a pen, signed the order, and handed it back to Vaughan.

"Do you have anything, Bob?" Truman asked, turning to Brigadier General Robert B. Landry, his Air Force Aide, who was in the chair next to Vaughan's. Landry, who is forty-one, commanded groups of both fighters and heavy bombers in Doolittle's Eighth Air Force in England. "Nothing," Landry said, "except Nick Bez sent you some fresh salmon, but the plane was held up and the fish spoiled. He just wanted me to tell you that he would try to send some more along to you, and he'd hope it would get through."

"That's too bad," the President said. "Thank Nick for me."

Now, having gone once around the figurative council table, the President centered himself at his desk. For a few moments, he shifted papers back and forth and straightened a pair of scissors and two paper cutters lying on the leather margin of his desk pad. He had suddenly drooped a little; it appeared that something he would have liked to forget was back in his mind, close behind his hugely magnified eyes.

"We've got a terrific situation on our hands," Truman said in a very quiet, solemn voice. "General Bradley called me at six-fifteen this morning. He told me that a terrible message had come from General MacArthur. MacArthur said there were two hundred and sixty thousand Chinese troops against him out there. He says he's stymied. He says he has to go over to the defensive. It's no longer a question of a few so-called volunteers. The Chinese have come in with both feet."

The President paused. The shock of this news—for this was the first that any of the other men in the room had heard of the all-out intervention of the Chinese Communists in the Korean war—made everyone sit stiff and still. The success in Korea that had seemed to be so nearly achieved was abruptly snatched away by that word "defensive." The entire policy since June, which had seemed to be turning out for the best, was now to be more heavily tested than ever; hopes of imminent peace were gone; the willingness of the Chinese Communists, and therefore, obviously, of the Russian Communists, to risk a general war for the stake in Korea was suddenly palpable. All of the staff must also have realized instantly what this news meant to the President, who would be answerable, quite alone and inescapably, for the outcome in Korea. Yet he had dealt patiently, throughout this conference, with each man's affairs, holding back his dreadfully heavy knowledge until all had had their say.

"Now," the President went on, "I'm going to meet with the Cabinet this afternoon. General Bradley will be there to discuss the situation. General Marshall is going to meet with the State and Treasury people. Acheson is informing the Congressional committees. It may be necessary to deliver a special message in a few days declaring a national emergency. When things are settled down a bit and we know exactly what our policy in answer to this thing will be, we'll talk to the people—a simple, four-network hookup from right here, about ten days from now, I would say. I want to have that meeting with the Congressional leaders you were talking about, Murphy. Let's not wait till Monday; let's arrange it for Friday. I don't think a personal appearance before the Congress would be desirable just now; the military-appropriations message will give us a chance to say whatever needs to be said to the Congress."

In outlining his concrete plans and acts, the President had hidden, as indeed he had all through the staff meeting up to this point, his feelings about this new development, with which he had lived for only about four hours. Now he paused for a few seconds, and suddenly all his driven-down emotions seemed to pour into his face. His mouth drew tight, his cheeks flushed. For a moment, it almost seemed as if he would sob. Then, in a voice that was incredibly calm and quiet, considering what could be read on his face—a voice of absolute personal courage—he said, "This is the worst situation we have had yet. We'll just have to meet it as we've met all the rest. I've talked already this morning with Bradley, Marshall, Acheson, Harriman, and Snyder, and they all agree with me that we're capable of meeting this thing. I know you fellows will work with us on it, and that we'll meet it."

Quickly, again, and characteristically, the President brought himself back to thoughts of concrete plans. "I'll have to ask you all to go to work and make the necessary preparations—the declaration of emergency, if we decide to go ahead with it; the appropriations message; the speech to the people. Matt, I may have to cancel all my appointments tomorrow. You be ready for that, will you?"

"Sure," Connelly said.

"Did you say two hundred and sixty thousand Chinese troops?" Landry asked incredulously.

"That's right," the President said. "They have something like seven armies in there. Of course, what they call an army isn't the same as ours. Their armies are about the same as our corps."

"I don't suppose you want me to announce anything yet," Ross said.

"Charlie, there's nothing to announce," the President said. "I don't know what can be said. We don't have to say anything about the Cabinet meeting, because it's our regular Tuesday meeting."

"That's true," Ross said. "We wouldn't want to call special attention to it, since it's a regular meeting."

The President nodded to William J. Hopkins, his Executive Clerk, who was sitting next to Steelman, and Hopkins, a self-effacing, taciturn man of forty who has been a clerk in the White House since 1943, stood up and handed across the desk to the President a pile of documents for signature. Truman pulled out the left leaf of the desk, put the papers on it, and began to sign them. (Most of them were letters drafted by Hassett, answering expressions of regret at the assassination attempt, which had taken place not long before; there was one official document, on the public-housing matter.) While the President was signing the papers, he said, "Well, the liars have accomplished their purpose. The whole campaign of lies we have been seeing in this country has brought its result. I'm talking about the crowd of vilifiers who have been trying to tear us apart in this country. *Pravda* had an article just the other day crowing about how the American government is divided, and how our people are divided, in hatred. Don't worry, *they* keep a close eye on our dissensions. We can blame the liars for the fix we are in this very morning. It's at least partly the result of their vicious lying campaign. What has appeared in our press, along with the defeat of our leaders in the Senate, has made the world believe that the American people are not behind our foreign policy—and I don't think the Communists would ever have dared to do this thing in Korea if it hadn't been for that belief. Why, J—— [a newspaper publisher] had an editorial just yesterday claiming that he was personally responsible for the defeat of our foreign policy. He *boasts* about it! And the result is this news we got this morning."

The President handed the papers he had signed back to Hopkins. Then he sat squarely in his chair again, and again his mood quickly changed. He suppressed every sign of the anguish that had been so visible on his face a few minutes before and of the irritability and disgust he had shown during his last remarks; his voice, though still quiet, took on a confident tone, and as he spoke now he struck an intensely personal note, seeming by his use of the first-person-plural pronoun to be remembering and resummoning the deep loyalty of these men around him. "We have got to meet this thing just as we've met everything else," he said. "And we will. We will! Let's go ahead now and do our jobs as best we can."

Then the President, with still another sudden shift of mood, closed the meeting with a playful formula he was then using, with slight variations, nearly every day, and as he did so he appeared to have recovered at least a measure of the exuberance with which he normally confronts life. "Well!" he exclaimed pleasantly. "If none of you gentlemen have any more noncontroversial items, I'll declare myself satisfied, and the meeting can adjourn."

Forty-eight Hours
JOHN HERSEY

The President of the United States lives and moves, mostly alone, in one of the most awesome jungles in the world—a rank, deep-shadowed, trackless, threatening, majestic, strangely beautiful tangle of dreadful responsibilities and bewildering trivialities; a place no man should go knowingly, yet one where many seem to want to wander. Some time ago, in order to learn how Harry Truman makes his way through the thickets of his power, I followed closely several days of his official life.

Reprinted by permission: © 1951 John Hersey. Originally in *The New Yorker* (April 21, 1951), pp. 36–51.

Two of them, January 9th and 10th of this year, were typical days for the President in most respects, neither more complex nor simpler than the average. On the first morning, Tuesday, January 9th, Truman awoke in his upstairs bedroom in Blair House at five-thirty, assaulted not by an alarm clock but by a habit of early rising that dates back to the ten years of his young manhood he spent on a farm. He arose, shaved ambidextrously, bathed, dressed, and descended to his study. There, for two hours and a half, he worked on the tremendously important Economic Message to the Congress that he was to send to the Capitol on the following Friday morning; this was a document containing the administration's estimates and plans, which could guard or break the economic health of the country, and it was full of verifiable data and untested theories and ideas on taxation, inflation, price controls, and wage controls—for all of which, in execution and in the long run, only the President himself could answer to the citizenry. The President's effort that morning was mainly to simplify the language of the message. (Whenever he can, he spends an hour in his study, reading the papers, perusing documents, and writing letters, and then goes for a walk and a swim in the White House pool; this morning the demands of the Economic Message forced him to give up his exercise.)

At eight-thirty, the President sat down to breakfast alone, as Mrs. Truman and Margaret had not yet returned from a holiday in Independence; they were both due that day in New York, where Margaret has an apartment. At a few minutes before nine o'clock, the President was taken by car to a private entrance to his office, in the West Wing of the White House. For an hour, he dictated personal letters to his shy, quiet private secretary, Rose Conway; he also read various documents that were put before him, and decided, and noted on them, the courses of action to be taken, if action was required. One of the papers was his schedule for the day, with a typed line or two briefing him on each appointment.

At exactly ten, the President got up from his desk and went to the door separating his office from its anteroom, the office of his Appointments Secretary, Matthew J. Connelly, and told those members of his staff who were waiting there for his summons to their daily conference with him that he was ready for them. They went into his office. Present were the President's three Executive Secretaries (one for appointments, one for correspondence, and one for the press), the Assistant to the President, the President's Special Counsel, three of his Administrative Assistants, his three Aides (military, air, and naval), and his Executive Clerk. The President handed out the papers he had for some of his staff members, and then called on each of them to bring up his business. The subject matter of the staff conference was as varied as the Presidency itself, and disposing of it consumed thirty-six minutes. During the conference, the Executive Clerk put on the President's desk a pile of documents that needed his signature—a pile which the Clerk would supplement during the day, and to which Truman would turn from time to time all day long, in moments snatched between appointments, until he had signed his name, altogether, more than four hundred times.

When the President had dismissed his staff, he received James S. Lay, Jr., Executive Secretary of the National Security Council. This Council is an inner cabinet, whose function, according to its directive from Congress, is to "advise the

President with respect to the integration of domestic, foreign, and military policies relating to the national security." It consists of the President, the Vice-President, the Secretaries of State, Defense, and the Treasury, the Chairman of the National Security Resources Board, the Director of the Central Intelligence Agency, and others designated by the President. Lay, who heads the Council's staff, sees the President every morning. On this morning, as on every other, Lay spent fifteen minutes briefing him on developments in this country and all over the world that affected, or might affect, the security of the United States. Much of the knowledge on which the President is obliged to base tremendous policy decisions comes to him by ear; during such lectures, he cannot let his attention stray for a second.

The President was due to meet at ten-forty-five, for a kind of pep session, with the Committee on Mobilization Policy of the National Security Resources Board, an advisory group composed of three leaders each from the fields of business, labor, and farming, and three representing the public as a whole. Chairman W. Stuart Symington of the NSRB had requested the meeting not to transact any business but to clarify the status of the Committee. Charles E. Wilson's Office of Defense Mobilization had been set up a few days before, and neither Symington nor the members of this policy committee knew whether their advice would still be wanted or needed. The President's talk with Lay began to run over, and the White House Receptionist, a huge, easygoing Southerner named William Simmons, who held the same position under Roosevelt and who, it is safe to say, has shaken the hands and can call out on sight the names of more famous people than any other living American, led the Committee members from the lobby of the West Wing into the long, narrow Cabinet Room, which abuts the President's office. The President entered the Cabinet Room by his private door at ten-forty-nine, and Chairman W. Stuart Symington took him around the room to shake hands with everybody. Someone asked Truman if he would mind sitting at one end of the long Cabinet table, to pose with the Committee for three press photographers who had just been admitted. He sat down and called cheerily to the others to gather around. "Here, pull that chair up!" he said. "Now! One on the other side. Who'll sit here on my right? Mr. Symbol!" (This nickname for Symington had apparently come to him on the spot; nobody around the White House had heard him use it before.) "Now, let's see—on my left I'd better have—our only lady! Come on, Anna!" He beckoned to Mrs. Anna M. Rosenberg, the then new Assistant Secretary of Defense, who from the start had been one of the three members representing the public on the Committee. The photographing took so long that by the time the President had moved to his regular seat, at the center of the Cabinet table, with his back to the row of French doors along the outer wall, and the others had settled themselves in their chairs, ready for business, the President was twelve minutes behind schedule. The session had been allotted only fifteen minutes all told.

Someone complimented the President on his State of the Union Message, which he had delivered before the Eighty-second Congress the previous afternoon.

"I'll tell you something," Truman said. "That's the first time since I've been President that I've lost sleep over a speech. For two or three nights there, I stayed awake over that one, and I'm not a man who loses sleep—never have been. It was just that I felt this was the most important declaration I'd ever been called upon to make. I felt it was terribly important to make the speech objective."

"It *was* objective," someone said.

"I tried to make it objective," Truman said. "It's not easy for me to be objective, you know. I'm a partisan fellow." Then, informally getting down to work, he said to the gathering, "This crowd's nothing new to me. I see a lot of faces around this table that I worked with when I was in the Senate, and especially during the war. I'm pleased to see all of you again. The reason we got together here today was that I wanted you to know that I'm glad to have the kind of advice you people can give. I want you to deal frankly with me. Talk things over, reach your conclusions, and make your suggestions to me just as frankly and bluntly as you want." With an explosive grimace of exuberance, the President added, "Maybe I'll even comply with some of them!" Everyone laughed. "Seriously," he went on, "I'm very much interested in your work. I just hope that all you busy people can take enough time to get the job done the way it has to be done. Stu, you take over now."

Symington began a little speech he had evidently worked out in advance. "Because of the reorganization of the government to meet the world situation," he said, "this group wanted to know whether to go ahead or not, and—"

"It certainly should!" the President broke in, with extreme earnestness.

Symington went on, "This is the only true advisory body we have that is free from politics and that draws its opinions from all levels and all occupations in the country. These distinguished people come here on a voluntary basis. They're giving their time generously and freely. All they ask in return is that their advice be carefully listened to. If they have suggestions, criticisms, or complaints, they want to be able to come straight to you, to the top executive power—"

"That's what I want, Stu," the President said.

"They will hold two meetings a month," Symington continued. "They want the President to be at one of those meetings."

"I'll be there," Truman promised.

Now ex-Senator Frank P. Graham, another of the members representing the public, spoke, more to Symington than to the President. "The sort of advice we unanimously agreed at the last meeting to hand along was typical of the kind we think can be useful."

"That's correct," Symington said. "I see the President regularly every Wednesday, so even though the President wasn't with us, I was able to pass our opinion on to him quickly and directly."

Looking around, Truman said abruptly, "I want you all to know that I need your help."

Anna Rosenberg spoke up. "Can I say something? Since I've been working down here in Washington, I can see things more clearly than I used to. Everybody down here is so tied up with operations—with getting things done—that they can't afford the luxury of stopping to think, and of trying to find out what people across the country are feeling about things. There's just too much to do. Out at the Pentagon, we start work at eight o'clock in the morning and we don't stop till midnight. I've always been a pretty hard worker, but I've never worked like this before. When I go to New York for the weekend, people ask me, because I've been in the Pentagon, 'What's going on?' 'What about Korea?' 'What's the war situation?' I find I don't know as much as they do from reading the papers. I've been too busy. That's why I'm glad I told General Marshall that I'd take the job with him only on condition that I could stay on with this body. Right at this very moment, the Armed Forces Policy Council is meeting out at the Pentagon, and nobody out there *dares* miss that, but I insisted on coming here, because I think nothing is so important as this, Mr. President. Here you have people from all over the country who *know* what their people are thinking. This Committee can stand off and assess the situation, because it's not immersed in operations."

"I'm sure that's so, Anna," Truman said.

"Mr. President," Symington put in, "I want to make sure you met our newest member, Mr. [Herschel D.] Newsom, the Master of the National Grange. As you know, he's taking Mr. Goss's place." Albert S. Goss, Newsom's predecessor as Master of the Grange, had died of a heart attack after speaking at the New York *Herald Tribune* Forum on October 25th.

The President said to Newsom, "I know you'll fill Mr. Goss's shoes all right, Mr. Newsom, from what I've heard about you." Then he said, to the Committee at large, "Along the lines of what Mrs. Rosenberg was saying, I think it's true: sometimes you can be too busy to think. You take my case. I was up till midnight last night on the Economic Message that has to go down to the Congress on Friday. Then I got up at five-thirty this morning and worked on it till eight-thirty. I had to take a forty-one-page, single-spaced document and try to get the gobbledygook out of it, so it would make sense to people who aren't economists—and yet still be true. We're just finishing the Budget Message; that goes down on Monday. So the next thing I have to face is an off-the-record budget seminar on Saturday morning. I have to get up in front of every blame expert in town over in the old State auditorium Saturday morning and tell them what our budget is all about. I have to know just about every figure in the whole budget, and it's going to be a printed document this thick." The President calipered an imaginary budget with his right thumb and forefinger, and found it about three inches thick. "After that, we have to spell out our program in detail to the Congress. That means at least ten special messages. So you can see that your President doesn't have much to do! That's why you people can be so useful."

"Mr. President," said William Green, president of the American Federation of Labor, "each and every one of us here gains a new sense of our obligation to meet together and discuss the nation's problems and to cooperate as fully as possible. Our only question is: How can we serve our people? This group represents all segments of our national life—labor, industry, farmers, private citizens. All have one mood and one common desire: to give the best we have to give. I feel sure that after this encouragement from you, we'll be able to do a better job."

"I know that's so," Truman said.

"Mr. President," said James G. Patton, president of the National Farmers Educational and Cooperative Union, "I noticed in your State of the Union Message you said that all nonmilitary expenditures would have to be cut back in favor of defense expenditures. We hope you realize that there are many apparently civilian expenditures, especially in the fields of agriculture and conservation, that it will be important to continue for the mobilization effort. We certainly learned that in the last war."

"Oh, I agree, Mr. Patton," Truman said. "I think you'll find that our budget takes that point into consideration."

Philip Murray, president of the Congress of Industrial Organizations, said, "Mr. President, do you think you can get support for the type of tax program you advocated in your message?"

"I think so," Truman said. "I hope so. The two tax bills we got through the last Congress were unprecedented in our history. By following along closely with the Senate Finance and the House Ways and Means Committees, I think we'll get what the country wants. What we're going to ask for is fantastic in figures. It will hurt everybody, rich and poor. Over the long haul, though, I think it will stabilize our monetary system and help to hold down this inflationary spiral we're in. Then, when we come out of this thing, we'll be a sound and solvent nation."

Marion B. Folsom, chairman of the Committee for Economic Development and treasurer of the Eastman Kodak Company, said, "Mr. President, I can say that by and large the business community was delighted to hear you speak of doing this thing on a pay-as-you-go basis. Otherwise, there would be nothing to do but let inflation take up the slack."

"Yes," the President said, "and you're sitting on hot lead when you do that. When the proper time comes, Mr. Murray, we'll ask for a tax increase to try to pay for our mobilization as we go along. All the economists seem to be agreed that's the soundest thing to do, and that's what we'll try to do."

Otto A. Seyferth, a steel man who is president of the United States Chamber of Commerce, said, "All of us were gratified to see the way you put your plea for unity yesterday. And I think you'll find there is unity at this stage."

"There is," the President said, "but there's not enough unity, considering the seriousness of the situation. I believe there's greater unity than there was a short while ago. Back in October and November, during the election campaigns, we had a bad situation. We had a personality campaign going on. We've got to argue the issues rather than personalities. If we can get some moral responsibility into this thing, we won't have any trouble at all."

"In discussing the issues," Graham said, "I hope the emphasis can be put on truth."

"You know that, don't you, Doctor?" the President said. "You got skinned in your primary by lies!"

Graham said, "Is there some way to get through to the peoples of the world—not behind the Iron Curtain; that has to come later, I suppose—to get over to the non-Communist world that we stand for equality and justice? We get all this propaganda from the Left, abroad, about America being the aggressor and the imperialist. We're not! Everyone who knows the truth knows we're not. When we went out to Indonesia [on a Good Offices Committee for the United Nations], we couldn't get anywhere at first, because the Indonesians were convinced that America was looking for an empire. But when we proved to them that we weren't 'agents of Wall Street' and 'economic imperialists' and all of that, they got into a mood to discuss things with us. The Communists beat the airwaves night and day with lies. Can't we stress the truth about ourselves? The truth is in things like the Point Four program."

The President said, "I'm of the opinion that we'll carry the votes of the world all right if we do what you've been saying, Doctor. If we preach the truth as loudly as they preach their lies, we'll be all right. Well," he said, standing up, "I've got to get back to my schedule!" Bidding the Committee goodbye collectively, he left by his private door.

It was eleven-eight. Though the President had shaved a few minutes off the quarter hour he had allowed himself to talk with the Symington Committee, he was running late, and when he returned to his office, he found a new complication: Dean Acheson was waiting for him, with a foreign-policy question that could not be put off. The Secretary of State took only eleven minutes to outline the problem and get an answer from the President, but by the time Acheson left, the next appointee, who had been told to be on hand promptly at eleven, had been waiting nineteen minutes. The heel-cooler was Representative Harry P. O'Neill, of Pennsylvania, who had three Scranton businessmen in tow. The note on the President's schedule pad, under the names of O'Neill and his entourage, read, "Congressman O'Neill asked for this a week ago, stating they wished to discuss question of getting a war plant located at Scranton, Penna." The President received the O'Neill party with great enthusiasm and with a distinct recollection of having met one of O'Neill's companions, a man named Rogers, on the campaign train in 1948, and of having said to Rogers then, "If I only get one vote, and that's yours, I'm still going to make a fight for this thing." He also recalled having stopped over in Scranton on his way to the Chicago convention earlier that year, to speak to the Irish-American Society. As for the defense plant, he told them that that was something they would have to take up with Charles E. Wilson, the director of the Office of Defense Mobilization. He said jokingly that the President of the United States isn't allowed to make any *important* decisions. The group left in good cheer.

At eleven-thirty-three, eighteen minutes late, the President received Congressman Frank L. Chelf, of Kentucky. The Congressman asked after the President's family. The President said they were fine, and added, with evident emotion, that he was particularly pleased that Margaret was getting such good crowds for her concerts. Chelf, who is something of a Southern gallant, was moved to remark that the President is a perfect father—"a regular Lord Chesterfield," he said. He then summarized a bill he had introduced into the Eighty-second Congress, H.R. 38, which had to do with the reapportionment of seats in the House of Representatives in line with the 1950 census; the President listened, and said he would study the effort Chelf was making to pick up marginal seats for certain predominantly Democratic states, in order to offset Republican California's great gain.

At eleven-forty-six, the President started on foot from his office, with his Press Secretary and his three Aides, for the auditorium on the fourth floor of the old State Department Building, where he had been due at eleven-thirty, to present five

Congressional Medals of Honor to the next of kin of dead or missing soldiers. The day was bitterly cold, and in Connelly's office, outside the President's oval office, someone said, "Don't you want to wear an overcoat, Mr. President?"

"It's only across the roadway," Truman said. "I'm in good condition; I couldn't catch cold if I tried."

On the way across the street, the President's Military and Air Force Aides, Harry H. Vaughan and Robert B. Landry, who were flanking him, teased him, and Truman talked fiercely back, in flamboyant, chuckling counter-attack. In the corridors of the old State Building, and all the way up to the fourth floor in a slow elevator, the two uniformed jesters carried on their hurried, earthy work and gave the heavily burdened Chief of State, their friend, four minutes of Old Times. Then, suddenly, in a little room off the auditorium, the party walked into an opposite atmosphere. There waited, solemn and proud, the bereaved next of kin of the five men whose memories were to be honored. At once, as if he had put off a Shriner's fez and put on the cap of Commander-in-Chief, and in changing hats had changed hearts, too, Truman silently shook hands with the five, and by a soft look in his enormously magnified eyes seemed to show that he shared their pain and pride. The relatives were then led into the auditorium. The President, spotting a carafe and a glass on a wide window sill in the small room, hurried to it, poured himself a glass of water, gulped it down, and then followed, sad-eyed, after the heroes' kin. Inside the auditorium, a battery of moving-picture cameras had been set up, and beside them a crowd of still photographers stood in an aggressive block. On the left side of the room, as the President entered, other relatives of the medal winners, including one young wounded soldier on a hospital wheel bed, were already gathered. The President stood behind a desk at the front of the room; the next of kin were seated in a row on his left; behind him were arrayed, at ease, his Aides and the Secretary of the Army, Frank Pace, Jr.; and to his right stood his Assistant Military Aide, Colonel C. J. Mara, with the citations in his hands and the medals lined up in front of him on the edge of the desk.

The first to be called forward was Mrs. Mildred D. Dean, the wife of Major General William F. Dean, who commanded the 24th Infantry Division in the early phases of the Korean campaign, and who is listed as missing in action near Taejon. While Mara read General Dean's citation, the President stood with his hands clasped in front of him, kneading them together. When Mara had finished reading, he handed Dean's medal to the President, and Truman gave it to Mrs. Dean, mumbling, so that those present could barely hear him above the snapping of the flashlight cameras, "I can't say this gives me pleasure, Mrs. Dean, because I know you'd a lot rather have General Dean back here than to have this medal. But he did a fine job, and he deserves this great honor."

After the second presentation, the President made another appropriate remark. The third recipient was Mrs. Madie S. Watkins, widow of Master Sergeant Travis E. Watkins, of Gladewater, Texas, killed near Yongsan. Mrs. Watkins, a very pretty girl of twenty-two, was obviously having difficulty keeping her face fixed in a proud smile, and while Mara was reading her dead husband's citation (". . . he rose from the foxhole to engage them with rifle fire. Although immediately hit by a burst from an enemy machine gun, he continued to fire until he had killed the grenade throwers. . . . Despite being paralyzed from the waist down, he refused all food, saving it for his comrades . . .") her shoulders began to shake spasmodically. Mara read, "Refusing evacuation, he remained in his position and cheerfully wished them luck. . . ." Mrs. Watkins broke into tears. The citation finished, the President handed Mrs. Watkins her husband's medal, took her hand, and, visibly affected himself, said, "I know this is hard for you, young lady, but never forget this as long as you live: this medal is the highest honor your country could give to a soldier. Never forget that." Next came an elderly mother, who cried, too, and whom Mrs. Watkins, with her emotions finally under control, comforted when she returned to her seat. Last was a father, who stood through the affair with a rigid face.

Still very much moved, the President looked up at the crowd in the room and spoke a few quiet words, not widely reported on, that gave the ceremony a significance broader than the honoring of five soldiers, words deliberately tossed into the so-called Great Debate—whether this country should send ground troops overseas or rely for security on geography, aircraft carriers, and long-range bombers. "I want to take this occasion," the President said, "to pay tribute to the infantry. You'll notice that all five of these Medals of Honor were awarded to ground soldiers. I don't think we ought to forget that they are the ones we depend on to hold the airfields and ports that our planes and ships operate from. They're the ones who fight from the holes in the ground and ridges and machine-gun nests. They're not the glamour boys of the services, but *they are the ones who win the wars"*—he bore down heavily on those words—"and they are the ones who make it possible for us to have freedom in this great nation of ours."

The ceremony was over, but that authority that is higher than the Presidency—the Public Eye—now took over; photographers, of both still and moving pictures, began commanding the Commander-in-Chief and his bereaved company where to stand and how to look. For almost as long as the ceremony itself had lasted, the cameras worked to catch an impression of what had happened, although the sharp emotions of the award ceremony were now already either dead or false. The President tried, especially when the newsreel cameras began to turn, to put the next of kin at ease, muttering to them that they should keep moving their faces around, look animated, like him—*he* was getting to be quite an actor, he told them. Once, in an effort to help both cameramen and the despairing relatives get the thing over with, the President suggested that the next of kin stretch out their hands, so that he could clasp them together in his; the result was a strange and stiff tableau, which the cameramen politely recorded. Then, looking straight into the Public Eye, the President spoke up again. "Today," he said, "I've given Congressional Medals of Honor only to men who didn't come back. This is the first time I've ever done that, even though I've awarded more Medals of Honor than all the other Presidents put together—but the reason I've given so many is just because of these terrible times that permit these medals to be earned and deserved." At last, at about twelve-twenty, the cameramen were satisfied. The President then went around and shook hands with every relative in the auditorium. It was nearly twelve-thirty when he hurried back across the street to his office.

In the meantime, back in the West Wing, Matt Connelly, the President's Appointments Secretary, had been rearranging things. Connelly is the Cerberus of the President's personal hell. Cerberuslike, he has three heads, which he uses all at once: one for planning Truman's schedule up to three weeks ahead; one for greeting visitors and getting them through appointments on the current schedule; and one for dealing, tactfully, firmly, and finally, with those who will not get in to see the President but who, for various reasons, must be allowed close to the presence of power—i.e., as far as the anteroom. All three of these heads, it happens, are deceptively enveloped in a single, well-formed skull. Since Connelly controls, to a great extent, the access to the highest center of authority in the government, he himself has immense indirect power, which he wields with craft, caution, loyalty, and also—because he has been close to Truman ever since 1941, when he became an investigator for the Truman Committee—with a shrewd understanding of the wishes of the Boss, as he and everyone else on the staff call the President. As a kind of insurance in his perilously powerful condition, Connelly has, literally behind him, at the only desk besides his own in the anteroom, the assistance of Miss Roberta Barrows, who sat at the same desk during Roosevelt's time, and who has the requisite tact and wisdom for one at the portals of authority. Not only does she see no evil, hear no evil, and speak no evil, but also, and just as valuably, she sees no good, hears no good, and speaks no good; she simply takes phone calls and keeps everyone who rings through aware of the impressive humility of the Presidency of the United States, which has (she makes the caller feel) time and courtesy to spare for every citizen, no matter how lowly or importunate. She also keeps a record of all appointments. During the medal ceremony, Connelly, seeing that the President was running late, had Miss Barrows put through a call to Frederick J. Lawton, Director of the Bureau of the Budget, who had a half-hour appointment for noon, and ask him to come in at two-forty-five instead. The first afternoon appointment had been scheduled for three-fifteen. Connelly tries to keep a dead spot in the early afternoon, to give the President a chance to get ahead with some of his desk work, which must otherwise be done at night or before breakfast. Today he had to put Lawton in the dead spot.

The President returned to his desk, picked up his phone at twelve-twenty-eight, and without the help of a secretary, put through a call to Senator Allen J. Ellender, of Louisiana, at the Senator's apartment. The conversation went like this:

Truman: I heard you were sick in bed, and I just wanted to tell you to hurry up and get well, and I wanted to thank you for that goose you sent me the other day.
Ellender: Did you eat it?
Truman: Certainly did. Best goose I ever ate.
Ellender: That was a banded goose. I'll bet you didn't know you were eating a banded goose.
Truman: No, I didn't know that.
Ellender: And I'll bet you couldn't guess in a thousand times where that goose came from.

Truman: That looked to me like a wild goose. I suppose it must have been banded in Canada. Those fellows migrate down here from Canada.

Ellender: You're wrong! That goose came from your home state. It was banded in Missouri on November 27th, and I shot it in the marshes in Louisiana on December 27th. That goose was one of your old Senate constituents.

Truman: *(delighted)* Can you beat *that!* If I'd known that, it would have tasted a lot better when I ate it!

Ellender: They have a new way of snaring geese out in Missouri. They lay out a little path of corn on the ground leading right into the snare, and the goose is so dumb he just puts his head down and eats his way into captivity.

Truman: Sounds like the way a woman traps a man—in more states than Missouri—doesn't it? *(in a kindly tone.)* You get yourself back on your feet soon—hear?

Ellender thanked the President for his solicitude, and the two men hung up.

The President signed his name a few times, and then Connelly opened the door and showed in Truman's twelve-thirty appointment. This was General George C. Marshall, the Secretary of Defense, for one of the President's "fixed appointments," which come at the same hours each week. His fixed appointments, besides his meetings with his staff and with Lay every weekday morning, included, at that time, sessions with the Democratic leaders of Congress, and later the Secretary of State, on Mondays; the Secretary of Defense, and then the Cabinet, on Tuesdays; the Chairman of the NSRB, and the Chairman of the Democratic National Committee, on Wednesdays; the press, the Secretary of State again, and the National Security Council, on Thursdays; and the Cabinet again, on Fridays. This time, because Marshall wanted to discuss Army manpower, he brought in with him Anna Rosenberg, his Assistant Secretary charged with that problem, who was seeing the President for the second time in one day but might not see him again for a month; and David Stowe, one of the President's Administrative Assistants, whom the President, at a staff conference some time before, had assigned as a watchdog over all manpower questions. Marshall reviewed the Defense Department's complicated plans for drafting men, which he and Mrs. Rosenberg were going to have to present to Congress in a few days. The President (with the citations for dead and missing soldiers not long out of hearing) was obliged, in the course of the following half hour, to make several decisions that would affect hundreds of thousands of young men and their families. For example, a decision he was asked to make, and did make, was this: A plan had been advocated to draft not only healthy eighteen-year-olds into the Armed Services but also (in order to distribute the burdens of defense fairly) young 4-F's into some kind of government service; should this plan be proposed to Congress now, because of its manifest fairness, or should it be put off, because adequate preparations could not be made to induct a large number of 4-F's before the summer? The President, while he approved the principle of spreading the load, finally decided not to propose the plan until its details had been more carefully worked out.

At one o'clock, the President went to Blair House for lunch. Afterward, he lay down and slept for half an hour. He was back in his office at two-forty-five, and started right in signing his name again.

By that time, two men had been waiting in the anteroom for some minutes: Lawton, whose morning appointment had been postponed, and William D. Hassett, the President's Correspondence Secretary, who, hoping the dead spot in the daily schedule had not been usurped, wanted to slip in and give the President something he had for him. Hassett had taken three dog-eared books of Truman's piano music—volumes of Beethoven sonatas, Mozart sonatas, and Mozart duets—and had had the Library of Congress trim the frayed pages, reinforce the torn ones, and rebind the books in hard covers. While waiting for the President to return from Blair House, Hassett had riffled through the books, making sure that in repairing them the Library of Congress had not obliterated any of the President's pencilled notes to himself. At the beginning of Beethoven's "Moonlight Sonata," for instance, which is scored in four sharps, he found a rather petulant reminder in Truman's hand: "*C # Minor!*" There was also, on the second page of the same piece, where an F-double-sharp made its second, and therefore unmarked, appearance in one measure, a big, hortatory "X" beside it; and there were as well some quite angry, incoherent pencil marks between the clefs of the Allegretto, which is scored in five flats. Hassett satisfied himself that the Library had practiced its usual discretion. Connelly came in just before two-forty-five, and when Hassett saw him, he said, "Pshaw! I was hoping to get in with these before *you* got back."

"Not today, Bill," Connelly said firmly. "We got behind this morning."

Hassett, and the bound volumes of music, retired for another, better day.

Connelly showed Lawton in to the President. There followed the fifteenth, and last, meeting between the director of the Budget and the President on the Budget Message, which was to be sent to Congress on the following Monday. As each section of the federal budget had been blocked out, Lawton had taken it to the President and discussed it with him; the President kept the typed drafts of all the sections in shiny brown cardboard folders, in the lower right-hand drawer of his desk, and occasionally, between appointments, he would take out one section or another and go over it. By now, he had memorized nine-tenths of the summary figures and had a fair idea of the rest. The budget had reached the page-proof stage, and this afternoon Lawton went over corrections and additions with the President. During the conference, a question came up on which the President wanted the opinion of his friend Secretary of the Treasury John W. Snyder, so, at three-two, he picked up the telephone and, again without benefit of secretary, put a call through. A little later, the President asked Lawton to spend some time with him on Friday afternoon, to help him prepare for the budget seminar Saturday morning. Lawton, who understands the pressure of time on the President, left at three-twelve. The President signed his name some more.

Connelly slipped George McK. Elsey, one of the President's Administrative Assistants, in at three-fifteen. Elsey, who studied at Princeton and Harvard to be a historian, has, among many other duties, the job of helping the President keep his papers in order. He talked with Truman now for seven minutes on a matter involving the President's personal file.

At three-twenty-two, Elsey stepped out and Connelly swung the President's door wide open for Senator James E. Murray, of Montana; Congressman Michael J. Mansfield, of the same state; and Senator Murray's son and assistant, Charles A. Murray. Senator Murray pointed out to the President that, according to the 1950 census, Montana was losing population, and that this was because both the mines and the farms of the state had been progressively mechanized; that the state was building new plants for aluminum, chrome, and manganese; and that Montana therefore needed new power facilities, over and above those of the Fort Peck and Hungry Horse Dams. The President said he would take the matter under advisement and discuss it with the Interior Department.

The Senator from Montana and his companions were replaced, at three-forty-two, by Senator Brien McMahon, of Connecticut, chairman of the Joint Committee on Atomic Energy, who, after touching briefly on some atomic matters, asked the President whether there had been any decision on a request—previously discussed with Truman by Chester Bowles, when Bowles was Governor of Connecticut—for authorization to locate a big new steel mill at the Connecticut port of New London. The President told McMahon that the matter had been cleared by the proper agencies and that the first steps could be taken in getting the plant set up.

At three-fifty, the President had an off-the-record appointment.

At four-six, the President went into the Cabinet Room and called a meeting of the Cabinet to order. [Cabinet meetings are for the most part informational sessions, at which general problems are discussed but big decisions are seldom made. Cabinet members dare not throw on the table, for mauling by their colleagues, projects that are dear to their Departments. They take up such matters in private with the President.] Truman usually goes around the table for opinions on matters that are important to him. This day he also read his latest draft of the Economic Message and asked the Secretaries, one by one, to comment. The meeting adjourned at five-thirty.

At five-fifty, after signing his name nearly a hundred times, and after reading some documents, the President packed a stack of papers five inches thick into a briefcase and was driven to Blair House. There he put in more than an hour's work in his study on the papers, interrupting himself only to call Mrs. Truman and Margaret at the New York apartment at exactly six o'clock. At seven-thirty-five, he left by car for the home of James M. Barnes, a former congressman and Administrative Assistant to Roosevelt, to attend a small birthday dinner for Speaker of the House Sam Rayburn. There were about twenty guests, mostly senators and congressmen. After dinner, the President played the piano for the company; later, he cut into a game of poker. He went home shortly after midnight, got into bed, and for more than an hour studied the federal budget.

After four and a half hours' sleep, the President awoke, dressed, and went to work again on his Economic Message, forgoing his exercise for the second morning in a row. He breakfasted alone, went to his office at nine, dictated letters and worked on papers, and admitted his staff promptly at ten. During this morning's staff meeting, he made some points about the Economic Message to his Special Counsel, Charles S.

Murphy, who is the head of a team of document-drafters, and gave Murphy his marked-up copy. After the meeting, Murphy retired for the day with his team to rework the entire message.

Congressman Overton Brooks, of Louisiana, who had an appointment for eleven-thirty, had appeared at ten-thirty. (An extraordinarily large number of people show up at the wrong hour for their appointments with the President, and as many come late, and therefore miss seeing him, as come early.) The President dismissed his staff at ten-thirty-five and since he wasn't to see Lay, of the National Security Council, until ten-forty-five, Connelly slipped Brooks in. Brooks discussed what had been marked on the President's appointment pad as "Louisiana matters"; i.e., politics.

After Lay's briefing, which followed, the President received, in succession, two hollow-eyed lame-duck Democratic congressmen, defeated men hoping for preferment in the Party. As head of the Party, the President cannot afford to spurn Party men who have been beaten in elections; there is always the future to be thought of. Each of the two men left the President's office looking somewhat less hangdog than when he came in, for Truman, who had been a lame duck in a small way himself once (in 1924, when defeated for reelection as Judge of the Eastern District of the County Court of Jackson County, Missouri), was able to show, by his own example, that perseverance can pay off. One of the lame ducks, displaying a lack of tact that may account in part for his having been defeated, said he had heard some rumors that the President was not feeling well—whispers that various events, such as the speeches by Senator Robert A. Taft on foreign policy, had reduced the President to a low state of mind and health. To this, Truman replied exuberantly, "I never felt better in my life. I can take these Republicans on, one by one, with one hand tied behind my back. Don't worry about me!"

At eleven-forty-five, after some paperwork during the blank quarter hour for which Brooks' appointment had been scheduled, the President received Robert Butler, his Ambassador to Cuba. Butler had called up from Havana eight days before, asking to see the President. On January 2nd, the President of Cuba, Dr. Carlos Prio Socarras, had made a statement binding his country with astoundingly unqualified allegiance to the United States. Butler wanted to make sure that the President knew about and understood the entire significance of this unusual obeisance. To his surprise, the Ambassador found that Truman had read President Prio's statement in full and was well aware of its implications.

At precisely noon (for, so far that day, everything had gone like clockwork), Simmons, the Receptionist, showed into Connelly's office, and Connelly conducted into the President's office, a party of about thirty distinguished men and women who were to witness the presentation to the President of the Woodrow Wilson Foundation Award. This award, for outstanding efforts for peace, had not been previously given to a President of the United States. The party, whose members now trooped by the President, shaking his hand, was headed by Dr. Harry D. Gideonse, president of the Brooklyn College, who was to present the award, and Mrs. Eleanor Wilson McAdoo, Wilson's daughter. (During the Brooks gap, Connelly had brought in to the President a letter from Mrs. Woodrow Wilson saying that ill health would keep her away from the ceremonies but paying Truman—both as President and as recipient of an award in her husband's memory—her respects.) After all the guests had shaken hands with the President, they formed a stiff line around the wall of his oval office. Some of the President's staff came in.

An awkward pause followed, while moving-picture cameras and recording equipment were set up. Dr. Gideonse laid on the front of Truman's desk a huge, flat jeweller's case he had been carrying, and opened it, to show the President the bronze plaque, a foot in diameter, that was to materialize the award. On one side of the plaque, Gideonse showed the President a symbolical bas-relief by the Yugoslav sculptor Mestrovic; then Gideonse turned it over and showed the President an inscription, which noted that the award was being given to Harry S. Truman "who, through his devoted support of the United Nations, and his courageous reaction to armed aggression on June 25, 1950, has sought to strengthen the United Nations in its defense of democracy against tyranny." The President bent over the desk and admired the plaque for some time, then called Mrs. McAdoo over to discuss it with her. Then he tested its weight and remarked on its heaviness. Then, because the sound technicians were still fussing over their equipment, he picked the plaque up and walked over to a group of ladies in the line of guests and held it out in front of them, showing them first one side and then the other, and the ladies exclaimed over it with exaggerated surprise and delight. "Oh!" cried one lady above the ohs and ahs. "That thing's heavy! Don't drop it on your foot!" The President, who had been warned by Gideonse against that very accident, showed that he had a good grip on the huge medallion, and shook it, to demonstrate that in his arms, conditioned on a rowing machine and by setting-up exercises, the plaque seemed as light as a dinner plate.

At last the cameras were ready. The President went back to his desk and put the plaque down on it, and he, Mrs. McAdoo, and Gideonse assumed ceremonial postures; the latter two faced their Chief of State, in formal attitudes, as if they had just walked up to him on a grave errand and had not been chatting and chuckling familiarly with him for several minutes. Gideonse, who was trembling, held up a written speech and began to read it. The President stood, as he had during the reading of the citations for the Medals of Honor the day before, clasping and unclasping his hands in front of him. He wore an expression of keen and humble interest, but he could not help glancing quizzically from time to time at the shaking pages Gideonse held. During Gideonse's speech, Joseph Short, the President's Press Secretary, walked around behind the President's desk and slipped into Truman's hand a folded piece of paper; the President unfolded it, glanced at it, nodded gratefully to Short, and folded it up again. Gideonse read on for nearly ten minutes. When he was finished, he picked up the plaque and handed it to the President. The President put it right back where it had been, opened the piece of paper Short had given him, and read a statement of about two hundred and fifty words that had obviously been prepared for him by a speech-writer. When he came to the words "The seeds Wilson planted are now bearing fruit," he lifted his head and smiled at Wilson's daughter. He ended with a statement, whose graceful turn of modesty was somewhat vitiated by the palpable fact that he had not phrased it himself, to the effect that he accepted the award not in his own name but in that of the American people. "It is *their* award," he read carefully. "It is *they* who have made this decision—that while peace is precious to us, freedom and justice are more precious."

The President dropped the hand that held the paper, looked around, and seemed to realize that the statement he had just read was not adequate to his part of the occasion. He then turned to Gideonse and Mrs. McAdoo and said slowly, "I myself as an individual feel entirely unworthy of the honor you have conferred upon me." He paused, then, still groping, added, "As President of the United States, I highly appreciate the honor that has been conferred upon me by the Woodrow Wilson Foundation." He paused again, then suddenly broke his formal stance, smiled with an easy candor, and became himself. "I was in a field on July 2nd, in the year 1912, driving a binder and binding wheat," he said, "and there was a little telegraph station about a quarter of a mile from one corner of that field, which, being a hundred and sixty acres, was a mile around—no, more than that: it was half a mile long on each side, so it was two miles around it altogether—and when I had driven around it every time, I would tie the horses and run over to the telegraph station to see how the convention in Baltimore was coming along. That was the convention that nominated Mr. Wilson for the Presidency. And from that minute on, I was a fan of Woodrow Wilson, who I think is one of the five or six great Presidents that this country has produced. And to receive an honor like this from a foundation dedicated to him is about the highest honor that any man can achieve. And I thank you very much for giving it to me."

An oval of applause broke out, and the President seemed to see that he had finally acquitted himself well enough. At once, the imperative cameramen moved forward and began to tell the President to look like an honored man: Closer to Gideonse and McAdoo! . . . Lift the plaque higher! . . . Head up, please, Mr. President! . . . Hold that! . . . Look this way! . . . Look that way! . . . Just one more!

When the photographing was over, knots formed, and the crowd broke up slowly. Several of the guests approached the President with cordial messages from mutual friends, and others offered him some thoughts on how to run the country. The President listened attentively to all, smiled, agreed, thanked, and seemed in no hurry (though in fact he must have known, so time-conscious is he, that he was already late for his next appointment). Finally, Connelly came in, and, with the effrontery and gallantry of Lord Nelson sweeping the sea of French and Spanish ships of the line, quickly threw everyone out.

There followed a half-hour fixed appointment with W. Stuart Symington, of the NSRB, who discussed with the President the relative importance of various minerals and metals to the national security, talking particularly about the steps necessary to guarantee the continued importation of certain raw materials from abroad. Symington also briefed the President on several matters that were to come up before a meeting of the National Security Council that afternoon. (The NSC, previously a fixed appointment on Thursdays, was this afternoon moved up one day, and has since remained a Wednesday appointment.)

The President went to Blair House at one o'clock for lunch and a nap. He appeared back at his office a few minutes before three, and worked on papers. At three o'clock, his Executive Clerk, William J. Hopkins, brought in a fresh pile of documents to be signed, and for nearly fifteen minutes the President wrote his name, over and over.

Shortly after three, Republican Senator Wayne L. Morse, of Oregon, arrived in the anteroom, expecting to see the President at three-fifteen. Connelly pointed out to Morse that his appointment was not until Friday afternoon, but, since he was a United States senator, Connelly told him to hang around; he said he would squeeze him in soon.

At three-fifteen, the President received the Secretary of the Interior, Oscar L. Chapman, who had requested an appointment a week before. Chapman outlined plans for new legislation on submerged coastal lands—the so-called tidelands—in the light of Supreme Court decisions on the matter. The President, whom Chapman found amazingly well informed on the subject, suggested a few changes in Chapman's proposed laws, and the Secretary said he would incorporate them into the drafts. Chapman then talked over with the President the status and scope of the Echo Park power development on the Colorado River. And, finally, he outlined some new Indian legislation his Department wanted to get through Congress. Chapman talked overtime, and at three-thirty-seven it was necessary for Connelly to open the door and nod to the President across Chapman's back. Truman stood up and tactfully adjourned Chapman at the end of his next paragraph.

The National Security Council was waiting for the President in the Cabinet Room. (Murphy's team, which had been working on the Economic Message there, had been shifted, in order to make room for the Security Council, into another large conference room, called the Fish Room because of a small, bubbling aquarium in one corner of it.) The Security Council discussed with the President some matters that are still Top Secret.

The Security Council adjourned at four-nine. Lawton, the Budget Director, had come into Connelly's office at three-fifty-five, asking to see the President on an urgent point regarding the budget, and the President had a fixed appointment with William M. Boyle, Jr., the chairman of the Democratic National Committee, at four o'clock. Out of inter-party courtesy, however, both Boyle and Lawton now deferred to the premature Republican senator from Oregon. The President listened to a report from Morse on the findings of a Senate subcommittee on Alaska, which were soon to be made public; an outline of a difference Morse had with the Civil Aeronautics Board in connection with airlines to Alaska; certain suggestions by Morse for Republican appointments to defense posts; and a protest against the overlooking of Oregon as a site for regional offices of the federal defense agencies. The President took notes on all of Morse's points and promised decisions on them.

At four-twenty-five, Morse gave way to Boyle, who had been busy in recent days on Capitol Hill and now had for the President's private ear a compendium of political recommendations from Democratic senators and congressmen. The President also talked over with Boyle some general Democratic Party policies.

At five-two, Boyle retired and Lawton came in. Lawton's business, one final set of changes in the Budget Message, took only nine minutes.

Next, Hopkins brought in a fresh fall of the never-ending downpour of documents to be signed, and the President worked on them, and on other papers, until five-twenty-three, when he stuffed his briefcase full of unfinished work—including an entirely new draft of the Economic Message, which Murphy's team had sent in. He put on his hat and coat, stepped out to the anteroom to say good evening to Connelly and Miss Barrows, and went to Blair House. There he settled down at once to work on the new draft of the Economic Message. At five-forty-five, he called Snyder, to ask him to have supper with him and talk over the new version of the message. At exactly six, he called Mrs. Truman and Margaret in New York. Snyder showed up a few minutes before seven. The President and his old friend had two Old Fashioneds each, had their supper, and then discussed the Economic Message until nine o'clock. At nine-five, the President telephoned Clark M. Clifford, his former Special Counsel and message-drafter, who had retired to practice law, and talked over some aspects of the message with him. Then the President called the Secret Service, to arrange to have his walk and swim the next morning. After that, he sat in his study and worked over the message until a few minutes before twelve. He went to bed at midnight and put himself to sleep by rereading a couple of sections of the budget.

3
DWIGHT D. EISENHOWER

1953-1960

In the context provided by the activist Presidencies of Roosevelt and Truman, the much more passive Presidency of Dwight D. Eisenhower looked weak and uninteresting. Later, in the context of the hyperactive Johnson Presidency, analysts were prone to look back on the Eisenhower era with a newly discovered nostalgia. But some clung to the view that an eight-year pause in addressing some of the pressing problems of the nation merely permitted little problems to grow into big ones, and thus the domestic crises of the late 1960s—especially in the area of racial conflict—have been laid at President Eisenhower's doorstep. This seems a harsh judgment; it is unlikely that eight years of the most frenetic presidential activity during the period from 1953 to 1960 could conceivably have undone the work of decades and centuries in American race relations. And so we must look elsewhere for the causes of domestic tension in the last half of the sixties.

Nevertheless, it is beyond dispute that Eisenhower's was a Presidency devoted to discovering the passive virtues of executive leadership. Many contemporary analysts took a dim view of this, although they could not argue with the massive majorities that Eisenhower piled up each time he ran for office. To understand Eisenhower's Presidency, in any event, one must understand how he organized the presidential office. This entailed avoiding operating details, making large grants of authority to subordinates—especially Governor Sherman Adams, for most of the eight-year period Eisenhower's trusted chief of staff—and concentrating upon what President Eisenhower conceived of as broad issues of national policy. This led, in the eyes of some observers, to a curiously theoretical, even doctrinaire approach to many problems of public policy. The virtues and the costs of this approach are explored in the four articles that follow, all by contemporary reporters.

Eisenhower's White House
CHARLES J. V. MURPHY

The story is told that shortly after his inauguration Dwight D. Eisenhower took a telephone call from the Chairman of the Joint Chiefs of Staff, General Omar Bradley, over in the Pentagon. As the new occupant of the White House put down the receiver, he remarked to his secretary in some bewilderment, "He called me Mr. President, and I've known Brad all my life."

The presidency has evoked in Mr. Eisenhower, as it did for a time in Mr. Truman, a searching sense of humility—he has commented on this privately to friends. But the White House has not overawed him as it did his predecessor. Accustomed to grave responsibility as the Supreme Commander of great coalition armies, equipped with cosmopolitan experience in a wide variety of state affairs, Eisenhower has fitted himself into the presidency with a calm assurance that in some respects is reminiscent of Franklin D. Roosevelt's regime. "FDR was always in command," says one of Eisenhower's aides. "So is Ike."

The description is not entirely accurate. The habit of command remains, but the habitual exercise of its prerogatives has been put aside. The skill with which the President has detached himself from the superficial implications of his past is evidenced by the virtual disappearance of the term "military mind" from the commentaries of his critics. This has been a studied psychological divestment on Eisenhower's part. His staff was instructed, even before the move from the Hotel Commodore to Pennsylvania Avenue, to avoid any partiality to the military idiom or military analogies. An occasional slip of the tongue will still betray a preelection associate into addressing the President as "General"; otherwise the rule has been faithfully observed.

The galaxy of ribbon-bedizened two-star aides that flanked Truman and Roosevelt on official occasions has disappeared. Eisenhower's senior military aide is a lieutenant colonel, the President having declared that generals should be doing a general's work, not acting as flunkies. Except for a small portrait of Lee on the wall (side by side with one of Lincoln), only the tidiness of Eisenhower's office suggests a soldierly past. On the wall opposite the President's desk in a bright painting of an *Alpenhutte* on a windy ridge, which the President admires for the painter's success in producing the luminous haze of the high mountains—a trick that eluded his amateur's resources when he tried painting mountain scenes last summer in the Colorado Rockies.

But ridding oneself of the working habits of a lifetime is quite another matter. There has unmistakably descended upon the White House a formality, an orderliness, and a quietude reminiscent of SHAEF and SHAPE. Moreover, the President in his approach to the machinery of government employs much the same methods that he perfected as the Supreme Commander of highly variegated forces. To a degree unknown to the presidency since Calvin Coolidge's Administration, Eisenhower practices decentralization and delegation of authority. Between him and

Reprinted from the July 1953 issue of *Fortune Magazine* (p. 75) by special permission; © 1953 Time Inc.

the heads of government departments and agencies is a definite understanding established forthrightly in advance: "You have full authority. I expect you to stand on your own feet. Whatever you decide goes. The White House will stay out of your hair."

It was with such an understanding that the President delegated to Herbert Brownell the heroic task of reorganizing the inchoate affairs of the Department of Justice; to George Humphrey an unqualified charter for management of fiscal policy; and to Charles E. Wilson the responsibility for the Pentagon. Eisenhower has accepted their decisions. The President as an impresario, an all-knowing virtuoso, governing by lightning riposte at press conferences or swift judgments at suddenly called meetings of his lieutenants, has no place in Eisenhower's scheme of things.

It is, for that matter, perhaps too early to judge precisely the kind of President he intends to be. Nevertheless a new conception of the presidency is beginning to emerge. The outline is still amorphous, and the pressure of events may dwarf the concept short of fulfillment; but the idea, as explained by a senior presidential adviser, is about like this:

> The chief reason why the White House lost dignity is that through the last twenty years it became an operating branch of the government. Labor disputes, CAB decisions, administrative and operational details of all varieties, not to mention the dispensing of patronage, all ended up in the White House. More often than not, decisions of responsible agencies were reversed by White House whim or the exigencies of the hour, until it became impossible to tell which part of the government was really responsible for what.

Ike's idea is that the President should rid himself of such pressures. His White House is a place where national policies will be worked out and all else excluded.

LIFE ALONG THE "CHANNELS"

Whether the presidency can ever be successfully disengaged from "operational" politics and administration remains to be seen. But there is no doubt that Mr. Eisenhower is working toward that end with patience, perseverance, even idealism. His purpose is visible in the attempted transfer of the dispensation of patronage from the White House to the Republican National Committee, under Chairman Len Hall. It is apparent, too, in the President's executive relationship with the heads of the departments and agencies of government—a relationship marked, on the one side, by an unprecedented delegation of operational authority and, on the part of the President, by a nose-to-the-grindstone concentration on issues of national policy.

Certainly the machinery now installed at the White House is strikingly different from that which served Roosevelt and Truman. There are no Republican counterparts of a Harry Hopkins, or a Clark Clifford, or a John Steelman flitting thither and yon on presidential errands. Nor does much survive of the easy camaraderie that in both Roosevelt's and Truman's time accorded the staff ready access to the presidential presence, and in Truman's time saw the President, daily, in congenial confabulation with his top assistants. The specialist has replaced the brain-truster, the trouble shooter, the triple-threat man, and the foot-loose plenipotentiary without portfolio. The iceboxes and bourbon caches have disappeared from the offices; nobody ever suggests that it might be a good time to "strike a blow for Liberty," and seeing the President means going through "channels."

The President's staff consists, with a few exceptions, of people who worked closely with him during the campaign, either at the Hotel Commodore headquarters or on the campaign train.* The most significant figures are the eight men in the gallery below.

In charge, as Assistant to the President, is Sherman Adams, former Governor of New Hampshire, and an experienced businessman. "My function," says Sherman Adams, "is neither to functionalize or institutionalize, but rather to departmentalize." Adams actually conducts himself as presidential Chief of Staff, although the term itself, because of the President's distaste for military analogies, is not encouraged around the White House.

Practically everything that concerns the President funnels through Adams. If the staff as a whole wishes to discuss some point of business with the President, request is made through Adams who decides whether the matter is sufficiently important to be carried beyond himself.

All the men below, however, have the privilege of seeing the President on their own, and Press Secretary James Hagerty enjoys a special quasi-autonomous status. He alone is authorized to speak publicly for the President. He is also one of the privileged few—Sherman Adams, Secretary of State John Foster Dulles, his brother Allen Dulles of Central Intelligence are the others—who can wake the President at night on a matter of national consequence. (So far the President's sleep has not been disturbed. The news of Stalin's death, which reached Washington about midnight, was a hairline case. The President's advisers decided, after anxious consultation, that it would keep until morning.)

The staff assembles in Adams' office, at eight-thirty every morning (except Monday, when Adams may be in attendance at the President's conference with the congressional leaders). Adams does not convene these meetings merely to farm out the work. "The White House staff," Adams observes, "is a clearing house for policy matters. These meetings are to make sure that these policies are properly coordinated." The staff also has another function. "Our job," says Maxwell Rabb, Adams' assistant, "is to compress the President's work into essentials—to sharpen everything up for discussion with him." Practically all the staff and, for that matter, government papers come to the President with a one-page synopsis on top. "If a proposition can't be stated on one page," goes a (somewhat questionable) Eisenhower maxim, "it isn't worth saying." The President insists that the White House staff, as well as the department and agency heads, produce for him, with their outlines of policy problems, precise recommendations of their own.

"The change in the White House," says Bernard Shanley, Special Counsel to the

*Governor Dewey, General Lucius D. Clay of Continental Can, Senator Duff, and others who loomed large in the campaign "Kitchen Cabinet," have receded into the background. They are seldom consulted on government questions by the President. "The President," Lucius Clay notes, "has an unusual capacity for walling off the social from the official. You'll never find 'cronies' mixed up in his business."

President, "is not just in the way of doing things, but even more in concept and attitude. There is no longer a one-man or one-clique show. It is an Administration at work."

This is not to say that the White House machinery is running to the complete satisfaction of the President. The "channels" still get clogged occasionally, and sounds of half-checked impatience continue to detonate around papers that the President judges "mediocre" or "overloaded" or simply "trivial." But, by and large, staff relations are harmonious, considering the inevitable counterplay of ambitions around a President.

This stability is in large measure an expression of Adams' own personality. Gray, austere, principled, he is determined to restore to the day-to-day transactions of the White House a dignity and a sense of national, as distinct from party, responsibility that had all but eroded away. If the atmosphere in the West Wing is suggestive of a New Hampshire bank, it is because Adams himself conveys that flavor. His associates find him brusque and withdrawn and outsiders who would like to make the White House a wailing wall complain that he is isolating the President. That he is rough on the staff, driving them through ten- and twelve-hour days, is self-evident. But the President's own working habits, his insistence that the staff block out all problems for him in advance, leaves Adams no choice.

The pent-up frustrations of the Republican party beat remorselessly against Adams' door. Its representatives in Congress especially, after two decades of heel-cooling, expect the White House to yield at once to their knock. Because it is not the President himself but Adams who answers, there is scattered suspicion that Adams is quietly gathering power into his own hands. Nothing could be further from the truth. Adams is a man devoid of mystery. He is no Richelieu or Colonel House. A simple rule guides him: to see that the President's job is done the way the President wants.

THE PRESIDENTIAL DAY

The President's workday goes something like this:

Awakened at seven o'clock by the faithful Sergeant Moaney, his Army orderly, the President takes breakfast half an hour later in the family dining room on the first floor—usually grapefruit and coffee. Because the President is accustomed to doing business at meals, there usually will be several guests—either members of his staff, or perhaps Congressmen, or a mixture of both. He is at his desk at about eight o'clock. He then skims through the New York and Washington newspapers, and signs the letters dictated the afternoon before. (Of the average 3,000 letters that arrive daily at the White House, from fifty to 100 reach the President's desk.)

His appointments begin at eight-thirty and run through until four to four-thirty in the afternoon, with five minutes for a perfunctory call to half an hour for serious business. The schedule of appointments is charted on a large card on the President's desk, each entry accompanied by a one-sentence identification of the visitor, the reason for the interview, and often a note suggesting the possible line of discussion. Eisenhower *thinks* much as Franklin Roosevelt used to do, by discussion rather than by reading, and his pleasure in batting around ideas with a cooperative visitor sometimes gets the better of his sense of punctuality. "I could make the schedules work," Appointments Secretary Tom Stephens once exclaimed to a staff associate fidgeting outside the President's office, "if you fellows wouldn't start him talking."

During his first three months in office, when the President was carrying out his plan of having all the ninety-six Senators and 435 Representatives in for a meal, most of his luncheons, as well as many breakfasts, were reserved for this formidable undertaking. Freed from this self-imposed duty, the President now has a somewhat more catholic choice of luncheon guests. Among the more recent, not including staff members: Bernard Baruch; the Class of 1915, West Point; the Canadian Prime Minister, Louis St. Laurent; all forty-eight Governors; Heavyweight Champion Rocky Marciano and some three dozen other athletes.

Requests for meetings with the President run into the hundreds every week—and Tom Stephens devotes the equivalent of a full day of his working week to expressing the President's regrets. On any given date, there are always at least one or two business or social organizations in convention in Washington, whose leaders reason that the President would be delighted to meet them. Or it might be Jim Farley, in the capital on a business trip, who would like to pay his respects; or Chief Yellow Tail to register the fealty of his tribe; or Darryl Zanuck of Twentieth Century-Fox to discuss his ideas for a motion picture about the Foreign Service.

WHO GETS IN

"Our responsibility," confides the harassed Mr. Stephens, "is to save the President's day for national business." Eisenhower has laid down a rule that, except for an occasional friend, he will see only people who *(a)* have government business to talk over with him or *(b)* are connected with national organizations or affairs to which the White House can properly impart the prestige of its endorsement. Under this reasoning the Cotton Queen and the Citrus Queen lost out while the heads of the Red Cross, the American Cancer Society, and the National Safety Council were welcomed.

There are three fixed conferences on the President's weekly calendar—the Monday meeting with the congressional leaders at eight-thirty; a Thursday meeting with the National Security Council at ten; and the Friday Cabinet meeting at ten. In addition two so-called "briefings" are regularly scheduled. An hour a week is set aside for the Chairman of the Joint Chiefs of Staff. Secretary of Defense Charles E. Wilson has a similar claim. In his hour Omar Bradley, soon to be succeeded by Admiral Arthur Radford, gives the President a comprehensive rundown of the world military situation. The meeting with Wilson serves the double purpose of informing the President about developments in the defense establishment while permitting him to coach "Engine Charlie" in a highly complex field where the Secretary's bull-in-the-china-shop behavior continues to distress the White House staff.

At odd moments during the day, in the chinks between visitors, the President tosses off short letters and notes. His habit, however, is to save more important dictation until the late afternoon, after he has disposed of the last caller. He feels more relaxed then, with the worst of the day behind him, and is able to reach deeper inside himself. It is during this reflective interval, for example, that he composes his letters to Sir Winston Churchill, thus continuing through a Republican Administration the historic exchange begun by FDR and the Former Naval Person.

OFF DUTY

The President has no fixed quitting time. But he tries to wind up the day not later than six o'clock. In contrast with Truman, who was preceded to his bedside by an armful of memoranda, dispatches, and intelligence reports, Eisenhower tries to walk out of his office with a clean desk behind him. "He is most definitely a 'day' man," in the judgment of a close associate, who attributes the fairly rigid compartmentation to a lifetime in the Army, with its early risings and quiet garrison evenings.

So far the President has been moderately successful, except in the matter of golf, in drawing a veil of privacy around his relaxations. His press secretary, Jim Hagerty, says firmly: "I have deliberately made a point of remaining generally uninformed on the subject." But complete "security" is of course impossible. When there is no state or business dinner at the White House, the President and "Mamie" may have a few friends in, like Mrs. Howard Snyder, wife of the White House physician, or Special Assistant Robert Cutler, who may telephone Mamie to make sure there is nothing "interesting," i.e., formal or serious, going on, and if there is not, invite himself over. Once or twice a week the President plays bridge in the solarium with other experts, among them Chief Justice Vinson, William E. Robinson, publisher of the New York *Herald Tribune,* Harold E. Talbott, Secretary of the Air Force, and Clifford Roberts, an investment banker and golfing companion. Other evenings he may do a little painting in a study next to his bedroom; or join Mamie and friends watching TV or the movies on the ground floor; or retire to bed early with a couple of "westerns," a soporific he commends to sleepless associates.

The President, six nights out of seven, will be in bed by eleven-thirty. There is method in this relaxed, somewhat withdrawn regime. He scolds his staff for driving themselves too hard. Speaking of the pressures that converged on him during the war, he says: "I dared not—I could not—get sick. Staying well became a serious business with me." His interest in golf is partly therapeutic—partly unashamed fascination with the game.

All in all, allowing for the well-publicized golf, the less-publicized business luncheons and breakfasts, the political and ceremonial duties that intrude on some evenings, it probably adds up to an average work week of about fifty to fifty-five hours, less than Truman's sixty-five to seventy, but considerably more than the thirty-five to forty of the CIO, whose leaders recently announced that they were going to keep a record of presidential appearances on the golf links.

THE NEW NSC

Much of the President's work revolves around the three landmarks on his weekly calendar, the meetings with the legislative leaders, with the National Security Council, and with the Cabinet. With each of these institutions, Eisenhower's methods differ from those of his predecessor, and in the case of the National Security Council the institution itself has changed as well. His use of the NSC as the strategic planning body at the apex of government may well become his most significant contribution to the executive technique.

The Council was established under Mr. Truman in 1947. Its statutory members were the President, Vice President, the Secretaries of State and of Defense, the MSA director, and the chairman of the National Security Resources Board (which the President is merging into the new Office of Defense Mobilization). The Director of Central Intelligence and the Chairman of the Joint Chiefs of Staff were, as they are today, in attendance as the Council's intelligence and military advisers. The founding idea was to bring continuously before the President all the complex considerations—political, economic, military, and scientific—that in their ever changing interplay determine the nation's strategic situation. Because the Council's role is advisory, its deliberations result only in recommendations to the President. Hence, as a policy generator, it is whatever the President wishes to make it.

Whatever Truman may have wished for the Council, he never willed the means. Last fall Dr. Vannevar Bush criticized it as "a meeting place of departments for compromise, rather than of chiefs of departments for momentous decision." It was meagerly manned. Its meetings were intermittent, and Truman himself seldom attended them until the outbreak of the Korean war. Even then the members might convene to find that the President had more pressing business elsewhere.

After election day Eisenhower asked Robert Cutler, a Boston banker (president of the Old Colony Trust) and a campaign adviser, to come up with a plan for reorganizing the Council, and to manage the Council thereafter. Having been a brigadier general on Stimson's staff during the war, Cutler began with a considerable lay knowledge of Pentagon ways. His stooped figure, mordant wit, and almost eccentric New England forthrightness represent, in many ways, the Administration's most sophisticated adornment—a kind of Oliver Wendell Holmes of the Cold War.

Among the new features of the NSC is a Planning Board, composed of senior experts from State, Defense, Treasury, CIA, MSA, JCS, and PSB, with Cutler as chairman. This board has become the central switchboard of security planning in the government. Cutler's ambition is to support it with a permanent staff of specialists modeled on the British system. The Planning Board meets three times a week, and the Council itself at least once a week.

THE FISCAL APPROACH

Another significant change, requested by the President, is the addition to the Council, as *ad hoc* members, of both the Secretary of the Treasury and the Director of the Budget. The idea was to introduce into the perspective of national strategic planning a form of fiscal checks and balances that had somehow been overlooked. But the most important single thing that has happened to the Council has been the unfailing attendance of the President, and his lively participation in its momentous transactions.

The day before the Council meeting Cutler usually lunches or breakfasts with the President—or rather, as Cutler puts it, "He eats, I talk." The President is informed of the topics on the agenda, and of the particular positions of the different departments whenever a divergence of view has developed.

CUTLER AT BAT

The Council meets in the Cabinet Room at the White House. Its deliberations ordinarily last from ten o'clock until twelve-thirty but on occasion they have continued through lunch and the afternoon. The first item on the agenda, almost invariably, is a report by Allen Dulles, director of Central Intelligence, on "the big picture" or a particular aspect—perhaps the situation in Egypt, or certain developments in Communist China. Then, as Cutler steers the discussion down the agenda, Dulles, Humphrey, Wilson, or whoever bears primary responsibility, leads off the discussion. A "precipitation" of the issues is meanwhile jotted down for Cutler, who summarizes the prevailing view with the statement, "Mr. President, the sense of the Council on this issue is, as I see it . . ."

The President encourages the other Council members, most of whom are as inexperienced in grand strategy as he is experienced, to speak their minds; and to challenge him if they disagree with his position. But even here he leans over backward to prevent national strategic decisions from bearing too heavy an impress of his own personality. He insists that Cutler's Planning Board pass up to the Council, with its own recommendations, a precis of all dissenting opinions and alternative solutions.

It was by this general method that the current military budget was constructed. Under Truman the military budget was worked up by the Defense Department and the final sum to be requested of Congress was settled between Truman and the Bureau of the Budget; the budget as such never figured directly in NSC deliberations. This year, by Eisenhower's direction, the Council was exposed, before it took up the broad question of strategy, to "a budget exercise." Secretary of the Treasury Humphrey and Joseph Dodge, Director of the Budget Bureau, outlined together, in plain terms, the government's financial and budgetary positions and their ideas on what the nation could afford for defense. This exercise occupied a part of almost every NSC session from the first meeting in February until the middle of May.

There was no detailed discussion within the NSC of the separate service programs; these were settled off stage between Wilson and Dodge and between the President and Wilson. What the Council did, under the President's guidance, was to reanalyze American strategy in terms of striking a viable balance between the external military and internal economic threats, or, as the President put it, of contriving "a respectable posture of defense that can be maintained for the long pull."

The President's chief contribution was to provide the philosophical approach to the problem—an approach conservative in both the military and economic sense. His reasoning that the nation could not allow its economic stability to be jeopardized by the possibility of war was responsible for the discarding of a strategy based upon a *fixed* date of maximum danger in favor of a *floating* date. In May this judgment, having been crystallized in the NSC, was submitted to the Cabinet, then to the legislative leaders, then to Congress.

THE CABINET'S MORNING

The revived prestige and vitality of the Cabinet is an equally striking phenomenon of the new administration. Franklin Roosevelt did not particularly fancy a "strong" Cabinet, and treated his Secretaries much as a sovereign might treat his court. Harry Truman was more considerate, but because he appointed mainly mediocrities, and because he used the Cabinet very much as he used the NSC—as a generator of policy recommendations that he could take or leave alone—it never recovered its lost prestige. Mr. Eisenhower entered the presidency determined to make the Cabinet amount to something.

By virtue of his example the Friday Cabinet sessions are animated by the same brisk purposefulness that characterizes the NSC sessions. The President always starts the meeting with a prayer—never spoken, but rendered with bowed head. Dr. Gabriel Hauge, the staff economist, monitors the agenda in much the same fashion that Cutler develops material for the NSC meetings. Vice President Nixon, Henry Cabot Lodge Jr., US Representative to the UN, Harold E. Stassen, Director of MSA, and Budget Director Dodge sit with the Cabinet by the President's invitation. Seated along the wall are half a dozen members of the White House staff—Cutler, Jackson, Persons, Hauge, Shanley, and Philip Young, Civil Service Administrator.

What has impressed the former corporation executives in the Cabinet is the President's ability to size up a problem, his instinct for judging whether it is ripe for decision, and the ease with which he is able to transfer his mind from one item of business to another. "The President," observes Secretary Humphrey, "is always quick to jump in with a suggestion. He almost never jumps in with a decision." If it develops that preparation for an agenda item is incomplete, or the basic facts are in conflict, or that the responsible official has failed, in the popular Federalese, to "do his homework," the President will proceed impatiently to the next item.

HUMPHREY'S RISE

Humphrey and Dodge have emerged as the dominant minds of the Cabinet. It is their counsel, not just in fiscal affairs but over a broad range of domestic policy, that the President usually follows, rather than the less orthodox viewpoint asserted by Lodge and Stassen. The President admires Humphrey's lucidity of mind, his forthrightness, the speed with which he has mastered the details of his vast office, and, most important, his sure-footedness. Humphrey, in turn, has been greatly influenced by Eisenhower.

"I'm not quite the same man I was last November," he concedes. He ranged himself alongside the President during the prolonged discussions over the budget and the tax program, though military spending, total spending, and total taxes are all higher than the Humphrey of last year could have imagined himself recommending. Humphrey went even further. He sought out his old friend, Senator Taft, to persuade him that the President's decision was right.

Nixon plays a much more important part in Cabinet deliberations than traditional usage has assigned the Vice President. It is, on the whole, a politically inexperienced Cabinet, and there has been a lamentable tendency, most conspicuously on Wilson's part, to talk down to Congress and to brush aside public opinion. The President looks to Nixon, in Cabinet discussions, to keep reminding the others that they are not working in a vacuum; that whatever they decide must be painstakingly justified before Congress and the public.

The most serious matter that has come before the Cabinet was the budget, which it threshed over for weeks. In mid-May there still survived a residual conviction that a deeper cut could be made in foreign aid and that some tax reduction was essential in order to mollify Republican leadership on the Hill. The President finally chose the occasion to set forth his views as to why tax reductions would have to be postponed, and foreign and military aid maintained at the determined levels. He spoke at length and with unexpected eloquence. When he finished, the Cabinet cheered. "It was all quite emotional," Brownell recalls, "something that you'd never expect to hear in a Cabinet."

ENVOYS FROM THE HILL

To the President's Monday-morning conference on legislation come Vice President Nixon, Senators Taft (until his recent illness), Bridges, Saltonstall, Knowland, Millikin, Speaker Martin, and Representatives Halleck and Arends. If some special bill or legislative situation is up for discussion, the committee chairman directly concerned is usually invited. Some of the White House staff are on hand, and certain Cabinet members may also be present depending on the agenda.

These meetings start precisely at eight-thirty and last, as a rule, from one to two hours. To legislators accustomed to the wandering interests of the committee chamber, the rather rigid order of business was at first slightly disconcerting. But as the unfamiliarity wore off, the visitors from the Hill were generally agreed that, by and large, the method had its advantages. "The work gets done," says Charlie Halleck, "and we're not forever getting bogged down in side issues."

The technical success of these meetings is due in large measure to the play of the President's own personality. Earnest in the advocacy of his own ideas, he is equally earnest about listening to others. "You go away with the impression," Joe Martin has decided, "that the President has at least made an honest effort to listen to you, without trying to make you swallow his ideas as gospel." The general impression on the Hill is that the President possesses an unexpected understanding of the legislative process—a gift that has won from Joe Martin the grudging tribute that "Army politics must be a better training ground than most of us had realized."

But the mechanics of assembling and maneuvering coalitions in support of legislation—the practical exercise of politics that brought out the gusto and genius of FDR—so far seems to have small appeal for Eisenhower. This chore he leaves to Adams, who in turn looks to Major General Wilton B. Persons, USA, retired, and his three assistants. Few men outside that body have a better knowledge of the workings of Congress than "Jerry" Persons, who twenty years ago went to the Hill as the War Department's liaison with the House Military Affairs Committee. When Eisenhower went to NATO, Persons traveled with him to maintain the channel back to the Hill. Well liked and trusted, he is diligent in keeping the legislative leaders informed about appointments and policy actions of interest to Congress. The faulty communication that, for example, left Taft without advance notice of the Bohlen appointment has been repaired.

WHO'S IN CHARGE?

The President has gone to extraordinary lengths to cultivate friendly relations with Congress—and in the process has alternately fascinated, puzzled, and alarmed Washington observers. A Washington columnist recently observed, half incredulously, that the President "acts as though he preferred to win Congress by kindness rather than force." Part of the explanation lies in the President's confidence in his own considerable talents for conciliation and persuasion and a belief that patience and reasonableness will tide him over situations where a Franklin Roosevelt, a Harry Truman, or a T. R. Roosevelt would resort unhesitatingly to coercion, guile, or threats.

But there is a deeper motivation, too—Eisenhower's almost devout adherence to the concept of Congress as a truly coordinate branch of the government. "Congress," he told a senior Senator, "is closer and more readily responsive [than the President] to the people." Congress is not only close to the people; it is very closely divided. With the Republicans holding a majority of only one in the Senate and eleven in the House; and the Republican majority itself divided into loose and unstable coalitions, the President, already looking to the 1954 elections, has embarked upon a deliberate course of avoiding party friction, if he can, while holding the support of conservative Democrats through the critical period of consolidation of power.

On the tax issue, for example, the President delayed and muffled the inevitable conflict with the Reed-minded Republicans to the last possible hour. He promised Joe Martin and other Republican leaders that he would not "jam legislation down Congress's throat." He took up the case with his legislative leaders in an atmosphere of patient and tactful negotiation. The impression he gave was that he was still examining the facts; that he was sympathetic to countervailing argument; that there was still a chance of his changing his position. The men from the Hill became aware of a recurring phrase of rebuttal: "I agree with you 100 per cent. But you in turn must bear in mind . . ."

The President's slowness to close with this crucial issue deepened the doubts of many who had begun to question his qualities of leadership after his side-stepping of Senator McCarthy. Some of his own staff were troubled by his noncombativeness, the tendency to postpone taking a firm position, the apparent lack of incisiveness and the classical attributes of positive leadership. They did not breathe easily again until he decided, late in May, to carry the issues to the people via television and the radio and to stump the Middle West. But this flanking move, though introducing a temporary change in tactics, does not necessarily connote the President's abandonment of the strategy of conciliation, in the view of his closest advisers.

One says: "You must understand that Eisenhower is a new kind of President using new methods. He does not intend to satisfy the people on the extreme edges of any given controversy. He is trying above everything else to create a community of interest, a community of mind, within the canopy that is the Republican party. It is by no means certain that the method will work. But the President is determined to give it a try."

The Day We Didn't Go to War
CHALMERS M. ROBERTS

Saturday, April 3, 1954, was a raw, windy day in Washington, but the weather didn't prevent a hundred thousand Americans from milling around the Jefferson Memorial to see the cherry blossoms—or twenty thousand of them from watching the crowning of the 1954 Cherry Blossom Queen.

President Eisenhower drove off to his Maryland mountain retreat called Camp David. There he worked on his coming Monday speech, designed, so the White House said, to quiet America's fears of Russia, the H-bomb, domestic Communists, a depression. But that Saturday morning eight members of Congress, five Senators and three Representatives, got the scare of their lives. They had been called to a

From *The Reporter* (September 14, 1954), pp. 31-35. Copyright 1954 by Fortnightly Publishing Company, Inc. Reprinted by permission.

secret conference with John Foster Dulles. They entered one of the State Department's fifth-floor conference rooms to find not only Dulles but Admiral Arthur W. Radford, chairman of the Joint Chiefs of Staff, Under Secretary of Defense Roger Kyes, Navy Secretary Robert B. Anderson, and Thruston B. Morton, Dulles's assistant for Congressional Relations. A large map of the world hung behind Dulles's seat, and Radford stood by with several others. "The President has asked me to call this meeting," Dulles began.

URGENCY AND A PLAN

The atmosphere became serious at once. What was wanted, Dulles said, was a joint resolution by Congress to permit the President to use air and naval power in Indo-China. Dulles hinted that perhaps the mere passage of such a resolution would in itself make its use unnecessary. But the President had asked for its consideration, and, Dulles added, Mr. Eisenhower felt that it was indispensable at this juncture that the leaders of Congress feel as the Administration did on the Indo-China crisis.

Then Radford took over. He said the Administration was deeply concerned over the rapidly deteriorating situation. He used a map of the Pacific to point out the importance of Indo-China. He spoke about the French Union forces then already under siege for three weeks in the fortress of Dienbienphu.

The admiral explained the urgency of American action by declaring that he was not even sure, because of poor communications, whether, in fact, Dienbienphu was still holding out. (The fortress held out for five weeks more.)

Dulles backed up Radford. If Indo-China fell and if its fall led to the loss of all of Southeast Asia, he declared, then the United States might eventually be forced back to Hawaii, as it was before the Second World War. And Dulles was not complimentary about the French. He said he feared they might use some disguised means of getting out of Indo-China if they did not receive help soon.

The eight legislators were silent: Senate Majority Leader Knowland and his G.O.P. colleague Eugene Millikin, Senate Minority Leader Lyndon B. Johnson and his Democratic colleagues Richard B. Russell and Earle C. Clements, House G.O.P. Speaker Joseph Martin and two Democratic House leaders, John W. McCormack and J. Percy Priest.

What to do? Radford offered the plan he had in mind once Congress passed the joint resolution.

Some two hundred planes from the thirty-one-thousand-ton U.S. Navy carriers *Essex* and *Boxer,* then in the South China Sea ostensibly for "training," plus land-based U.S. Air Force planes from bases a thousand miles away in the Philippines, would be used for a single strike to save Dienbienphu.

The legislators stirred, and the questions began.

Radford was asked whether such action would be war. He replied that we would be in the war.

If the strike did not succeed in relieving the fortress, would we follow up? "Yes," said the chairman of the Joint Chiefs of Staff.

Would land forces then also have to be used? Radford did not give a definite answer.

In the early part of the questioning, Knowland showed enthusiasm for the venture, consistent with his public statements that something must be done or Southeast Asia would be lost.

But as the questions kept flowing, largely from Democrats, Knowland lapsed into silence.

Clements asked Radford the first of the two key questions: "Does this plan have the approval of the other members of the Joint Chiefs of Staff?"

"No," replied Radford.

"How many of the three agree with you?"

"None."

"How do you account for that?"

"I have spent more time in the Far East than any of them and I understand the situation better."

Lyndon Johnson put the other key question in the form of a little speech. He said that Knowland had been saying publicly that in Korea up to ninety per cent of the men and the money came from the United States. The United States had become sold on the idea that that was bad. Hence in any operation in Indo-China we ought to know first who would put up the men. And so he asked Dulles whether he had consulted nations who might be our allies in intervention.

Dulles said he had not.

The Secretary was asked why he didn't go to the United Nations as in the Korean case. He replied that it would take too long, that this was an immediate problem.

There were other questions. Would Red China and the Soviet Union come into the war if the United States took military action? The China question appears to have been side-stepped, though Dulles said he felt the Soviets could handle the Chinese and the United States did not think that Moscow wanted a general war now. Further, he added, if the Communists feel that we mean business, they won't go "any further down there," pointing to the map of Southeast Asia.

John W. McCormack, the House Minority Leader, couldn't resist temptation. He was surprised, he said, that Dulles would look to the "party of treason," as the Democrats had been called by Joe McCarthy in his Lincoln's Birthday speech under G.O.P. auspices, to take the lead in a situation that might end up in a general shooting war. Dulles did not reply.

In the end, all eight members of Congress, Republicans and Democrats alike, were agreed that Dulles had better first go shopping for allies. Some people who should know say that Dulles was carrying, but did not produce, a draft of the joint resolution the President wanted Congress to consider.

The whole meeting had lasted two hours and ten minutes. As they left, the Hill delegation told waiting reporters they had been briefed on Indo-China. Nothing more.

This approach to Congress by Dulles and Radford on behalf of the President was the beginning of three weeks of intensive effort by the Administration to head off disaster in Indo-China. Some of those at the meeting came away with the feeling that if they had agreed that Saturday to the resolution, planes would have been winging toward Dienbienphu without waiting for a vote of Congress—or without a word in advance to the American people.

For some months now, I have tried to put together the bits and pieces of the American part in the Indo-China debacle. But before relating the sequel, it is necessary here to go back to two events that underlay the meeting just described—though neither of them was mentioned at that meeting.

On March 20, just two weeks earlier, General Paul Ely, then French Chief of Staff and later commander in Indo-China, had arrived in Washington from the Far East to tell the President, Dulles, Radford, and others that unless the United States intervened, Indo-China would be lost. This was a shock of earthquake proportions to leaders who had been taken in by their own talk of the Navarre Plan to win the war.

In his meetings at the Pentagon, Ely was flabbergasted to find that Radford proposed American intervention without being asked. Ely said he would have to consult his government. He carried back to Paris the word that when France gave the signal, the United States would respond.

The second event of importance is the most difficult to determine accurately. But it is clear that Ely's remarks started a mighty struggle within the National Security Council, that inner core of the government where our most vital decisions are worked out for the President's final O.K. The argument advanced by Radford and supported by Vice-President Nixon and by Dulles was that Indo-China must not be allowed to fall into Communist hands lest such a fate set in motion a falling row of dominoes.

Eisenhower himself used the "row-of-dominoes" phrase at a press conference on April 7. On April 15, Radford said in a speech that Indo-China's loss "would be the prelude to the loss of all Southeast Asia and a threat to a far wider area." On April 16, Nixon, in his well-publicized "off-the-record" talk to the newspaper editors' convention, said that if the United States could not otherwise prevent the loss of Indo-China, then the Administration must face the situation and dispatch troops. And the President in his press conference of March 24 had declared that Southeast Asia was of the "most transcendent importance." All these remarks reflected a basic policy decision.

It is my understanding, although I cannot produce the top-secret NSC paper to prove it, that some time between Ely's arrival on March 20 and the Dulles-Radford approach to the Congressional leaders on April 3, the NSC had taken a firm position that the United States could not afford the loss of Indo-China to the Communists, and that if it were necessary to prevent that loss, the United States would intervene in the war—*provided* the intervention was an allied venture and *provided* the French would give Indo-China a real grant of independence so as to eliminate the colonialism issue. The decision may have been taken at the March 25 meeting. It is also my understanding that this NSC paper has on it the approving initials "D.D.E."

On March 29, Dulles, in a New York speech, had called for "united action" even though it might involve "serious risks," and declared that Red China was backing aggression in Indo-China with the goal of controlling all of Southeast Asia. He had added that the United States felt that "that possibility should not be passively accepted but should be met by united action."

The newspapers were still full of reactions to this speech when the Congressional leaders, at the April 3 secret meeting with Dulles and Radford, insisted that Dulles should line up allies for "united action" before trying to get a joint resolution of Congress that would commit the nation to war.

The Secretary lost no time. Within a week Dulles talked with diplomatic representatives in Washington of Britain, France, Australia, New Zealand, the Philippines, Thailand, and the three Associated States of Indo-China—Vietnam, Laos, and Cambodia.

There was no doubt in the minds of many of these diplomats that Dulles was discussing military action involving carriers and planes. Dulles was seeking a statement or declaration of intent designed to be issued by all the nations at the time of the United States military action, to explain to the world what we were doing and why, and to warn the Chinese Communists against entering the war as they had done in Korea.

In these talks Dulles ran into one rock of opposition—Britain. Messages flashing back and forth between Washington and London failed to crack the rock. Finally Dulles offered to come and talk the plan over personally with Prime Minister Churchill and Foreign Secretary Anthony Eden. On April 10, just a week after the Congressional meeting, Dulles flew off to London and later went on to Paris.

Whether Dulles told the British about either the NSC decision or about his talks with the Congressional leaders I do not know. But he didn't need to. The British had learned of the Congressional meeting within a couple of days after it happened. When Dulles reached London they were fully aware of the seriousness of his mission.

The London talks had two effects. Dulles had to shelve the idea of immediate intervention. He came up instead with a proposal for creating a Southeast Asia Treaty Organization (SEATO). Dulles felt this was the "united front" he wanted and that it would lead to "united action." He thought that some sort of *ad hoc* organization should be set up at once without waiting for formal treaty organization, and to this, he seems to have felt, Churchill and Eden agreed.

Just what the British did agree to is not clear, apparently not even to them. Dulles, it appears, had no formal SEATO proposal down on paper, while the British did have some ideas in writing. Eden feels that he made it plain that nothing could be done until after the Geneva Conference, which was due to begin in two weeks. But he apparently made some remark about "going on thinking about it" in the meantime.

At any rate, on his return to Washington Dulles immediately called a SEATO drafting meeting for April 20. The British Ambassador (who at this point had just read the Nixon off-the-record speech in the newspapers) cabled London for instructions and was told not to attend any such meeting. To cover up, the meeting was turned into one on Korea, the other topic for the Geneva Conference. Out of this confusion grew a thinly veiled hostility between Dulles and Eden that exists to this day. Dulles felt that Eden had switched his position and suspects that Eden did so after strong words reached London from Prime Minister Nehru in New Delhi.

EDEN AT THE BRIDGE

A few days later, Dulles flew back to Paris, ostensibly for the NATO meeting with Eden, France's Georges Bidault, and others during the weekend just before the Geneva Conference opened.

On Friday, April 23, Bidault showed Dulles a telegram from General Henri-Eugene Navarre, then the Indo-China commander, saying that only a massive air attack could save Dienbienphu, by now under siege for six weeks. Dulles said the United States could not intervene.

But on Saturday Admiral Radford arrived and met with Dulles. Then Dulles and Radford saw Eden. Dulles told Eden that the French were asking for military help at once. An allied air strike at the Vietminh positions around Dienbienphu was discussed. The discussion centered on using the same two U.S. Navy carriers and Philippine-based Air Force planes Radford had talked about to the Congressional leaders.

Radford, it appears, did most of the talking. But Dulles said that if the allies agreed, the President was prepared to go to Congress on the following Monday, April 26 (the day the Geneva Conference was to open) and ask for a joint resolution authorizing such action. Assuming quick passage by Congress, the strike could take place on April 28. Under Secretary of State Walter Bedell Smith, an advocate of intervention, gave the same proposal to French Ambassador Henri Bonnet in Washington the same day.

The State Department had prepared a declaration of intentions, an outgrowth of the earlier proposal in Washington, to be signed on Monday or Tuesday by the Washington ambassadors of the allied nations willing to back the venture in words. As it happened, there were no available British or Australian carriers and the French already were fully occupied. Hence the strike would be by American planes alone, presented to the world as a "united action" by means of the declaration of intentions.

Eden, on hearing all these details from Dulles and Radford, said that this was a most serious proposition, amounting to war, and that he wanted to hear it direct from the French. Eden and Dulles thereupon conferred with Bidault, who confirmed the fact that France was indeed calling desperately for help—though no formal French request was ever put forward in writing.

Eden began to feel like Horatius at the bridge. Here, on the eve of a conference that might lead to a negotiated end of the seven-year-old Indo-China war, the United States, at the highly informal request of a weak and panicky French Government, was proposing military action that might very well lead to a general war in Asia if not to a third world war.

DULLES'S RETREAT

Eden said forcefully that he could not agree to any such scheme of intervention, that he personally opposed it. He added his conviction that within forty-eight hours after an air strike, ground troops would be called for, as had been the case at the beginning of the Korean War.

But, added Eden, he alone could not make any such formal decision on behalf of Her Majesty's Government. He would fly to London at once and put the matter before a Cabinet meeting. So far as I can determine, neither Dulles or Bidault tried to prevent this step.

Shortly after Eden flew off that Saturday afternoon, Dulles sat down in the American Embassy in Paris with his chief advisers, Messrs. MacArthur, Merchant, Bowie, and McCardle, and Ambassador Dillon. They composed a letter to Bidault.

In this letter, Dulles told Bidault the United States could not intervene without action by Congress because to do so was beyond the President's Constitutional powers and because we had made it plain that any action we might take could only be part of a "united action." Further, Dulles added, the American military leaders felt it was too late to save Dienbienphu.

American intervention collapsed on that Saturday, April 24. On Sunday Eden arrived in Geneva with word of the "No" from the specially convened British Cabinet meeting. And on Monday, the day the Geneva Conference began, Eisenhower said in a speech that what was being sought at Geneva was a "modus vivendi" with the Communists.

All these events were unknown to the general public at the time. However, on Sunday the *New York Times* printed a story (written in Paris under a Geneva dateline) that the United States had turned down a French request for intervention on the two grounds Dulles had cited to Bidault. And on Tuesday Churchill announced to a cheering House of Commons that the British Government was "not prepared to give any undertakings about United Kingdom military action in Indo-China in advance of the results of Geneva" and that "we have not entered into any new political or military commitments."

Thus the Geneva Conference opened in a mood of deepest American gloom. Eden felt that he had warded off disaster and that now there was a chance to negotiate a peace. The Communists, whatever they may have learned of the behind-the-scenes details here recounted, knew that Britain had turned down some sort of American plan of intervention. And with the military tide in Indo-China flowing so rapidly in their favor, they proceeded to stall.

In the end, of course, a kind of peace was made. On June 23, nearly four weeks before the peace, Eden said in the House of Commons that the British Government had "been reproached in some unofficial quarters for their failure to support armed intervention to try to save Dienbienphu. It is quite true that we were at no time willing to support such action . . ."

This mixture of improvisation and panic is the story of how close the United States came to entering the Indo-China war. Would Congress have approved intervention if the President had dared to ask it? This point is worth a final word.

On returning from Geneva in mid-May, I asked that question of numerous Senators and Representatives. Their replies made clear that Congress would, in the end, have done what Eisenhower asked, provided he had asked for it forcefully and explained the facts and their relation to the national interest of the United States.

Whether action or inaction better served the American interest at that late stage of the Indo-China war is for the historian, not for the reporter, to say. But the fact emerges that President Eisenhower never did lay the intervention question on the line. In spite of the NSC decision, April 3, 1954, was the day we *didn't* go to war.

The Presidency: The Effect of Eisenhower's Illness on the Functioning of the Executive Branch.
JAMES RESTON

WASHINGTON, June 17. The illness of President Eisenhower has focused attention here not only on the personal well-being of the President but also on the workings of the institution of the Presidency during his absence from the White House.

The two illnesses in the last nine months have coincided with two important events that influence all interpretations of the subject. These are:
- The Presidential election, in which Republicans are trying to retain and the Democrats to regain control of the White House.
- The atomic revolution, which has confronted all major governments with major adjustments in their policies, and a new political and economic offensive by the Communist powers for control of the uncommitted or neutral nations.

These two events, involving not only the political control of the most powerful nation in the free world but the balance of power in the world struggle with Communism, have sharpened and distorted all comments on the subject and raised a number of specific questions.

From *The New York Times* (June 18, June 19, June 20, June 21, June 22, 1956). © 1956 by The New York Times Company. Reprinted by permission.

TWO CONTRADICTORY ANSWERS

Have the President's illnesses affected the efficient conduct of the nation's business? Has the Eisenhower staff system strengthened the institution of the Presidency to the point where it can make up for his prolonged absences from the White House?

So far, the public has been given two contradictory and politically inspired answers to these questions. They are:

1. The official Administration answer is that the President's illnesses have not affected the efficient operation of the executive. But this answer contains an obvious contradiction.

When the President was well, his closest associates made a great deal, and justifiably, of the profound effect of his character and personality on Administration leadership, particularly in the deliberations of the National Security Council, the Cabinet and the Tuesday morning meeting with Republican legislative leaders.

When the President was unable through illness to carry on these personal and institutional meetings, however, the same officials maintained that the President's absence did not affect the Administration's efficient conduct of business.

2. The Democratic line has been equally contradictory. The Democrats have tended to argue from the first that General Eisenhower was an absentee President a good deal of the time, even when he was well, and that he relied almost wholly on his White House staff and Cabinet. But when he was taken out of action, they rejected the argument that the Cabinet could carry on effectively and contended that his loss tended to cripple the Government.

PRESIDENCY STRENGTHENED

No reporter can say with assurance where the truth lies between these two points of view, especially since the Administration is not in a mood to cooperate with anybody trying to get at the facts. But some points are fairly obvious, among them the following:

• This Administration has strengthened the institution of the Presidency by more effective staff work in the White House office headed by former Gov. Sherman Adams of New Hampshire; in the National Security Council, which is a Cabinet committee recommending coordinated security decisions to the President on the basis of carefully prepared staff papers, and in the Cabinet, which now deals primarily with domestic questions and has, at last, an operating Cabinet secretariat.

• In the first 115 weeks of this Administration, the National Security Council met 115 times, usually for about two hours each time, with the President in the chair. During that period before the President's heart attack it reduced to writing basic security policies that undoubtedly continue to provide policy guidance to the Administration leaders during the President's absence.

• From the start, the President gave extraordinary power to Governor Adams to bring questions to the point of decision, just as he had given unusual power to his wartime chief of staff, Gen. Walter Bedell Smith, and his North Atlantic Treaty Organization Chief of Staff, Gen. Al Gruenther.

He gave similar latitude to his Cabinet members, just as he gave wide latitude to his theatre commanders in the war.

• Meanwhile, an elaborate system of secretaries, special assistants and administrative aides was established to try to keep up with the rapid growth of the President's responsibilities. A competent Staff Secretary, Col. Andrew J. Goodpaster, was appointed to supervise the paper work and maintain personal contact for the President with the Pentagon.

THE NEW AND THE OLD

It is generally agreed here that these things were all to the good, that they were necessary and useful refinements of the system that was originally put into operation at the White House in the late Forties after years of prodding by the late James Forrestal.

A sharp distinction should be made, however, between the operation of this system on the administration of established policies, which the President had personally reviewed and settled, and the effectiveness of the system in producing new policies or modifications of old policies when the President is absent.

The Cabinet can carry on, for example, the established policy of this Administration toward Latin America or Japan or Canada. Everybody knows what it is: the policies have been reduced to writing and kept up to date.

It is the range of new problems—created by the new weapons, the new post-Stalin, post-hydrogen bomb policies in Moscow and Peiping, the rising strength and importance of the neutral nations and the new political and legislative factors on Capitol Hill—that highlights the absence of the President.

What happens when a fundamental question such as United States disarmament policy has to be hammered out without the personal participation of the President?

What happens when sincere differences between the Army, Navy and Air Force over their missions and their development and use of the new atomic weapons and guided missiles reaches such a point that official documents are leaked out of the Pentagon to bring public opinion into the dispute?

It is reasonable to suppose that the President's personal intervention was not missed last Tuesday in the White House when the legislative leaders came to discuss the $1,100,000,000 cut made by the House of Representatives in the Administration's foreign aid program?

QUESTIONS ARE POSED

What happens when the evidence piles up that the country is still unconvinced about the importance of a foreign aid and liberal foreign trade policy that the President himself regards as vital to the success of his whole "cold war" policy?

Who is to straighten out the confusion over the Administration's policy toward the neutrals when Secretary Dulles says precisely the opposite from General Eisenhower and then merely proclaims that there is no difference?

What is there in the impressive big black policy books that the Cabinet members take to the National Security Council about the reorganization and redirection of the North Atlantic Treaty Organization?

The answer to all these questions is that they remain to be settled, that they have been in need of prolonged discussion and revision for many months and that the illnesses of the President have had a profound effect in delaying necessary decisions.

This Administration, bound together by loyalty to the President, has been far less guilty than any of its Democratic predecessors in the last generation of squabbling in public. But it does not follow from this that its leaders are agreed on what to do about many of these questions.

On the contrary, there are basic differences about the new disarmament policy now under discussion, about the whole question of foreign trade and foreign aid, about the attitude the United States should take toward the new Soviet policy of subversion, capital development and political resiliency, and about the meaning of the Soviet military manpower reduction.

Ever since the Geneva conference, where agreement was reached not to use the ultimate weapons to settle the "cold war," it has been almost unanimously agreed among foreign policy experts here that the United States had to review its propaganda effort, its diplomacy and its foreign economic policy if it were to avoid a steady deterioration of the free world's position.

NEED FOR REVISION DENIED

For months it was denied that any need for revision existed. From early August until late in September, the President was in Denver on vacation. Thereafter, he suffered his first illness and did not get back to his full duties until January 9.

Meanwhile, there was divided counsel within the Administration about how to respond to the new Soviet economic and political offensive. The "spirit of Geneva," had faded and the Communist arms deal with Egypt had been completed but it was not until January 19 that the President called his principal aides to the White House study to try to settle the differences over the foreign aid budget. And then this was compromised in the budget and a decision made to have Joseph Dodge, the President's foreign economic adviser, study the meaning of the whole Soviet economic drive.

Some progress was beginning to be made on disarmament policy, East-West contacts policy and one or two others, when the President suffered his second illness. The backlog of unsettled questions and the divisions in the Government, therefore, remain.

The price of these divisions and of the President's absences has not been catastrophic or irretrievable. It cannot be said that any fundamental change has taken place in the world balance of power during these nine months, though the entrance and growing influence of the Soviets in the Eastern Mediterranean is a historical and disturbing fact.

The price, however, has been delay and a sense of uncertainty about the leadership of the United States. The Administration has reacted by saying that America's prestige is higher than at any time since the war, that European union is closer than ever in history, and that the Government, despite the President's illness, has lost none of its effectiveness.

All a reporter can do is to check these observations with responsible officials and diplomats. What he finds is simply that they do not believe it. In fact, they seem to be more conscious of the value of the President's leadership than many of his associates.

They think, in short, that the President is sorely missed, that his relations with Congress and with other governments have deteriorated and that no amount of staff work or orderly committee analysis makes up for the unremitting leadership of the President in the White House.

WASHINGTON, June 18. President Eisenhower was on a restricted diet of food and work today but "The White House Office," which carries the main work-load of the Presidency, was busier than Times Square on a Saturday night.

For example:

- More than 2,100 letters poured into the White House mail room for the President.
- The Special Assistant to the President for Atomic Energy, Lewis L. Strauss, who also is chairman of the Atomic Energy Commission, sent his monthly report on the peaceful uses of atomic energy to the President. It was put in his folder for tomorrow.
- William H. Jackson, Special Assistant to the President on Foreign Affairs, delivered a report to the White House on the Operations Coordinating Board.
- A group of local and state officials met in the Fish Room of the White House and was addressed by the Assistant to the President, Sherman Adams. The Fish Room is so called because it once housed a tank of tropical fish.
- There were staff discussions with the Bureau of the Budget about a legal snarl over funds to finance a research reactor for a foreign country and more discussions about when the President's plane would be available to bring visiting officials to the United States, among them Prime Minister Nehru of India.
- In addition—and this was only a small part of the day's work—the President's Staff Secretary, Andrew J. Goodpaster, had to route from the White House to the various departments and agencies a vast number of communications on all kind of things: A complaint from a citizen against allied acts of violence in the

Mediterranean, an appeal from a feed manufacturer in Chicago for drought relief in Iowa, a complaint from a citizen that he could not get a Federal job and a proposal to send the National High School band and chorus overseas on a goodwill tour.

"GREATER THAN ANY MAN"

Anyone who studies the flow of work in "The White House Office" will soon understand what President Wilson meant when he said:

"The office [of the Presidency] is so much greater than any man could honestly imagine himself to be that the most he can do is to look grave enough and self-possessed enough to seem to fill it."

In the first of these articles, the work that cannot be delegated to the President's staff was enumerated. But there is a mountain of additional work that can and does go on, regardless of the President's absences from the White House.

The duties and responsibilities of the Presidency have grown as vigorously as the growth of the nation itself. For example, in 1790, under President Washington, there were nine executive departments, each doing with fairly simple duties. This had grown to only eleven under President Lincoln in 1864. Today, President Eisenhower is responsible for fifty-seven agencies and departments, many of them much larger than the whole Federal executive establishment in the Nineteenth Century.

In 1789, President Washington approved twenty-seven laws and three Executive Orders; in 1955, President Eisenhower signed 390 public laws, 490 private laws, sixty-five Executive motions.

Similarly, in 1789, Washington transmitted twenty military and sixty-five civilian nominations to the Senate, while last year, President Eisenhower sent up 37,467 military and 3,219 civilian nominations. The civilian personnel of the Federal Government in 1789 numbered 1,000, the military 1,300, while today the civilian personnel totals 2,371,421 and the military 2,935,107.

This has, of course, meant a vast change in the bureaucracy of the White House, particularly since the beginning of World War I. President Washington had one full-time secretary, Lawrence Lewis, his nephew. Even at the turn of this century, President McKinley had less than a dozen personal aides working with him in the White House.

Today, "The White House Office"—as distinguished from the executive office of the President, which includes the Bureau of the Budget and several other large arms of the Presidency—numbers 398 persons with an annual budget of $3,375,000. In President Truman's last year, "The White House Office" had a total of 279, but since then, certain special projects on disarmament, psychological warfare, foreign economic policy, etc., have added 128 employes.

To think of the President, therefore, is one thing, but to think of the Presidency is something quite different. Who runs this vast establishment? Where did they come from? And how good are they?

ADAMS HEADS THE STAFF

The central figure in the coordination and direction of "The Office" is Gov. Sherman Adams, the Assistant to the President. His principal assistants are Gen. Wilton B. Persons, who, as Mr. Adams' deputy, worries primarily about legislation; the three major "secretaries," Bernard Shanley, who keeps the appointments and directs the flow of people in and out of the President's office; James C. Hagerty, who deals with the press, and Col. Andrew J. Goodpaster, who, as Staff Secretary, keeps the right papers going to their proper destination.

The core of this White House staff moved right into the White House with the President from his campaign train in 1952. This was true of Governor Adams, General Persons, Mr. Shanley and Mr. Hagerty. It was also true of two of the President's main Administrative Assistants, Gabriel Hauge, a magazine writer who wrote speeches in the 1952 campaign, and Fred Seaton, a Nebraska newspaper publisher, who recently moved from the White House to be Secretary of the Interior.

Others on the campaign train who are now in the White House are Kevin McCann, a 1952 speech writer who is doing the same job as a Special Assistant; the military aide to the President, Col. Robert L. Schulz, who was with General Eisenhower in Paris and at Columbia University, and Maxwell M. Rabb, a Boston lawyer, who worked with Henry Cabot Lodge Jr. on the campaign train and is now Secretary to the Eisenhower Cabinet.

The two innovations President Eisenhower has brought to the functioning of "The White House Office" are (1) a much clearer line of authority and delegation of authority to and through Governor Adams and (2) the introduction of a corps of special assistants to the President on special subjects (disarmament, foreign affairs, foreign economic policy, etc.).

Both are still controversial, probably because they are new. There is general agreement that Governor Adams has produced a tidier and more efficient administration of the White House staff. During the President's illnesses he has been both a rallying point and a source of continuity for the whole Administration.

Even his critics in this political community, who are numerous (particularly in the vicinity of Capitol Hill), agree that he is a diligent, clear-headed man of character. But he is exercising vast powers beyond the scrutiny of Congress in a position where he is not accountable to anybody but the President. And the question about him is whether he is not establishing precedents that other men, of lesser character, might exercise in the absence of some other President.

ASSISTANTS IN CONTROVERSY

The appointment of special assistants for disarmament (Harold E. Stassen), foreign affairs (Mr. Jackson), atomic energy (Mr. Strauss), foreign economic policy

(Joseph M. Dodge), public works (Gen. John S. Bragdon) has raised questions of conflict with the statutory authority of the heads of the established departments and agencies of the Government.

For example, Mr. Stassen has reacted in one way to the Soviet disarmament and arms-cut proposals and Secretary of State Dulles in another. There have been differences, too, between State and the special assistants on questions of wider technical and cultural contacts with the Soviet Union. These have inevitably brought the concept of the special assistants into controversy.

In general, however, there has been far less controversy between this White House staff and the departments than existed in previous administrations when powerful secretaries and White House favorites, such as the late Harry L. Hopkins, were at odds with the established Cabinet officials.

The main criticism of the White House staff is not that it has been at odds with the departments but simply that it is not as good as it could be or ought to be at a time when the responsibilities of the Presidency touch on the security of the whole free world.

The White House staff, it is generally agreed here, is loyal, technically efficient and industrious, but not brilliant. If the top men in it—those who work constantly in the White House—were compared, say, with the top men surrounding the president of any of the great industrial or commercial organizations in the United States, it is doubtful that they would be regarded as superior.

It compares well with any previous White House staff, but whether that is good enough today is a question that Washington, preoccupied with the President and indifferent to the Presidency, seldom raises.

WASHINGTON, June 19. Tuesday is legislative day at the White House, and Maj. Gen. Wilton B. Persons, who runs interference for the President on Capitol Hill, was in his office this morning at 7:40 A.M.

He looked decidedly unmilitary—a tall, ruddy, 60-year-old man with receding gray hair, sportily dressed in a rough raw silk tan sports jacket, tan trousers, braided sports belt, two-toned shoes, white shirt and a maroon tie figured with Republican elephants.

On his desk, in keeping with the medicinal quality of Washington these days, was a large sign:

While in this office speak in a low, soothing tone of voice and do not disagree with me in any manner.
Please be informed that when one has reached "my age" noise and non-concurrence cause gastric hyperistalsis, hyper secretion of hydrochloric acid and rubus of the gastric mucosa . . . and I become most unpleasant.

"Slick" Persons has seldom been unpleasant to anyone in his life, which is why he is the President's liaison man with Congress, and he wasn't unpleasant this morning. In fact he was entirely relaxed, for the normal Tuesday morning routine had been canceled.

TUESDAY'S SIGNIFICANCE

To anyone interested in the responsibilities of the modern American Presidency, the normal routine of Tuesday morning at the White House is significant.

It is a reminder that the President is not only Commander in Chief, principal administrative officer, ceremonial head, and keeper of the public conscience, but that he is party leader and legislative leader as well.

Coincidentally, the Tuesday morning meeting illustrates President Eisenhower at his best. It clashes with the illusion, now being carefully projected here, that everything goes on as before, regardless of the President's illness.

Normally, the President presides over the legislative council meeting at 9 A.M. in the Cabinet room. (It was moved up from 8:30 A.M. at the suggestion of the physicians after the President's heart attack last September.)

Usually in attendance are the Republican leader in the Senate, William F. Knowland; the Republican leader in the House of Representatives, Joseph W. Martin Jr.; the chairman of the Senate Republican policy committee, Senator Styles Bridges of New Hampshire; the Republican whip in the Senate, Senator Leverett Saltonstall; the Republican deputy House leader, Representative Charles Halleck of Indiana; and the Republican whip in the House, Representative Leslie C. Arends.

In addition to the President, Sherman Adams, the Assistant to the President; General Persons; Gerald D. Morgan, the White House special counsel, and the other White House Congressional liaison officers—I. Jack Martin (Senate) and Bryce N. Harlow (House)—represent the executive branch.

Depending on what is up for discussion, the ranking Republican members of the Congressional committees handling the topics on the agenda and the Cabinet members principally concerned will also attend.

President Eisenhower's leadership in these meetings was at first tentative and respectful toward the Congressional leaders. For the first year of his Administration, he reigned but did not rule. Then slowly, until his first illness, he changed his tactics.

Unlike Franklin D. Roosevelt, who tended to use the rubber-truncheon approach to Congress, and Harry S. Truman, who increasingly tended to taunt his former associates on Capitol Hill, President Eisenhower always has used the cooperative approach.

He put the legislative program on an organized basis. General Persons prepared for the Tuesday morning meeting by calling a session every Saturday morning of all the principal legislative representatives of the various departments and agencies. Here proposals for the Tuesday agenda were drafted.

On Monday, after consultation with the Republican legislative leaders, General Persons then prepared the agenda, briefed the President on it early Tuesday morning, and left the leadership to the President.

PRESIDENT ENJOYS IT

This is precisely the type of meeting that the President enjoys. He runs it informally, and tends to take the judgment of the legislators on what can and cannot be achieved in Congress. But more and more he had tended to be assertive, to put all his powers of persuasion into the meeting, and to work personally with recalcitrant members in the hope of persuading them to back the Administration's requests.

Much more than is generally realized, the President has been in private contact with members of the Senate and House of Representatives by telephone, letter and in unpublicized meetings at the White House on legislative matters. The general impression here is that these personal contacts have paid off.

For much of the last nine months, however, the President simply has not been available to carry on this role as legislative leader. It was, of course, impossible during much of the time from his heart attack in September until he resumed his "full duties" in January. And while he has tried to carry on during his present illness by issuing public statements this week from his hospital bed, the all-important Eisenhower personal touch has been missing.

These absences have also, inevitably, cut the President's contacts with other members of the Administration more than is generally realized or officially admitted.

For example, he used to have a regular meeting every Monday with Arthur F. Burns, chairman of the Council of Economic Advisers, and Gabriel Hauge, the administrative assistant who keeps an eye on the growth of the national economy.

These meetings are no longer held on a regular basis, as part of the system of conserving the President's strength. Messrs. Burns and Hauge still do see the President if something of unusual importance comes up. But today, for example, they held a breakfast meeting at the White House not with the President but with Mr. Adams, General Persons and Mr. Martin of the White House staff.

CONFLICT OF CONCEPTS

The history of the Presidency, as Prof. Edward S. Corwin of Princeton has pointed out, reflects a struggle between two different conceptions of how the President should conduct his office.

First is the conception that the executive ought always to be subordinate to the supreme legislative power.

Second is the conception that it ought to be, within generous limits, autonomous, self-directing and assertive in initiating and pressing for the legislation it wants.

President Eisenhower tended at the beginning of his Administration to adopt the first concept. For a time he tended to subordinate himself in the legislative process to the Congress.

In his second, and particularly in his third year, however, he moved close to the second concept, at least to the point of adopting Theodore Roosevelt's conviction that "the action of the executive [often] offers the only means by which the people can get the legislation they demand and ought to have."

President Eisenhower never did go so far as to agree with the first Roosevelt that the Presidency was "the bully pulpit" of American life. But he did seek more and more to use the Tuesday meeting, the personal contacts and occasionally the persuasive power of patronage on the Congress.

The trouble is that this is an endless battle, requiring the unremitting attention of the President. And unfortunately his illness and absences from the White House have made this impossible.

WASHINGTON, June 20. President Eisenhower came into American political life in a convulsive era as a symbol of unity. Fortunately he has tried to extend the principle of unity into the machinery of the Presidency.

The essence of his personal power is that nobody is mad at him. Men may differ with him, or feel sorry for him, or ridicule his ingenuous copy-book-maxim approach to life and government, but even then they seldom regard him with personal hostility.

This is a powerful factor that has contributed to his record as Chief Executive, legislative leader, mentor to a divided party, head of a mighty coalition and even as negotiator with the Russians.

But what happens when he is stricken twice within nine months and cannot use all his personal powers of persuasion?

The answer to this is that his leadership is seriously weakened by absence and doubts about the future. But while the President is temporarily on the sidelines, the Presidency as an institution has not been uninfluenced by his passionate interest in unity and teamwork.

For example, promptly at 12:30 this afternoon, eight men walked into the Secretary of State's dining room on the fifth floor of the New State Department Building on Virginia Avenue.

The host at luncheon was the Under Secretary of State, Herbert Hoover Jr. The others were William H. Jackson, the special assistant to the President for foreign affairs; Reuben B. Robertson Jr., Under Secretary of Defense; Harold E. Stassen, the President's special assistant for disarmament; Lieut. Gen. C. P. Cabell, deputy director of the Central Intelligence Agency; John B. Hollister, director of the International Cooperation Administration; Theodore C. Streibert, director of the United States Information Agency, and one of their aides, Elmer B. Staats.

OPERATIONS BOARD MEETING

This was the weekly Wednesday meeting of the Operations Coordinating Board, the least-known but probably the most important Eisenhower contribution to the machinery of the Presidency.

The O. C. B. is not a policy-making committee. It has nothing to do with the operations of the Government within the United States. Its sole function is to see that the overseas operations of the Government are being carried out by all departments and agencies in accordance with the policies recommended by the National Security Council and approved by the President.

In short, it is an anti-confusion device. It was grafted on to the Presidency to see that a big government that is getting bigger does not have one department carrying out overseas policy one way and several other departments carrying it out some other way.

There are now so many officials from so many departments operating overseas— on information, agriculture, atomic energy, commerce, labor, immigration, intelligence and defense—that harassed United States Ambassadors have trouble recognizing them all, let alone keeping tabs on what they are all doing.

Consequently, the O. C. B. was created under the President and the security council to coordinate and follow their overseas operations and see that they stayed coordinated.

This is a big job, roughly equivalent to seeing that all mortals operate in accordance with the Ten Commandments. But the idea is clear; it is to carry out Eisenhower's passion for teamwork.

It would be wrong to suggest that this was a wholly original idea. In September of 1939, a week after Germany invaded Poland, President Franklin D. Roosevelt established the Executive Office of the President.

This was Mr. Roosevelt's realization, after almost seven years in power, that the President, without an elaboration of Presidential staff services, could not possibly supervise and unify both executive policy formulation and execution.

Truman Set Up N. S. C.

This was greatly improved under President Truman with the creation of the National Security Council, a committee of the Cabinet, ably staffed and charged with coordinating security policy.

Since then, however, it has become increasingly (and sometimes painfully) evident that coordinating policy was not enough. Carrying out of that policy had also to be coordinated if United States officials, who have a weakness for thinking in narrow departmental terms, were not to interpret the coordinated policies in a dozen different uncoordinated ways.

The O. C. B.'s headquarters are at Jackson Place and Pennsylvania Avenue in an old house once owned by Gen. William T. (If nominated I will not accept, if elected I will not serve) Sherman. It has subcommittees working all over this town.

There are, in fact, more than forty of them, some watch-dogging information operations overseas, some studying certain countries, others following whole regions, some checking on atomic energy operations.

At least once every six months, each of these committees produces a "progress report" which goes to the National Security Council and the White House.

Whenever they find that a policy is so obscure that it defies coordinated execution, they yell to the security council for a better one. When they find some eager beaver overseas conducting his own private foreign policy, they blow the whistle on him.

That, at least, is the theory. The O. C. B., of course, has its critics. There are some officials here who think it is the greatest time-killer since the invention of golf. Others blanch at the thought of all those committee meetings, all those bootless, vainglorious speeches, and all those "progress reports," which, they charge, are never read by the President.

Nevertheless, the O. C. B. is by general consent a useful new device of the Presidency that is developing authority and coming out of its early development stage.

OLD QUESTION ARISES

It has not managed to keep the officials it is intended to serve from making countless contradictory statements. And since its members have vastly different ideas about many operations, the old question arises:

"Who will coordinate the coordinators?"

Just the same, in any study of the President and the Presidency, the Operations Coordinating Board is bound to interest the historians. It cannot make up for the absences of the President. It cannot persuade the Congress to vote the President's foreign aid funds; it cannot coordinate policy (that is the function of the N. S. C.); it cannot provide the leadership necessary to get the United States into an effective international trade organization. But it can help produce some unity in the operations of policies that are already on the books.

Thus, it draws attention to a fact that is seldom noticed, namely that the President has tried to institutionalize his concept of teamwork. And institutions such as the O. C. B., while far from perfect, are helping carry on as best they can while the President is away from the White House.

WASHINGTON, June 21. The American Presidency, like most other national institutions, is in a race with the pace of American history.

So swift is that pace and so vast the growth of the American Republic and its responsibilities, that all national institutions—and the habits of the men who run them—inevitably lag behind.

This is true in a special sense of all political institutions. It is true, regardless of the party in power, not only of the Presidency but of the Congress with its multiplicity of overlapping committees and its cult of seniority.

It is true not only of the machinery for electing Presidents but also of the methods of selecting powerful assistants to the President. And the problem of change in Washington is especially difficult. For change depends most of the time on the men who have benefited by the political habits and machinery of the past.

In this series of articles, of which this is the last, an effort has been made to draw a distinction between the President and the Presidency, and to report on some of the men and institutions that carry on the burdens of the office during the President's illness.

All these men are caught in this race with the fierce transition of the time. They are all conscious of the need of change. And while they do not change as fast as events, it does not follow that progress has not been made.

CABINET MEETING DAY

This, for example, was Cabinet meeting day in Washington (it is usually on Fridays). The only resemblance it bore to Cabinet meetings of Franklin D. Roosevelt's time was that it was held in the White House Cabinet Room.

The Cabinet under F. D. R. was a story-telling bee—informal, unprepared, and unrecorded. When, after the war, officials and historians wanted to know what happened in these Cabinet meetings, they had to go to the late Henry L. Stimson's personal diaries. For no official record was kept, no agenda was prepared, no catalogue of decisions was preserved. And the only consolation for the historians was that it probably didn't matter, for the Cabinet was not the place where the main business was conducted.

Today, the Cabinet (minus John Foster Dulles, Secretary of State, who was off in California scalding Nikita S. Khrushchev, his favorite target) arrived at the White House, each with his black Cabinet diary.

The secretary to the Cabinet, Maxwell M. Rabb of Boston, had prepared an agenda. For each item on the agenda there was a background memorandum, setting out the points at issue, and a financial statement, indicating what the various proposals would cost, if adopted.

When Vice President Richard M. Nixon, pinch-hitting for the President, called the meeting to order, the Cabinet members did not have to be told the background of the problem (this took up most of the time in the Roosevelt meetings). The problems had been defined and the papers circulated to the members by the Cabinet secretariat earlier in the week.

Furthermore, a record of the meeting was kept by Mr. Rabb. And as soon as Mr. Nixon ended the meeting to go to Quantico, Virginia, for a survey of problems with the lords of the Pentagon, representatives of all the Cabinet members met at the White House. They recorded whatever decisions had been taken so that they could follow up on the action promised.

DIFFERENT FROM BRITISH

This is not to say that the Cabinet is now an agency of the Presidency comparable, say, to the British Cabinet. It does not have the power of decision, as the British do under the system of Cabinet responsibility. Nor does it deal with national security matters.

Its responsibility is to report and recommend policy on home matters—agriculture, natural resources, justice, etc. National security questions are dealt with in the National Security Council. The council is now the most powerful agency of the Government under the President, and the most important arm of the Presidency.

This came into being under President Harry S. Truman on the basis of the experience of the war. It was the result of many years of anguish over the burdens of the White House, and was finally given statutory authority in the National Security Act of 1947, as amended in 1949.

This act did four things:

1. Established the Department of Defense (instead of separate departments of Army, Navy and Air Force).
2. Created the Central Intelligence Agency for the collection and appraisal, at a central point, of world intelligence relating to national security.
3. Set up the National Security Resources Board (now the Office of Defense Mobilization).
4. Established the National Security Council.

The purpose of the N. S. C. was to advise the President on the integration of domestic, foreign and military policies relating to national security; to "assess and appraise the objectives, commitments, and risks of the United States in relation to our actual and potential military power"; to consider policies on matters of common interest to the departments and agencies of the Government, "and to make recommendations to the President in connection therewith."

ANTI-FREE-WHEELING DEVICE

This was intended to keep the separate departments dealing with security matters from running off in all directions—sort of an anti-free-wheeling device. And while nobody can ever hope to coordinate as many people as now work in the security field, it has done extremely well.

The statutory members of the N. S. C. are the President, who normally chairs the weekly meeting on Thursday mornings; Vice President Nixon, the Secretaries of State (Mr. Dulles) and Defense (Charles E. Wilson), and the director of the Office of Defense Mobilization, Arthur S. Flemming.

Others who attend are the director of the Central Intelligence Agency, Allen W. Dulles, who opens each meeting with a world intelligence report; the chairman of the Joint Chiefs of Staff, Admiral Arthur W. Radford; the Secretary of the Treasury, George M. Humphrey; the assistants to the President for disarmament (Harold E. Stassen) and foreign affairs (William H. Jackson); the director of the Bureau of the Budget, Percival F. Brundage, and such other officials as the President wishes to invite.

The difference between the N. S. C. and the Cabinet, other than that one deals with home affairs and the other with security affairs, is that the N. S. C. is far more formal. It does everything on the basis of carefully prepared staff work, and almost always deals with questions that require a specific recommendation to the President for policy action.

If the President has something he wants studied, he refers it to his special assistant for security affairs, Dillon Anderson. Mr. Anderson is a conservative lawyer from Texas who has a gift for wry verse, which he does not use on N. S. C. papers.

Mr. Anderson may then refer the question to the department concerned, or to several departments for their observations. And when the papers are then taken by the N. S. C. permanent staff (most of whose top members have been there from the start of the agency), the staff prepares them for the consideration of the National Security Council's planning board.

POWER OF PLANNING BOARD

Much has been written, though little is known, about the N. S. C. What is more important is that even less is known about the council's planning board, which does most of the pick-and-shovel work for the N. S. C. and a great deal of its thinking.

It is, therefore, the principal planning and coordinating interdepartmental committee in the issues of war and peace and one of immense power. This, of course, is flatly denied by all its members, who are not only "anonymous" but practically invisible.

The planning board met this afternoon in Room 382 of the Old State Department Building—nine men whose names are almost unknown beyond the top level of official Washington.

Mr. Anderson, the aforementioned writer who normally is chairman of the planning board, was not present this afternoon. He was away on Kwajalein Atoll with Lewis L. Strauss, the atomic energy chief, presumably listening to bangs. His place was taken by the man who has been staff secretary of the N. S. C. from the beginning, James S. Lay Jr.

The other members on hand today were Robert R. Bowie, the Harvard teacher who is Assistant Secretary of State and head of that department's policy planning staff; Robert Amory Jr. of the Central Intelligence Agency; Maj. Gen. Francis W. Farrell, representing the Joint Chiefs of Staff; Jarold A. Kieffer of the President's Advisory Committee on Government Organizations; C. Dillon Glendenning of the Treasury; Robert E. Mattison of the White House disarmament staff; Ralph W. E. Reid, assistant director of the Bureau of the Budget, and Karl Harr of the Department of Defense.

BASED ON PAPER WORK

The famous men who sit on the N. S. C. base their discussions, like the Cabinet, on carefully prepared papers, and they are not restrained in their criticisms. But the men in big government who prepare the papers for Cabinet members, who have a thousand other things to do each week, are in the key spot, regardless of how much they may deny their authority.

These instruments of departmental cooperation—the N. S. C., the N. S. C. planning board, and the Operations Coordinating Board, which sees that the N. S. C. policies are carried out by all concerned—provide the President with solid staff services, but they cannot substitute for the President.

As Sidney W. Souers, the first executive secretary of the N. S. C., wrote about interdepartmental committees of the past:

> [They] suffered for lack of a definite mission . . . and most of all, from authoritative direction.

This is true to a certain extent today in the N. S. C. The council and its planning board can recommend, but the constitutional responsibility of the President is still the duty to decide.

When he is available he works hard at the N. S. C. papers. And even now he is beginning to send his observations to the staff from the hospital. But he is not able, and has not been able during his two illnesses, to go through the long, hard task of arguing out the N. S. C. problems and hammering them into the policy he wants.

"The powers and duties" of the Presidency, mentioned in Article II, Section 1, Paragraph 6 of the Constitution, do not refer only to those simple acts of signing papers that have to be signed so that the public business can go on.

They refer not only to the President but to the whole of the Presidency: to the direction of these staffs, to the hard decisive business of choosing between dangerous courses.

This is why there is apprehension in Washington about the illness of President Eisenhower. There are institutions behind him that carry on better than his political opponents would have the public believe, but these institutions do not work so well without him as his political supporters pretend.

Eisenhower as President:
A Critical Appraisal of the Record
WILLIAM V. SHANNON

Across a divided and militarily defenseless Europe, the shadow of Stalin's armies fell; in Korea, Communist Chinese forces pushed American armies back toward the sea; in the United States, Joseph McCarthy scored his first major political triumph,

Reprinted from *Commentary* (November, 1958), pp. 390-398, by permission: copyright © 1958 by the American Jewish Committee.

and the Fulbright Committee investigation began to uncover a vein of corruption in the national administration. It was a grim time for Americans. It was November 1950.

When President Truman summoned General Dwight D. Eisenhower to his private study in the White House one afternoon that month to ask him to return to active duty and become chief of the NATO forces in Western Europe, he called upon one of the few Americans who commanded universal respect and admiration. The image of Eisenhower, the liberator of Nazi-occupied Europe, stood bright and untarnished. He was a symbol of the nation's triumphant and united national purpose in a time when the national consensus was fracturing and the national mood becoming querulous and ugly. Eisenhower's acceptance of his new military assignment ended his brief civilian career as president of Columbia University. It restored him to the center of the public scene where in the decade to follow he was to be the dominant figure. His dominance of the age did not derive from any personal mastery of its diverse forces. A central personality may epitomize the spirit of an era and symbolize its prevailing balance of political forces without necessarily transforming the one or controlling the other. As the decade of the 20's is inextricably linked with Calvin Coolidge and the 30's with Franklin Roosevelt, the 1950's in our political history is likely to be known as the age of Eisenhower.

Although Eisenhower has two years still to serve, his place in history and the significance of his presidency are already becoming clear. Eisenhower is a transitional figure. He has not shaped the future nor tried to repeal the past. He has not politically organized nor intellectually defined a new consensus. When he leaves office in January 1961, the foreign policies and the domestic policies of the past generation will be about where he found them in 1953. No national problem, whether it be education, housing, urban revitalization, agriculture, or inflation, will have been advanced importantly toward solution nor its dimensions significantly altered. The Eisenhower era is the time of the great postponement. Dwight Eisenhower, the executor and trustee of the programs of his two Democratic predecessors whose contemporary he was (Eisenhower is only eight years younger than Franklin Roosevelt and six years younger than Harry Truman), already looms in history not as the first great figure of a new Republican age but the last of an old Democratic generation.

In assessing Eisenhower's status, it is worth recalling the somber, impassioned national mood which the sudden, savage turn in the Korean war created eight years ago this autumn. The emotions aroused by that war endangered the great double consensus on foreign affairs and domestic affairs which had been in the making since 1933. Eisenhower's historic function when he entered political life two years later was to end the war and preserve that consensus against the attacks of its enemies.

The domestic consensus had emerged out of the violent political struggles and intellectual gyrations of the New Deal period from 1933 to 1938. It rested on an irreversible common agreement that the Federal government has a responsibility to maintain the rudiments of a welfare state. Social security, unemployment compensation, and minimum wages were the basic features of this program, and its chief guarantors were the trade unions to whom the Wagner Act of 1935 had given firm legal status. The unionists and their unorganized but sympathetic fellow workers were the guarantors of the consensus because they were the most numerous and, compared to the farmers, the old-age pensioners, and other groups, the most politically dependable of all the New Deal beneficiaries. The Full Employment Act of 1946, the first year of the Truman administration, set a seal of official approval on this consensus but did not extend its range.

The other half of the national consensus, the half on foreign policy, had also begun under Roosevelt but had reached its more significant development during the Truman years. Roosevelt, by his aggressive championing of an internationalist position during the bitter isolationist-interventionist debate of 1940-41, established the basis for a national policy. His actions and his education of the public were essential first steps. He carried it further in his negotiations during the war with various Republican party personalities, looking toward our entry into a world organization. Truman completed this undertaking by leading the country into the United Nations. A genuine bipartisan collaboration during the next five years carried through the Marshall Plan, the Greek-Turkish program, the Berlin airlift, the Point Four program, and other achievements abroad. By 1950, the consensus on foreign policy was well established. It rested on the concept of containment. If Russian aggression in all its forms was firmly resisted, if the military and economic strength of the West were maintained and increased, and if the neutral, underdeveloped countries were not lost to Communism, it would be possible to avoid a third war and to leave the resolution of the cold war to the slow working of history.

Communist China's entry into the Korean war put the foreign policy consensus in jeopardy. The shocking defeats, the capture of thousands of our troops by the Communists, and the eventual bloody stalemate aroused many doubts and profound dissatisfaction. The scope of the war and its inherent nature intensified popular resentment and bafflement. It was clearly not a major war evoking the instinctive zeal and emotional commitment of the whole population; yet its duration and the thousands of dead and wounded made it more burdensome than the brief "brushfire wars" that the containment policy had seemed to postulate. If it was only "a police action," as President Truman called it, how could the government ask for wartime sacrifices? If it was a glorious struggle on behalf of the United Nations, why did the other UN members leave almost all of the fighting to us?

The anxieties were deep and shaking. The public, half-unconsciously and inarticulately, began the search for an alternative to the existing consensus. First, there was a brief, wild resurgence of the old isolationist impulse in early December 1950 when the drive to the Yalu turned into disastrous defeat. The momentary impulse to get our forces out of Korea and abandon the Asian mainland to the Chinese Communists receded once General Ridgway rallied our forces and stabilized the military situation. Second, there was the alternative of smashing our way out of the dilemmas of a containment policy by adopting a more venturesome course. This alternative drew upon feelings and posed choices ranging from the proposals for bombing across the Yalu in Manchuria to launching a preventive war "to get the whole thing over with." The popularity of this alternative policy of aggressive venturesomeness reached its height in the spring of 1951 when General MacArthur made his triumphant tour through the United States after his dismissal. This alternative began to fade during the prolonged, anti-climactic MacArthur hearings. There was yet a third alternative. Senator Joseph McCarthy and a few other senators propounded the view that the real source of danger was treason within. The tendency of those who propagated this alternative was to deprecate the importance of the Soviet Union's power and enormously inflate the real but limited and secondary dangers of Soviet espionage and political infiltration within this country. The minimizing of the Soviet Union's menace flattered many naively chauvinistic ideas about our own relative place in the sun; the exaggeration of the espionage-infiltration problem catered to a congeries of notions about foreigners, radicals, and Communists. And McCarthy's unexpectedly rich talents for political invention and propaganda gave this alternative a raging vitality which was only beginning in 1950 and did not lose force for more than four years.

As against the alarms and confusions of the isolationist, MacArthurian, and McCarthyite alternatives, Harry Truman and Dean Acheson, the two chief official exponents of the containment policy, made an ineffective defense. Truman was without the resources of rhetoric and the mastery of a grand style which would have enabled a Roosevelt or a Wilson to make an early and overpowering counterattack. Acheson was impaled by his own verbal indiscretions and his starchy public manner. They could only mechanically repeat the familiar platitudes about collective security, the United Nations, and the importance of having allies.

The times called for a man who could restate national purposes, reassert in more winning terms the basic truths underlying the foreign policy consensus, and thereby make possible once again the full concentration of national energies. The situation seemed to require a political figure who would personify the causes that united us rather than those which divided us. It was a situation, in a word, that was historically right for a conservative. The conservative aspiration in politics is always toward the ideal of unity, toward the assertion of proved values and established rationales, and directed toward the deliberate blurring of economic and political conflicts. Even more, the times were right for a certain kind of conservative whose appeal had proved valid in the American past. This was the military hero who had a conservative social background but was basically apolitical and who, although a military man, had the plain, even drab, style suitable in the chief of state of a profoundly civilian country. No "fancy Dans" like the elegant General George Brinton McClellan in 1864 or the imperial, proconsular General Douglas MacArthur in 1952 need apply. What was wanted was another Washington, another Grant. What was wanted, and what was so splendidly and self-evidently available for the asking, if the asking were insistent enough, was Dwight D. Eisenhower.

The connection between the conservative aspiration (one can scarcely call it, at least in this country, an ideology or a philosophy) and the military hero candidate is more than an expedient alliance. The ideal of national unity dominates the military ethos. Soldiers are trained to defend the existing social order rather than to examine it critically. Military officers see social and economic groups as components in the great design of national strength, not as dynamic participants battling one another in the social arena. If Eisenhower found the conservative Republicans with their dedication to the status quo and their resistance to rapid change more intellectually congenial than the liberal Democrats with their reformist tradition, he was no different from the great majority of his fellow officers. The military services are not a training school for liberals.

The natural affinity between political conservatives and a military hero has deep roots in the American past. George Washington, our first conservative president and also our first soldier president, set the mold. The conservative Whigs managed to elect only two presidents, General William "Tippecanoe" Harrison in 1840 and General Zachary Taylor in 1848. The Republican politicians seeking to consolidate their hold on the country after the Civil War chose General Grant. Each of these men was relatively innocent of political ideas. Their appeal was based on the exploitation of their personality as a symbol of integrity and unity. Their campaigns were usually keyed to a simple idea. Grant, for example, said in 1868: "Let us have peace." Eisenhower, with the air of a man expressing a crystal clear idea, said repeatedly in 1952: "I believe our test should be—what is good for 155,000,000 Americans."

In the fall of 1949, Senator Arthur Vandenberg wrote in a private letter to a friend that he might support General Eisenhower in the next presidential contest. "I think the specifications call for a personality of great independent magnitude who can give our splintering American people an 'evangel' instead of an ordinary campaign," he wrote.

Three years in advance, Vandenberg had forecast Eisenhower's "Great Crusade." It was as the candidate of the more responsible Republicans interested in protecting the foreign policy consensus that the General entered politics. (In 1948 he had privately favored Vandenberg's own nomination with Harold Stassen as a running mate.) Lacking any alternative to Senator Taft, the Eastern Republicans successfully and plausibly argued with Eisenhower that he would only be carrying out his NATO mission in a different way. By blocking the coming to power of Taft and his neo-isolationist backers, Eisenhower would make certain that a foreign policy oriented toward the defense of Europe and aligned with the principles of the UN would continue to prevail.

Once nominated, Eisenhower necessarily took into account the three principal strains of Republican party criticism of existing foreign policy. Speaking about the Korean war in Peoria, Illinois, he projected the goal of the ultimate withdrawal of American troops from mainland Asia. If there had to be wars there, "let Asians fight Asians." This remark delighted the devout readers of the Chicago *Tribune*. It evoked glowing words of praise from troglodyte politicians like ex-Senator C. Wayland "Curly" Brooks. But it was meaningless. As army chief of staff in 1946-48, Eisenhower had repeatedly and successfully recommended the withdrawal of American troops from Korea. Moreover, it was settled national military policy to avoid stationing troops on the Asian mainland. But this was quite different from disengaging ourselves completely from our interests and responsibilities on that continent. The Peoria speech was only a fugitive gesture to the isolationists.

Eisenhower made more ambiguous gestures in the direction of the aggressive alternative symbolized by General MacArthur. He allowed himself the liberty of condemning the "negativism" of the containment policy and of referring vaguely to the "liberation" and the "rolling back" of the Communist empire. He promised to go to Korea but he left open the question whether he would end the war by extending it to gain a decisive military victory, or try to end it by continuing the armistice negotiations. The campaign rhetoric unfortunately persisted after election day. In his first State of the Union message, Eisenhower "unleashed" Chiang Kai-shek. Secretary of State Dulles wordily threatened the Communists with "massive retaliation" at times and places of our own choosing. The administration strengthened the government's propaganda forces to wage psychological warfare, seize the strategic initiative, liberate the satellite states by radio broadcasts, and attain various other doubtlessly worthy if uncertain ends. Two crises in the Formosa Straits have demonstrated Chiang Kai-shek is not a free agent; the Hungarian revolution proved the United States had no intention of risking anything to liberate the satellite peoples.

Eisenhower, during the 1952 campaign and for a period thereafter, accommodated himself in small, symbolic ways to the emotional thrust of McCarthyism. He deleted a brief word of praise for General Marshall, his patron, from his Milwaukee speech; he affirmed vigorously his determination to clear the Communists out of government, to encourage the work of the Federal Bureau of Investigation, and to cooperate with the investigating committees of Congress, clearly implying the Truman administration had been remiss, if not treasonable, in these matters. He did not avow belief in the McCarthyite conspiracy theory of the origin of the country's troubles but, to the dismay of some of his admirers in both parties and former colleagues in the Roosevelt and Truman administrations, neither did he disavow it.

Eisenhower's strategy in waging the "Great Crusade" was the only one possible for him given the plasticity of his temperament, his unintellectual cast of mind, and his confident, optimistic nature. He did not separate the sheep from the goats; he welcomed all dissidents to his cause, committed himself in an irretrievable way only to invulnerable platitudes, and hinted genially that in his new synthesis a reconciliation of all divergent elements would be possible. This may not have been the internationalist "evangel" that Vandenberg and his other original supporters had in mind, but it is typical of successful party leaders in our country. Franklin Roosevelt, for example, was able in 1932 to hold the loyalty and quicken the hopes of Huey Long and Bernard Baruch, of Harry Byrd and George Norris. Roosevelt organized his coalition with care and calculation while Eisenhower, gifted with some of the instincts if not the insight and expertise of a successful politician, apparently only did what came naturally to him. If his tactics did not rally a newly broadened and better informed support for the foreign policy consensus, they served at least to deaden and to dissipate the pressures for any serious change from that policy. Eisenhower's fabian tactics carried through successfully the defensive holding action which Truman and Acheson after 1950 could no longer sustain.

As against this negative but vitally important accomplishment, Eisenhower's own positive initiatives in foreign affairs dwindle into insignificance. The Baghdad pact in the Middle East and the SEATO pact in the Far East are pale imitations of the NATO pact in Europe. They have proved irrelevant, if not noxious, diplomatic devices. The administration's ambivalent attitude toward Nasser brought the Atlantic Alliance almost to the breaking point in the Suez affair, but our common interests with Britain are so strong they can survive almost any shock; under Prime Minister Macmillan's soothing ministrations, the alliance re-formed itself. Eisenhower has given hospitality in his administration to MacArthurite tendencies in the persons of Assistant Secretary of State Walter Robertson and Admiral Arthur Radford, but he has heeded their counsel scarcely more than his predecessor did the words of MacArthur himself. Eisenhower has tried the "great man theory" of diplomacy at the summit in Geneva and Dulles has subjected himself to innumerable conferences and journeyings, but no new approaches to the Soviet monolith have developed and none of the old has availed much. Eisenhower settled for truces in Korea and Indo-China, leaving those countries divided and their future unsettled. This is the kind of minimum accommodation between the Communist and non-Communist worlds which the original containment concept had envisaged.

Holding the line and protecting the gains of the past worked well enough in Europe where in the Eisenhower years the situation has remained virtually stable. Secretary Dulles threatened the French with an agonizing reappraisal, but the French were supremely indifferent. So in the end was the Secretary of State. The European Defense Community died, the British and French patched up a reasonable substitute, and the only agonizing was done by the Secretary's Democratic critics. Career diplomats worked out a compromise solution of the Trieste affair, the Russians relinquished their grip on Austria, and the United States kept the line open to Tito in Belgrade. Germany remained divided. Europe remained divided.

In the Middle East and the Far East, however, creative policy making was called for. The situations were less stable and the inherited guide lines of policy were less well developed. Eisenhower had no contribution to make to the hard problems of Arab and Israeli, of African nationalism, of Communist China's menace to Southeast Asia, of Indonesia's interior decay, and of India's economic viability. He held the line and beyond that he could not go. When he got in trouble on a foreign policy issue in these areas of the world, it was usually because he applied the lessons of the postwar past rigidly and almost mechanically. He reacted to the Anglo-French-Israeli war with Egypt as if it were the Communist invasion of South Korea all over again. When the Chinese Communists shelled Quemoy and Matsu in 1958, he again reacted: hold the line. When Democratic critics attacked him for a lack of discrimination in applying the principle of resisting Communist pressure, Eisenhower responded only with a stubborn reiteration of the principle. At his press conference on October 15, 1958, a reporter asked him if he believed the expression of opposition views on Quemoy "actually weakens the administration's position or ability to negotiate." Eisenhower replied:

No, not always, but I will tell you: there is a very clear distinction to be made with respect to foreign policy as I see it. One is the policy and one is its operation.

Every single day there are new and tough decisions that have to be made within a foreign policy, but if you go back to 1947 [the date of the Truman Doctrine and the beginning of the Marshall Plan] and see the statements that are made about opposing the territorial expansion of Communism by force, when you go back and see what our policy went into in the effort to develop collective security, mutual aid, technical assistance, that kind of thing that . . . at least will help to make the free world stronger collectively and each individual nation as opposed to Communism, that when you come down to it are the basic parts of the policy.

At times, humans, being human, are going to make errors. And therefore I do not, by any means, decry intelligent questioning and criticism of any particular point. But when it comes to the policy that is being established, *I think it has been standing pretty well on its own feet for a long time* (italics added).

Eisenhower's clear distinction between a policy and the carrying out of that policy may be simpleminded, but future historians are not likely to find a better or more revealing extemporaneous tribute to the foreign policy consensus. Eisenhower's caretaker attitude is clear. His and Dulles's day-to-day decisions do not matter; only the policy matters, and it has an autonomous life of its own not really greatly dependent on their daily actions and judgments.

When Harry Truman ordered American troops into Korea in June 1950, he did not know that he was killing his Fair Deal domestic program. War and liberalism always go ill together, but when the Korean conflict began few foresaw how it would transform the domestic economic scene and jeopardize the national consensus on domestic policy. When the war broke the country was just pulling itself out of the mild recession of 1949-50. With more than 4,000,000 unemployed and farm prices drifting downward, the overriding problem seemed to be how to avoid a possible depression. The Truman administration was ready to adopt the familiar Keynesian solutions of deficit financing and easier credit. Meanwhile, Truman in the 81st Congress of 1949-50 pushed hard for an extension of the welfare state program. He recommended the Brannan farm plan, Federal health insurance, fair employment practices legislation, increased slum clearance, and Federal aid to education. The country seemed lethargic and a bit hesitant about these proposals. The Democratic congressional majorities elected in 1948 were not quite large enough to pass them. Except for the Wagner-Ellender-Taft Housing Act of 1949 which passed with Republican cooperation, all of these measures failed by a few votes. Yet it would require only small Democratic gains in the November 1950 elections to insure their passage.

The Korean war, however, not only benefited the Republicans at the polls and made the 82nd Congress of 1951-52 considerably more conservative than its predecessor, but also touched off a severe inflation. Unemployment vanished, farm prices soared, and the high cost of living replaced the threat of joblessness as a key domestic issue.

The emergence of the inflation issue played an important part in Eisenhower's first victory and has been significant in influencing the tone of his administration. The fear of inflation greatly helped him to organize a new majority coalition in the country

A Critical Appraisal of the Record 131

and end the Republican party's chronic minority status. Before 1952, the Republican party drew its strength principally from three groups. One was the more sophisticated Eastern industrial and financial community and its allies in the press, clergy, and universities; this was an elite group, small in numbers but important in terms of wealth, prestige, and influence in the mass communication industries. By a British analogy, these voters, overwhelmingly but not exclusively Republican, make up what might be called the American Establishment. These were the people who had organized the successful Willkie boom in 1940 and had subsequently more or less accepted Governor Dewey and his associate Herbert Brownell as their political agents. A second group was the less sophisticated, much more numerous but relatively less effective, hard-shelled conservative business and commercial people of the smaller cities and towns of the Midwest. Their idol was Robert A. Taft. These voters gave, at most, grudging acceptance to the great consensus; some hoped for a withdrawal into isolation, others resented labor unions. The strongest conviction they shared was that government cost too much, that the budget should always be balanced, and taxes reduced promptly. The third group were the farmers who had voted predominantly Republican since the midterm election of 1938. These three groups were not enough to make a majority. The Democrats were able to maintain themselves in power with the support of the captive South and the second- and third-generation immigrant community voters in the nation's dozen largest metropolitan areas.

Eisenhower cracked the Democratic big cities and the high cost of living was probably his most potent weapon. He made sharp gains among housewives. Moreover, he broke into the ranks of the young voters. During the 1930's and 40's, voters under thirty had been heavily Democratic. By 1952, however, many young war veterans bore a burden of fixed charges, in their mortgaged suburban homes, with appliances bought on the installment plan, driving cars purchased through a finance company. In abstract economic theory, debtors benefit from inflation, but as a practical matter many of these voters felt they were losing in the dollar race. They feared their wages and salaries would not keep pace with rising prices. They voted for Eisenhower.

However, there were other causes bidding for the allegiances of these voters being detached from the old Democratic urban coalition. One of them was McCarthyism. McCarthy had an entree to these voters because, like many of them, he was Catholic and of immigrant ancestry. He was also relatively young and a war veteran. He was a demagogue with a simple issue to exploit who made a biting, raucous, emotional appeal. For these voters, his appeal was quite a new and different experience contrasted to the stodgy, Chamber of Commerce rhetoric they had been accustomed to hear from Republican orators.

The only real threat to the domestic economic consensus established in the New Deal and perpetuated in Truman's Fair Deal would come from a genuine linkage between working-class- and lower-middle-class urban voters, attracted by a noneconomic issue like McCarthyism, and the regular Republican voters of the more hard-shelled, conservative, Midwestern school. If the Republican ticket in 1952 had been Taft and Knowland instead of Eisenhower and Nixon, this linkage might have had serious consequences. A right-wing Republican administration much indebted to the emotional dynamism of the McCarthyites for its victory might have attempted a genuine counter-revolution to reverse many of the verdicts of the 30's and 40's embodied in the economic consensus. Eisenhower's nomination forestalled this eventuality. He absorbed the McCarthyite frenzy into his own "Great Crusade" where in subsequent years it died of inanition.

In terms of the internal dynamics of the Republican party, therefore, Eisenhower's victory in November 1952 had several meanings. It meant much of the potential McCarthy following had been detached from his orbit and their fears, dissatisfactions, and status tensions given a different kind of political expression. "I Like Ike" was a harmless substitute for hating the targets McCarthy singled out. The Eisenhower victory meant that millions of lifelong Republican voters were doomed to a new frustration. The "hard-shells" hoping for a permanent cut in foreign aid, a crackdown on labor, or a big reduction in taxes and the budget had contributed to a victory that in terms of these objectives had no meaning. The Eisenhower victory also meant that there were now millions of voters momentarily enlisted in the Republican cause who had never been in the party before; they had been attracted by "Ike"'s personality, by his promise to bring down the cost of living, and by a desire to escape the Korean stalemate. And finally the victory meant that the predominant Republican wing of the American Establishment was, for the first time in a generation, in power in an administration of its own choosing.

The Eisenhower performance was bound to disappoint at least some of these divergent groups. In practice, it has disappointed them all, and for an odd reason. Upon taking office, Eisenhower, the choice of the more sophisticated Republicans, turned out to have many of the convictions of the most Tory adherents of Taft: he did not share their animus against union labor, but otherwise he was a true disciple of the Old Guard orthodoxy. He believed in the absolute primacy of thrift, he wanted to return government functions to the states, he believed deficit financing was sin, he believed high taxes and government regulations were "stifling free enterprise." Eisenhower in the White House was closer to an Iowa Rotarian than to a Wall Street banker. He was the man from Abilene, Kansas, not the man from Morningside Heights.

The Eisenhower administration vaguely disappointed many in the Eastern elite who had hoped for more positive leadership. Nelson Rockefeller symbolized this discreet discontent when he left the administration and financed a series of reports on public issues urging ambitious programs far more costly than Eisenhower would countenance. The blue-ribbon members of the committee which presented the Gaither Report on national defense filed, in effect, a dissent to Eisenhower's concept of the national interest.

Eisenhower and Agriculture Secretary Benson, committed to the view that subsidies were intrinsically wrong and that what farmers desired above all was the liberation from government marketing and production restraints, did not abolish subsidies, restraints, or surpluses, but they did manage to alienate the farmers, a dwindling but still sizable Republican voting bloc.

The newer Republicans, converted in 1952 in the cities and the suburbs, should have been reassured by the administration's preoccupation with the inflation problem and "the stable dollar." To some extent they were, but they had other tangible concerns such as the schools their children attended and the cost of medical care for their aged parents. The Eisenhower administration, penny-pinched and budget-obsessed, sabotaged the annual legislative drives for Federal aid to schools, cut back the slum clearance program almost to a nullity, and on the whole failed to demonstrate that it was vitally concerned with the needs of the urban and lower-income voters. The latter retained their "liking for Ike," but as early as 1954 and in increasing numbers they, like many farmers, began to re-identify their own economic welfare with the Democratic party. The gap between Eisenhower's popularity and that of the Republican party widened rather than narrowed as his years in the White House progressed.

The hard-shell Republicans who should have been most pleased at the President's unanticipated sharing of their convictions have been disillusioned by his lack of fighting zeal. If the budget were to be balanced at a modest level, income taxes substantially reduced, the balance of functions between the Federal and state governments shifted, and the trend to big government reversed, it would require as many violent political struggles as it took to pass the New Deal in the first place. It would probably be necessary, for example, to pass a national right-to-work law, forbid industry-wide collective bargaining, and break the political activities of the labor unions. On no front has Eisenhower undertaken a struggle of this magnitude. If his limited physical strength and his limited intellectual interest in this sort of problem were not sufficient to debar such a conflict, his desire for national unity and harmony would in any case prevent it. The domestic consensus rests secure in his hands.

Arthur Larson, the quondam philosopher of "Modern Republicanism," propounded the thesis in his book *A Republican Looks At His Party* (1956) that the Republican party under Eisenhower's leadership had "for the first time in our history discovered and established the Authentic American Center in politics." The Eisenhower administration expressed an "American Consensus." The steady decay of the Republican party at the state and congressional district level throughout the Eisenhower years is enough to discredit this thesis. Parties which have formulated a widely accepted consensus on the big contemporary issues and are united behind a great leader do not show these alarming signs of disaffection and disrepair.

There is an American Consensus on the issues, but it was developed by Franklin Roosevelt and developed further in some respects by Truman. Eisenhower has been content to leave it undisturbed. His few attempts to return to the "little government" of a bygone day have been abortive. Two statistics alone are enough to account for his defeat: there are 40,000,000 more Americans than there were twenty years ago and more than one-third of all Americans now live in states other than those in which they grew up. The growing population makes the pressure for increased government services irresistible and the mobility of that population makes it equally inevitable that the people look to the Federal government to supply those services as state loyalties disappear and state boundaries become unreal.

Eisenhower did disturb the old political balance of power as distinguished from the consensus on issues, but he had not the energies, the talents, nor the experience to exploit his personal triumphs for his party's advantage.

Eisenhower has been the great leader *manque*. His dignified bearing, his warm flashing smile, his easy manners made him seem a man with whom most voters could feel at ease, and his hero's reputation made him seem a man in whom they could safely trust their destiny. Has their trust been misplaced? The answer lies in America's margin for error. Eisenhower and his administration have lived off the accumulated wisdom, the accumulated prestige, and the accumulated military strength of his predecessors who conducted more daring and more creative regimes. If our margin for error is as great as it has traditionally been, these quiet Eisenhower years will have been only a pleasant idyll, an inexpensive interlude in a grim century. If our margin for error is much thinner than formerly, Eisenhower may join the ranks of history's fatal good men, the Stanley Baldwins and the James Buchanans. Their intentions were good and their example is pious, but they bequeathed to their successors a black heritage of time lost and opportunities wasted.

4
JOHN F. KENNEDY

1961-1963

Three years is not a long time in which to make a lasting mark on the broad sweep of public policy, even from a position as lofty as the Presidency. The Kennedy Presidency, which only lasted this brief time, made a new start in a number of areas, as one would expect of a Democratic President following on eight Republican years in the White House.

Most of all, there was an infusion of new energy and color into the Presidency, a spirit captured in several of the selections that follow. There was high morale in the Kennedy White House, a sense of urgency and purposefulness among the presidential staff, not unmixed with high self-regard. This was chastened, but not extinguished, by the early fiasco of the attempted Cuban invasion at the Bay of Pigs and by the Kennedy administration's problems in matching its priorities with those of a more slow-moving Congress.

President Kennedy himself was an alert and able man, wide-ranging in his curiosity, interested in the world and in making things happen. The organization of his Presidency was much influenced by Arthur Schlesinger's admiration for Roosevelt's administrative style and Richard Neustadt's critique of the Eisenhower White House. Kennedy made more substantive demands than Eisenhower, displayed a great eagerness to receive and a quickness to assimilate information. This tended, like a draft in a chimney, to pull decisions to the top.

Information is of course not wisdom, and nobody will ever know if Kennedy's preoccupations or decisions were the right ones. It was Kennedy who decided to invest heavily in the space program—and also to establish a Peace Corps. Kennedy placed major emphasis on achieving detente with Russia—an effort largely unrealized in his time—and on building a defense capability that could be used efficiently in conditions short of all-out nuclear war. In this he—and his brilliant Secretary of Defense, Robert McNamara—succeeded, but in so doing, of course, provided the United States with a capability to intervene in stepwise fashion in Vietnam. Thus does fortune smile and frown upon the memories of American Presidents long after they have left the White House.

To his contemporaries, what was impressive about the Kennedy White House was the sheer brains, the swiftness of thought, that dwelt there. More jaundiced eyes also noticed that high abilities were often turned to self-justification, occasionally leading to nasty scraps with an overwhelmingly approving press corps—a habit that in some cases has not abated as members of the Kennedy entourage have dispersed to private life. Thus, even today, it is sometimes hard to get an accurate picture of the Kennedy White House through the fog of nostalgia and self-esteem spread by many who worked there. The four articles that follow are written by three journalists and a political scientist who have succeeded in distancing themselves from the Kennedy glamour sufficiently to give an informative picture of a man and his staff at work.

A New Style, a New Tempo
DOUGLASS CATER

Last December, while consulting a senior statesman about the selection of a Secretary of State, President-elect Kennedy remarked that he had suddenly discovered he didn't know "the right people." During his campaigning he had, of course, met practically every politician in the country. But as far as picking a cabinet was concerned, his large circle of acquaintances seemed inadequate. The truth of these remarks, made matter-of-factly and with no suggestion of regret, was subsequently borne out when Mr. Kennedy appointed men not previously known to him to several key posts in his administration.

It was not the only handicap he had to overcome in a hurry. There are some who argue that running a legislative office was the worst possible preparation for one who must head the vast Executive establishment. During his fourteen years as congressman and senator, Mr. Kennedy never had more than thirty-five employees on his office payroll. As President, he has more agency heads than that reporting to him, and the Executive Office of the President, at last count, numbered more than twenty-eight hundred.

More significant than its numbers, there has been in recent years a steady build-up in the bureaucratic organization of the office. Under President Eisenhower particularly, it became a locus of councils and secretariats. Last fall certain Republicans even went so far as to suggest that the Presidency had grown too difficult except for someone—like, for example, Vice-President Nixon—who had served an apprenticeship.

If he has been awed by all this, Mr. Kennedy has not let on. As the youngest elected President following the oldest, he has not hesitated to carry out a bloodless revolution against the elder generations by staffing his office with associates whose average age is even less than his own. It has become an absorbing spectacle in Washington to watch venerable politicians kowtowing to these youthful Presidential assistants, some of them on the sunny side of thirty.

President Kennedy and his staff have brought a new style and tempo to the White House. Under the Eisenhower concept, teamwork was conducted much in the manner of a football game—frequent huddles, great attention to co-ordinating everybody, and interminable periods spent catching breath between plays. The Kennedy concept seems to be more along the lines of basketball. Everybody is on the move all the time. Nobody has a very clearly defined position. The President may throw the ball in any direction and he expects it to be kept bouncing.

Co-ordination has become merely a minor pastime. The White House morning staff conference, a routine in Mr. Eisenhower's day, has been dispensed with. Much of the co-ordinating machinery attached to the cabinet and the National Security Council has been junked. With obvious pride in the lack of formal organization, one Kennedy aide recently boasted that it would be impossible to draw up an administrative chart for the White House since there is practically no hierarchy. He

From *The Reporter* (March 16, 1961), pp. 28-30. Copyright © 1961 by The Reporter Magazine Company.

suggested that perhaps the best way to distinguish the more important members of the staff is to observe who arrives at work in a chauffeured car, who takes guests to dine in the White House mess, and—high in the pecking order—who gets to swim in the pool.

It was not by accident that for several weeks the spacious corner suite once occupied by Sherman Adams went vacant until, in order to relieve the congestion, two Kennedy assistants agreed to share it. It has been made explicitly clear that the job of *The* Assistant to the President no longer exists.

The Kennedy office works very much according to the views expounded by professor Richard E. Neustadt of Columbia, a former Truman aide who has become an adviser on organization for the new President. In *Presidential Power: The Politics of Leadership,* Neustadt argues that the President must wage eternal war to keep from becoming clerk rather than leader in his own office. The latter-day growth of Presidential bureaucracy, which is supposed to lift the burden from the Chief Executive, can actually make him a victim of other people's routines. According to the Neustadt theory, a President must keep his staff small and flexible if he intends to hold power firmly in his own hands.

Mr. Kennedy, as Neustadt readily concedes, did not have to read a book to understand all this. So far he has shown an intuitive grasp of what he must do to keep on top of things. He hasn't hesitated to cut across channels and down through echelons in seeking the information he needs or in communicating his interest in a particular problem. No bureaucrat can feel entirely safe from a Presidential phone call, no departmental meeting from a sudden Presidential visit. Mr. Kennedy hands out assignments with remarkable facility, frequently picking the man nearest at hand when a problem arises. It does not seem to concern him that his aides may find themselves duplicating or even competing with each other. It is *their* job to recognize and reconcile conflicts, not his.

All this could lead to chaos. But despite its youth, Mr. Kennedy's staff has had experience both in working together and working in the Washington milieu. At least a half dozen of his top assistants—Theodore Sorensen, Ken O'Donnell, Ralph Dungan, Larry O'Brien, Myer Feldman, and Pierre Salinger—have an understanding of their boss based on long and intimate association. By temperament they are not noticeably given to jealous rivalries.

THE PLACE ON TOP

Mr. Kennedy's approach to the Presidency was clearly evident in his Executive Order abolishing the Operations Coordinating Board, which had been employed by Mr. Eisenhower to "implement" the work of the National Security Council. In the opinion of its enemies, OCB had become a make-work affair, serving to impede rather than implement the conduct of an effective national strategy. While getting rid of the structure, however, Mr. Kennedy took care to retain a senior career official on the OCB staff who had proved himself an effective trouble shooter. "That fellow knows how to spot the scatter rugs on the polished floor of government," a Kennedy aide explained. Under McGeorge Bundy, what remains of the NSC staff will be involved in less routine and hopefully will offer more help to the President. The NSC itself will work more in task forces than as a formal council.

Another way to help the President, it has been proposed, will be to reestablish the State Department's primacy among the government agencies for all international matters. Mr. Kennedy intends the Secretary of State to be his first minister rather than, as Mr. Eisenhower once suggested, designating a new official to bear that title. State Department representatives will chair the interdepartmental committees and be held responsible for carrying out their mandates.

Mr. Kennedy's advisers admit that this is taking a calculated risk that the traditionally slow-moving State Department bureaucracy can measure up. It also presupposes that the Secretary of State will develop the kind of close relationship with the President that justifies his preferred status. But if it works, they feel, it will cut away some of the governmental superstructure that has grown up around the White House and obscured the President's place on top.

The President faces a peculiarly subtle problem in determining how to deal with the Vice-President. It is not a question for Mr. Kennedy of asserting his leadership but of finding ways to make proper use of the tremendous and restless energies of Lyndon Johnson. The two men's regard for each other has developed greatly since just before Mr. Kennedy's nomination, when neither considered it likely that Johnson would end up in second place on the ticket. Mr. Kennedy has reason to feel grateful for his running mate's dogged campaign performance.

Even with the best of intentions, however, the Vice-President's lot can be an unhappy one. Boredom being a more debilitating disease than fatigue, the present incumbent may have acquired a new understanding of why it is that almost twice as many Vice-Presidents as Presidents have died of natural causes while in office. For a politician like Johnson, accustomed to standing at the very center of the power struggle as Senate majority leader, the sudden release from pressure must produce symptoms akin to the bends.

President Kennedy is trying to keep Johnson intimately involved in Executive affairs, summoning him to the White House with great regularity and delegating to him the chairmanships of the National Aeronautics and Space Council and the Committee on Government Contracts. The Vice-President will now have a suite of offices in the Executive Office Building, something Nixon never had. In a private letter to Johnson, believed to be unique in Presidential literature, Mr. Kennedy has set forth his ideas about the Vice-President's place in the scheme of things and has authorized additional assistants to supplement Johnson's meager staff.

But both men realize there are limits to what a President can dispense, particularly when it cuts into his own hegemony. More important to Johnson's status in the Kennedy administration will be the role he can play as all-round expert in Congressional affairs. The challenge is formidable: a *Congressional Quarterly* projection of last year's voting would indicate that most of Mr. Kennedy's major measures lack a clear majority.

It is a delicate business, for Johnson now stands outside the jealous institution he ran so effectively. He is said to recognize that his powers as majority leader, even though created uniquely by him, cannot be transferred to his new office.

FOCUSED INTENSITY

Quite clearly, Mr. Kennedy's concept of a personal Presidency requires, first of all, an incumbent who has a wish to stay on top of things. If he is distracted by untidy details or confused by the multiplicity of problems requiring his attention, he could soon be run ragged. So far at least, Mr. Kennedy has shown no signs of strain. On the contrary, he has indicated, after the prolonged ordeal of campaigning, when a single misstep might have meant personal calamity, the rigors of the White House seem comparatively mild.

He appears to be having the same kind of love affair with his job that Roosevelt always had and Truman developed but Eisenhower never felt. It shows itself in matters both large and small. A man who never before paid much attention to where he lived, Mr. Kennedy has been giving meticulous attention to the White House, helping hang naval pictures in the President's study, selecting drapery material for the President's bedroom, and inspecting preparations for a diplomatic reception.

Despite the churn of White House activities, there has been a measured order to the President's own workday. So far the petitioners from Capitol Hill have not been showing up in great numbers. Mr. Kennedy has been scheduling discussions, of no fixed duration, with each of the committee chairmen who will shape his legislative fate. He held four long conferences with his ambassador to Russia, Llewellyn Thompson, who during his previous Washington visits had always been accustomed to a single twenty-minute audience with Mr. Eisenhower. On the morning of Khrushchev's attack on Dag Hammarskjöld, Mr. Kennedy found time for an unhurried discussion of the school situation in New Orleans with a journalist who had just returned from that city. He turns to each new subject with focused intensity. While he is talking and listening, he has a habit of writing notes to himself that have a way of spurring later actions.

It is still early to measure the real thrust of Presidential actions. In dealing with West German Foreign Minister Heinrich von Brentano, Mr. Kennedy was a cordial host who recalled a brief meeting fourteen years earlier that Brentano had evidently forgotten. The President chose to stress West Germany's obligations not to the United States but to the free world. Under no condition, he assured his guest, would U.S. troop commitments be made a bargaining instrument for getting German concessions. It was the soft sell but, some felt, a decidedly skillful one.

Mr. Kennedy has been capable of stiffer tactics with ambassadors from the various departments of his own government in Washington. Without much ado, he ordered the redrafting of a Medical Aid for the Aged bill prepared by the Health, Education and Welfare Department that had been prematurely disclosed to Congress. There are rumors of reprisals in the offing if enterprising cabinet members and agency heads forget their primary allegiance to the President's program and try to establish separate ententes on the Hill.

But these and his other acts so far are hardly measures of the President's ability to take the initiative. His response to Khrushchev on the Congo, while prompt and forceful, was nonetheless not action but reaction. His pronouncements on the New Orleans situation have undoubtedly helped ease that particular crisis, but it will take other steps to avert the school desegregation crises still in the making.

It is precisely here that Mr. Kennedy's capacity as President may meet its severest test. In junking the cumbersome machinery that never really helped the former President keep ahead of events, he has assumed a responsibility to provide better techniques of his own. He seems to have a canny awareness of this. By the variety of his close advisers, who are by no means of one mind on the critical choices confronting him, and by his apparent willingness to move along several lines of action at the same time, he may be able to avoid the immobility that can be fatal to Presidential power.

In his progression toward the Presidency, one close associate has pointed out, Mr. Kennedy displayed a remarkable capacity for concentrating on the task at hand. When he was in Wisconsin, he gave little thought to the problems of West Virginia. In West Virginia he was not concerned about the convention in Los Angeles. During the fall campaign, he took only the most elementary steps to prepare for the eventuality that he might be elected. He has gotten where he is, the associate argued, by not wasting his time or energy trying to look beyond the next horizon.

Undoubtedly, it was a sensible way for a politician working his way to the top to focus his attention. But a President who means to stay on top of his job had better have a range of vision that goes a great deal farther than the next horizon.

The Cabinet:
Index to the Kennedy Way
RICHARD F. FENNO, JR.

Every President of the United States recasts the relationship between the Chief Executive and his Cabinet. John F. Kennedy by now has been in office long enough for interested observers to draw some conclusions about how he deals with the men—both as individuals and as a group—who sit at his Cabinet table.

There are eleven men of formal Cabinet rank—ten department heads, who constitute the hard-core membership, and the Ambassador to the U. N. (Had Congress approved the President's recommendation for the establishment of a new Department of Urban Affairs and Housing, there would have been a twelfth.) President Kennedy has described his pattern of relationships with them in an

From *The New York Times Magazine* (April 22, 1962), p. 13. © 1962 by The New York Times Company. Reprinted by permission.

apparent paradox: "I think in the future that we will find the Cabinet perhaps more important than it has ever been, but Cabinet meetings not as important."

His system is to delegate copious responsibility to each Cabinet member for the management of his department and to rely heavily upon each Cabinet member for assistance in his own departmental area of competence. But he believes that the practice of calling them all together at the Cabinet table is "unnecessary and a waste of time"—of his time and theirs.

More openly than any other modern President, Mr. Kennedy has minimized the importance of Cabinet meetings in his decision-making process. He has convened only fifteen of them since his inauguration. "I can't remember when we had the last Cabinet meeting," remarked one of its most influential members a few weeks ago.

The President believes that the Cabinet is simply not the appropriate group with which to discuss most of his problems. "He hasn't downgraded the Cabinet," said a White House aide. "He has a great deal of respect for the members personally and he works with all of them. It's just that he doesn't think the subject matter requires all of them in a group. They each have their separate jurisdictions and their separate problems. When two or three of them have a common problem, he gets them together and works with them."

The nature of the problem determines the group with which the President works; the superior status of the Cabinet carries with it no special claim upon his time. "I can't imagine," agreed one sympathetic member, "why the President would want to hear Bob McNamara talk about price supports on cotton or Orville Freeman talk about sending troops to Vietnam."

The problems which the President has decided to bring before the Cabinet are Government-wide in impact and almost wholly on the domestic side. The group has concerned itself with the state of the national economy on several occasions, with budgetary policy, with Government personnel activities and with Congressional relations. The domestic flavor of Cabinet discussion is reflected in the fact that the Cabinet regulars in addition to the eleven who have Cabinet rank are Vice President Lyndon Johnson, Special Counsel to the President Theodore Sorensen (through whom all domestic problems flow on their way to Mr. Kennedy), Director of the Budget Bureau David Bell, Chairman of the Council of Economic Advisers Walter Heller, and Timothy (Ted) Reardon, the Special Assistant to the President handling Cabinet affairs.

A few meetings have been devoted primarily to foreign affairs, but even then to problems which have particularly direct implications for the domestic economy—one, for instance, on the balance of payments and another on foreign aid. Normally, however, Cabinet activity in the area of foreign relations has been confined to briefings by Secretary of State Rusk. When Mr. Kennedy wishes to canvass the widest range of opinion on foreign policy, he (like President Eisenhower before him) does so in the National Security Council and not in the Cabinet.

When the Kennedy Cabinet convened for its first meeting, each member received a thirteen-page compilation of commentary on the President-Cabinet relationship. A quotation on the cover summarized the possible uses of the corporate Cabinet as follows: "Collectively, they can provide him with a political sounding board, with a stimulating clash of policy alternatives, with a forum in which some coordination can be achieved, and with a gathering in which to kindle Administration *esprit.*"

Contrary, perhaps, to popular opinion, past Chief Executives have emphasized the first and the last of these usages. Thus far in the Kennedy Administration, only the last one has been very conspicuous.

When a President employs his Cabinet as a *political sounding board,* he seeks the members' experienced judgment as to the likely public reaction to a proposed decision and, hence, the political consequences thereof. President Eisenhower, for example, requested Cabinet assessment of public opinion prior to issuing some of his veto messages.

Occasionally, Franklin Roosevelt inquired as to whether the American people would or would not support a particular step—toward preparedness in 1940-41, for instance. But the perpetual agitation of his Cabinet members over the timing of both domestic and foreign decisions makes it clear that he rarely courted their judgment on popular attitudes.

President Kennedy's legislative and campaign experience has yielded a similar disposition to trust his own instincts in these matters. A close White House aide explained, "He doesn't need anyone to tell him what the public thinks. He's had more political experience than any of the members of his Cabinet."

Last fall, however, during the formulation of the Administration's first budget, the President utilized the Cabinet importantly as a sounding board. A major decision was whether to present a balanced or an unbalanced budget. Every Cabinet member would be affected by the decision and every Cabinet member had his ear to the ground in his departmental constituency. The President profited by hearing the fullest possible range of judgments as he moved toward his ultimate choice of presenting a balanced budget.

Cabinet meetings which provide the kind of *clash of policy alternatives* among informed individuals which would educate and assist the President are a rarity in every Administration. Neither Wilson nor Roosevelt nor Truman was in the habit of throwing out a problem and relying upon the ensuing debate to clarify it for him—much less decide it for him.

Even Eisenhower found his Cabinet meetings most useful as a forum in which members could present and explain programs which had already been carefully prepared and were ready for his decision. He could, and usually did, indicate his support of the policy as outlined—much in the manner of initialing a staff document. He held regular weekly meetings, but not more than eight or ten in eight years featured serious controversy.

In the tradition of his predecessors, President Kennedy proceeds well along the path to a decision before he broaches the subject in full Cabinet meeting. Cabinet members agree that he has usually made up his mind, though sometimes it is not possible to tell. Normally, however, they meet to "get the word" on policy. "And he's really emphatic about what he wants," exclaimed one member. Thus, at a meeting which followed two weeks after the budget discussion, he announced his decision to balance the budget and read a directive (later published) ordering all those present to cut back expenditures.

For reasons that the President obviously understands, Cabinet meetings have never fulfilled their potential as devices for *coordination among departments*. The problems to be coordinated rarely involve all the members. Those who have serious conflicts will avoid exposing them for collegial consumption.

Some minor coordination has been achieved in the past by turning the Cabinet meeting into a clearing house for informational reports by the members on their current problems. More than half of Roosevelt's and Eisenhower's Cabinet hours were consumed in this fashion. A more valuable purpose has been served by Presidential comments to the group—not in the sense that these can resolve open conflicts but in the sense that they foster a similarity of expression on the public face of the group.

In practice, the members of the Kennedy Cabinet have achieved a most informal but useful brand of coordination through regular luncheons. Members take turns inviting "the boys" (though not the President) to each department for "an hour and a half of fellowship and talk."

"You get to know the others on a first-name basis," said one participant. "You learn what kind of a person each is and how you have to deal with him—in a formal way or just by calling him on the phone. Our sessions have been lively, down to earth, no-holds-barred bull sessions."

Since George Washington created the Cabinet, its meetings have served one constant and indispensable function—the stimulation of *Administration esprit*. Mr. Kennedy's meetings are no exception. Some members feel that other contacts—business and social—are so frequent that Cabinet meetings are hardly necessary to knit the group together. But the majority of members, as well as key White House assistants, find Administration cohesiveness better served by a meeting of Cabinet and President than by any other device.

"The main purpose," said one Cabinet member, "is to give people a feeling of being part of a joint effort. You could get too far out from the center. You could get the idea that all you had to do was administer your own unit and didn't have to worry about anything else. That's not so; and that attitude wouldn't be good."

Every Cabinet tends to become a collection of warring feudal baronies. So far, the present Cabinet deserves credit for its lack of internal backbiting or public feuds.

In the opinion of seven department heads interviewed recently, two facts about the Kennedy Cabinet operation are noteworthy—the free rein which they have in running their own departments and the unrestricted informal access which they have to the Chief Executive. On the one hand, each knows that "I don't have to clear every little thing with the White House." On the other hand, each feels: "You've got one of the most accessible Presidents in history."

Franklin Roosevelt's Cabinet members prized Cabinet meetings as opportunities to buttonhole the President. Following each meeting, they scrambled unceremoniously for positions at F.D.R.'s elbow—a ritual known as "prayer meeting at amen corner." Mr. Kennedy commented adversely on this practice during one of his early meetings. The warning was quite unnecessary.

"I must talk with him in person or on the phone twenty times a week," said one Secretary. "I don't hesitate to call him if something important comes up—even at night or on Sunday. And it's the other way around, too. I get night calls and Sunday calls from him."

"I can pick up the telephone and call him any time," commented a second member. "I did it yesterday. I'll call up the White House and say, 'I want ten minutes tomorrow or the next day.' But I don't do that too often. None of us bothers him too much."

Most members work primarily through the President's assistants. "I believe the job of a Cabinet member is to take burdens off the President's back, not put them on," declared a member with executive experience. "If I have an idea, I may call Kenny O'Donnell or Ted Sorensen or Larry O'Brien and say, 'This is a thought I had. Would you pass it along to the President sometime?' I try not to add to his burden."

Still a fourth member called attention to the unique advantages in having the President's brother as a Cabinet colleague. "One of the things about this Administration is that you have Bobby as the alter ego of the President. You can take things to him that under other circumstances you might take to the President." The Attorney General is, along with Vice President Johnson, one of the President's two all-purpose advisers. His liaison activities can assist the Cabinet member and, at the same time, shield the President.

The way in which President Kennedy uses his Cabinet is a by-product of his temperament and experience. "The Cabinet expresses the personality of the President," says one White House aide, "and this one's an individualist. He doesn't work in committees or groups or things like that. He's much better when he's alone."

He functions, in his own expression, "bilaterally" with innumerable groups and individuals, taking in information and fresh points of view—but only from those people who are involved with a given problem and who can make contributions to its solution. Cabinet members often qualify, but, as one put it, "all kinds of people get into the White House who are outranked in their agency."

By reflection as well as by inclination, President Kennedy knows that the only way to preserve his power to make choices is to keep many channels to him open and maintain a fluid structure around him. He positively fears the diffusion of leadership through over-structured committee activity. This doctrine of the practical art of being President was doubtless confirmed and sharpened by his early reading of Richard Neustadt's book "Presidential Power."

But it is also a method of operation closely attuned to his Congressional experience. As a Senator, Mr. Kennedy functioned at the vortex of a decision-making process, listening to a great array of fact and opinion—from constituents, party leaders, colleagues, personal staff, pressure groups and administrative officials. Whatever structure was given to this vast intake came mostly from within his own mind.

"He can get to the point very quickly—just like that," a Cabinet member remarked. "He likes to hear different points of view. But he doesn't like to sit around in a group and ask, 'What do you think? What do you think?' and so on all around the circle."

"This is not a conversational Administration," said another. "The President likes doers, not talkers."

Kennedy's Working Staff
JOSEPH KRAFT

"No one man can fill the Presidency," Harry Truman once said. And in modern times at least, no one man has had to. For the past quarter-century the term "Presidency" has engrossed, besides the Chief Executive, a score of aides grouped in the White House Office. Their sole business is to help the President do his business. They are the President's Men.

Because they work behind the scenes, the functions and even the persons of the President's Men tend to be obscure. Not their importance. A survey of the federal bureaucracy made by a private management firm in 1960 found 75 dominant positions in the government—eight of them in the White House Office. Only two or three Cabinet members rival some members of the White House staff in influence and authority. Collectively, the White House staff probably outweighs any other group in the government, not excepting the Cabinet and the National Security Council.

Besides being important, the White House staff is peculiarly symbolic. Every President faces the problem of putting the imprint of his policy upon highly complicated problems that necessarily work their way up through a cumbersome bureaucracy which has its own momentum and direction. The chief means for bending the bureaucracy to the President's will is the White House staff. Its function is to move from the bureaucracy to the Presidency, reliably enough and soon enough to be effective, the elements of decision. More perhaps than any other aspect of government, the White House staff reflects the characteristic ways, means, and purposes of the President. It is his "lengthened shadow."

Thus under Eisenhower, the White House staff answered exactly the needs of a military man and national hero, with little appetite for detail, who deemed it his mission to harmonize discordant elements in the nation. In structure the staff was hierarchical, heading up in The Assistant to the President: first Sherman Adams; after 1958, General Wilton Persons. Co-ordination was a main feature, and there were thrice-weekly staff meetings and an elaborate machinery, including a staff secretary and a Cabinet secretary, to make sure that all bases were touched. Great stress was laid on agreed position papers (one for nearly every foreign country was prepared, and kept up to date, by the staff of the National Security Council) which, like field manuals, would pass the word from the President down through the ranks. Whether in the interests of protecting General Eisenhower or not, an unmistakable effort was made to resolve disputes below the Presidential level. "I count the day lost when I have not found some way of lightening the President's load," Sherman Adams once remarked. General Persons used to say: "We're not looking for business."

* Copyright © 1962, by Minneapolis Star and Tribune Co., Inc. Reprinted from the December, 1962 issue of *Harper's Magazine* (pp. 29-36) by permission of the author.

Under Kennedy, the staff has been shaped to meet the needs of a President with abundant stores of restless energy, with a great capacity for assimilating detail, and with a taste for tackling issues before the rough edges are planed away in coordination. "When things are very quiet, and beautifully organized," he once said, "I think it's time to be concerned." Extraordinary as it may seem, and despite many recommendations to the contrary, there has not been a single meeting of Kennedy's White House staff; nor is there likely to be. Neither is any single staff man the majordomo, though some members are senior to others. In structure, the staff is not a pyramid, but a wheel figuring a network of bilateral relations between the President and his aides. Staff members get together frequently on an *ad hoc* basis; but their characteristic relationship (despite talk of the Irish Mafia and the Harvard Clique) is neither partnership nor feud, but a kind of disengagement, reinforced by separateness of function and personality. Formal papers are at a minimum, but all staff members are encouraged to bring to the President all official problems. "We work for a President," one staff member says, "who *is* looking for business."

But how do they work? And what are the strengths and weaknesses of the system?

TWO MEN FOR ALL SEASONS

Twenty-two persons currently make up the White House staff—as against twenty-eight for Eisenhower through most of 1960. But the numbers mean almost nothing. While some persons who figure actively in White House activities are carried on the staffs of other agencies, others are in the White House for want of another suitable post, and still others attend more to personal, social, and secretarial than to governmental tasks. For operational purposes, the Kennedy White House Office breaks down into two all-purpose aides and five functional offices.

The two all-purpose men are Ralph Dungan, a veteran of the President's Senate staff, and Arthur Schlesinger, Jr., the Harvard historian and Pulitzer Prize winner. Dungan is chiefly responsible for personnel, or as he puts it, "headhunting." He maintains a permanent list of talent available for posts in the government; checks the job recommendations that come up from the Congress, the Democratic National Committee, and the Departments and Agencies; and keeps tabs on the expiration dates of term appointments. Though that function is heavily political, Dungan is personally a reflective and genial person, the very opposite of the hard-nosed operator supposed to thrive in the politics of the New Frontier. "He's the nicest guy I ever met in politics," a Connecticut job-seeker who didn't get the job once said of him. Though the personnel job is normally a full-time occupation, Dungan, because of his substantive interests, has taken on a wide variety of other tasks—for example, he is the Presidential overseer of the foreign-aid program and works on policy toward Latin America and Africa.

Schlesinger's assignment is more diverse. He has maintained liaison between the President and UN Ambassador Adlai Stevenson, has sat in on Latin American policy meetings at the State Department and White House, has taken an occasional hand at speeches, and functioned as a point of contact between the White House and the intellectual community. "Arthur," one other White House aide says, "has minimal operational responsibilities. He serves as a general gadfly." In his own view, Schlesinger has a special responsibility for innovation. He had a hand in the speech made by the President at the 1962 Yale Commencement which aimed at setting in motion an economic re-education of the nation. It was his idea to establish a White House cultural office, and to place in it August Heckscher.

FIVE SLOTTED BY FUNCTION

Of the five functional slots, one may best be described as staff assistant to the President. It is filled by Kenneth O'Donnell, thirty-eight, a former Harvard football star and member of Robert Kennedy's staff when he was counsel to the Senate rackets committee. O'Donnell handles most of the White House administrative chores: appointments for the President, arrangements for Presidential trips, and such matters as FBI clearance for the White House staff. Insofar as anyone keeps the rest of the staff systematically informed about the President's thoughts and actions, it is O'Donnell. He is also, in the words of one of his colleagues, "the chief White House official for party politics," and thus in constant liaison with the Democratic National Committee and local party groups across the country.

Probably O'Donnell sees the President more than any other staff member—some ten or twenty times a day. In an offhand way, his judgment is likely to be asked on any matter ranging from a tax cut to a candidate for Governor of New York. Personally, he does correspond to the image of a Kennedy type: highly intelligent, physically powerful, and with tight features. "Kenny makes a hundred decisions a day," one other White House aide says, "and without any flap." Better perhaps than any other of the President's Men, he can take and hold a negative position. "When I want a No decision," says an assistant secretary, "I take my problem to O'Donnell."

The second functional slot is the office of the Special Counsel, which might be called the office of Presidential programs. Invented initially for Samuel Rosenman in the Roosevelt Administration, then passed on to Clark Clifford and Charles S. Murphy in the Truman Administration, the post is now held by a thirty-four-year-old Nebraska lawyer, Theodore C. Sorensen, who has been with Mr. Kennedy since he came to the Senate in 1953. Sharing the office with Sorensen are a Deputy Counsel and an Assistant Special Counsel, respectively: Myer Feldman, a former Pennsylvania law professor with extensive experience in private business and the government; and Lee White, a classmate of Sorensen at the Nebraska law school who worked with him, as did Feldman, in the President's Senate office.

Sorensen's responsibility runs virtually across the board. He drafts most Presidential messages and speeches; sits in with Cabinet members and Agency heads in formulating the legislative program and the Budget; attends the President's weekly meeting with the legislative leaders, and the pre-press conference briefing of the President; and participates actively in handling virtually every major domestic issue and some major foreign issues. Feldman and White work—largely independently—in the same area, but generally on more detailed matters: Feldman on agriculture, transportation, communications, trade and tariffs, and much regulatory Agency business, as well as some Israeli affairs; White on civil rights, public works, and conservation. All three men have direct access to the President, though Sorensen undoubtedly sees him most often—and on the more full-blown issues.

While much has been said about Sorensen's liberal past—his father was campaign manager for Senator George Norris in Nebraska, and he himself has always been a liberal Democrat—what most characterizes his shop are the businesslike virtues: lucid grasp of complicated issues, good judgment, and staggering production. "Sorensen," says one of the permanent officials in the Bureau of the Budget, "can understand anything from sugar subsidies to bomb shelters. And he's the fastest good writer this place has ever seen. His office does what at least ten men did in the Eisenhower regime."

The third functional slot is the Special Assistant for National Security Affairs, a post created for—and to a large extent, by—the former Harvard Dean, McGeorge Bundy. Bundy—or in his absence his deputy, the Harvard economist Carl Kaysen—receives copies of virtually all the incoming cables to the Secretaries of State and Defense and the Director of the Central Intelligence Agency. These he sorts out, taking the most important, or those bearing on immediate business, direct to the President. Bundy has also made his office a workshop for putting together policies that cannot easily be constructed in any other single place—the American stand on bomb testing, for instance. And, of course, his shop is the clearing house for a wide variety of questions and proposals coming to the President from the national security Agencies. To handle this business, Bundy has built a small staff organized along geographic lines. It meets daily and includes a staff secretary; specialists in Far Eastern, Soviet, and Arab affairs; and Schlesinger and Dungan when they are wearing their Latin American or African hats. Decisions made by the President are registered, not in elaborate position papers, but in short memoranda—the NSAM or National Security Action Memoranda—which merely state the fact that the President has considered an issue and decided such and such.

Perhaps alone among the White House staff, Bundy is heir to a tradition—the tradition of leadership in American foreign policy that stretches from Theodore Roosevelt through Elihu Root to Henry Stimson, who worked with Bundy's father, Harvey, in the Hoover Administration and World War II, and who entrusted to McGeorge Bundy the writing of his official biography. Bundy's style is fully in keeping with that tradition. He has spoken and written extensively and dealt man-to-man with the likes of Harold Macmillan, Konrad Adenauer, and Andre Malraux. Confident mastery—not without disdain for those who don't have it—colors his expressions. A reference to "pompous nonsense" in a recent article in *Foreign Affairs*, for example, has left a sting in some parts of the Pentagon and some quarters at Harvard.

The fourth functional slot is the assistant for Congressional relations. Used only sporadically in the Eisenhower Administration and hardly at all by Truman and Roosevelt, this post has been given special weight under Kennedy. It is headed by one of the President's oldest associates, the forty-five-year-old Massachusetts public-relations man, Lawrence O'Brien, who has under him five aides—one Senate man, three House men, and a general assistant. O'Brien receives every Monday night written reports from the various Departments and Agencies on pending legislation; these form the basis of the breakfast meetings, usually held Tuesday morning, with the legislative leaders. O'Brien or one of his aides usually sits in on the meetings that precede formulation of the President's legislative program. As measures enter the critical stages in Congress, O'Brien and his men usually take over the lobbying task from the Departmental representatives.

While there has been much complaint of arm-twisting, the fact is that a great deal of O'Brien's work is a public-relations service job. He sees to it, for example, that the Departments and Agencies give advance notice to Congressmen of decisions affecting their districts. In one typical ten-minute interval, not long ago, he took three telephone calls from the Hill—one dealing with a pending bill, a second concerning money for a Senatorial campaign, a third involving a White House tour for a constituent of a Republican Senator. Supplying such services comes naturally to O'Brien, an engaging redhead, notably fair-minded, with an instinctive grasp of the other man's point of view. Of one Congressman who complained publicly of arm-twisting by O'Brien's office, O'Brien says: "I don't mind. He's a Democrat in a Republican district. It helps him if the voters think he's fighting the Democratic organization."

The fifth functional slot is the well-known office of Press Secretary, filled, with the help of two assistants, by Pierre Salinger, a thirty-seven-year-old California writer and editor who formerly worked on the staff of Robert Kennedy. Salinger presides over an inter-Departmental briefing session that precedes Presidential press conferences, and also acts as informal chairman over a weekly group of government information officers. But his chief job is getting out information to newsmen. He briefs the White House regulars twice a day—at noon and again at four in the afternoon. While no match for President Eisenhower's Press Secretary, James Hagerty, in keeping newsmen out of trouble by dispensing innocuous information in encyclopedic detail, Salinger has a special brand of comedy that works toward the same result. At a briefing on September 24, for example, after refusing comment on a question concerning Cuba, and another concerning the convicted Soviet spy Robert Soblen, Salinger plunged into this exchange:

Q. Is there anything to the story that the Green Room is going to be chartreuse and the Blue Room is going to be white on white?
Mr. S. I am glad that you brought that up.
Q. What was the question?
Mr. S. The question was whether the Green Room is going to be chartreuse and the Blue Room was going to be white on white.
Q. What is chartreuse?
Q. Could we file what we already have?
Mr. S. I would like to deal with this matter within the limits of the knowledge I have, but I can state equivocally that . . .

Q. You mean unequivocally.
Mr. S. Unequivocally that the Blue Room will continue to be the Blue Room.
Q. You didn't answer someone's question. What is chartreuse?
Mr. S. I couldn't tell you that. The Green Room will remain the Green Room, and the Blue Room will remain the Blue Room.
Q. You are talking about the name or the motif?
Mr. S. I am talking about the two rooms.

Several moments later a reporter asked: "Do you mind if we leave?" With perfect aplomb, Mr. S. replied: "Not in the slightest."

"AS FLUID AS IT CAN BE"

Virtually no piece of Presidential business, of course, fits cleanly into any single compartment. The slightest alteration in the Communications Satellite Bill, for example, involved O'Donnell, who was watching the political angles as they affected private business; O'Brien, who had a finger on the Congressional pulse; White, who did much of the drafting in co-operation with the Justice Department and Space Counsel; and Bundy's office which was concerned with international implications.

The course of events, moreover, dictates a continuous shifting of priorities and assignments. The recent Drug Bill, for instance, was initially Sorensen's ball, but when he had to do a major speech, it was passed on to Feldman who, when he had to go to Israel, passed it on to White. Civil rights, normally White's bailiwick, became the province of Sorensen, O'Donnell, Robert Kennedy, and the President when the admission of James Meredith to the University of Mississippi became an all-out test of strength between the federal government and Governor Ross Barnett. Thus, in action, what look like clear lines of well-defined jurisdiction blur into a kaleidoscope. "The White House operation," one aide says, "is as fluid as it can be."

Even amidst this organic process, however, there are fixed reference points—three dominant orientations—for the White House staff. Of these, the most important is the President himself. His day—in the office with the papers read at 9:15; back to the White House living quarters (or mansion) for a swim, lunch, and reading at around 1:00; back in the office around 2:30; back to the mansion with a sheaf of papers at around 7:30—sets the pattern for the staff's day. Generally they are in the office before the President, and generally they quit after he goes home. While staff access to the President is very easy, the custom is not to interrupt his formal appointments. Staff members usually catch him, singly or in groups, as he enters his office in the morning or after lunch, or just before he quits it for lunch or dinner. Written material for his attention is usually placed in a folder he takes home at night. Sometimes, just before dinner, the President will himself wander into one of the staff offices for a chat.

Casual terseness marks most of the exchanges between the staff and the President. "What have you got?" or "What's up?" is Mr. Kennedy's usual opening phrase. Then, as one aide says, "You're supposed to tell him—bang, bang, bang."

"Take care of that" or "Check that with so and so" is the normal Presidential response. Assignments are handed out in an equally informal manner. Often all the President says is: "I'd like you to think about such and such."

The ability to interpret laconic questions correctly is absolutely crucial in the Kennedy White House. General Maxwell Taylor was taken on as the President's Special Military Adviser last June in large part because, as one White House staffer says, "he was a military man who spoke the President's language." Now that General Taylor has become Chairman of the Joint Chiefs, there will be no need of a translator between the Chiefs and the President, and the odds are that he will not be replaced in this job.

Both the President's Scientific Adviser, Jerome Wiesner, and his Chairman of the Council of Economic Advisers, Walter Heller, have had troubles because they tended to be long-winded. It is generally acknowledged in the White House that much of the early confusion regarding the Administration derived from poor staff reading of the President's signs. "There were some new boys around," one of Mr. Kennedy's long-time assistants says. "They thought when he said, 'Take care of that,' he meant for them to do it personally. They were running around all over the place. Now they know he wants them to take care of it through the appropriate channels."

Some part of the White House staff enters into virtually all White House action. Three staff men (Bundy, Sorensen, and O'Donnell) were in on the Cuba quarantine plan from the very beginning. Sorensen and O'Donnell shared with the President and Robert Kennedy the tightly held secret that Anthony J. Celebrezze, who was originally being considered for a judgeship, would instead be appointed Secretary of Health, Education, and Welfare.

But the President keeps open a wide variety of other channels to the outside world. He reads extensively and is likely to take initiatives based on articles and editorials as well as staff memoranda. He has very close personal relations not only with the Attorney General, but also the Secretary of the Treasury, Douglas Dillon. He is apt to call personally any one of a dozen men in the State and Defense Departments, and he has hosts of close connections in the Congress and the press corps. In these relationships, the White House staff enters hardly at all; nor do they figure much in the President's social life. On the contrary, he generally takes his ease with what one White House aide calls—somewhat ruefully—"the swells" of the society world.

LINKS WITH THE OUTSIDE

For its part, the staff also has an important orientation toward the outside world of government and politics. Indeed, every member has a distinct focal point: O'Donnell with the Democratic National Committee and with local political leaders; Salinger with the press; O'Brien with the Congress; Bundy with Defense, State, and the CIA; Sorensen with the Bureau of the Budget, Treasury, and the Council of Economic Advisers; Feldman with Agriculture, Commerce, and the regulatory Agencies; White with Justice, Interior, and the housing Agencies. In those areas where the President himself has only a limited interest, the White House staff is likely to have wide latitude. Though Department and Agency heads can communicate directly with the President, those outside the range of his keenest interest are generally pleased to have a White House staff member present their case. "We usually try to go in to the President with Sorensen on our side," one Department head says. In the negotiations on the Trade Bill, Feldman tended to carry the ball for the Commerce Department, even negotiating certain agreements directly with various producer interests.

But in those areas where the President's interest is keenest, the staff role tends to be more narrowly confined. Sorensen, before giving his views on an important matter of economic policy, will see to it that the President has first the views of the Treasury and the Council of Economic Advisers. Bundy, just because he has so often been talked of as a Deputy President for Foreign Affairs, hews particularly close to the reporting line. Before the President meets with the Secretaries of State and Defense, say, Bundy will analyze for him the views of each, giving an estimate of the underlying reasons, and perhaps supplying a list of questions the President should have answered before reaching his decision. "Mac doesn't usually advise the President," one of his colleagues says. "He gives the President the means for assessing the advice that comes from others."

In that spirit, a key function of all White House staff members is to spot the weak points in the proposals generated by the other parts of the Executive Branch. White House staff members played a key part in heading off a tax increase at the time of the Berlin buildup of July 1961; in putting at least some public-ownership features into the Communications Satellite program; in knocking down a State Department proposal that the action on the Trade Bill be delayed until 1963; in blocking proposals made after the Bay of Pigs that there be established a Cold War Strategy Board, and a special office of Psychological Warfare in the State Department. It is generally agreed that the special forte of the Special Counsel's office is penetrating analysis. "When Sorensen gets into something," one of the permanent civil servants at the Bureau of the Budget says, "it gets a thorough scrubbing." It is also generally agreed that the biggest single failure of the White House staff lay in timidity in questioning the proposals for the Cuban invasion of April 1961. "At that point," a former White House aide says, "we just didn't have the confidence to tell the veterans of the bureaucracy, 'Look, you're crazy.'"

A similar and equally important role of the White House staff is pulling information and problems out of the Departments for Presidential decision. When the issue of control over West New Guinea was bogged down in an internal State Department dispute between the European bureau with its Dutch clients, and the Far Eastern bureau with its Indonesian clients, Bundy's office pulled it out for Presidential disposition. A great many of the issues between Commerce and State over the Trade Bill were forced to a head by Feldman. Such tactics inevitably grate hard on some people in some Departments. The more so as the White House staff people are not particularly gentle. Two officials who refused to yield up a document to

Bundy, on the grounds it wasn't yet ready, were told: "Well, I see it's still the same, old, Germanic, wrongheaded State Department."

Still the hurt feelings do not seem to get in the way of effective operational co-operation. The response to the Soviet protest over the U-2 plane which flew over Sakhalin Island last summer, for instance, was put out in a matter of hours, though it involved a temporary freeze on all other government mention of the issue, and close co-operation among Salinger, Bundy, and the State and Defense Departments.

A CERTAIN STIFFNESS

In the course of such operations, the Kennedy staff members develop still a third critical orientation: toward each other. There has been some written gossip, and much more talk, about a split among the Irish Mafia, the Senate group, and the Harvard Clique. It is true that the White House men dealing with patronage and politics are Irish; it is also true that the Special Counsel's office is filled by former members of the President's Senate staff; it is equally true that those most heavily engaged in foreign affairs are Harvard intellectuals. Inside each group, moreover, there are friendships that do not spill over: Sorensen, for example, often sees Feldman after hours, but not Bundy, who sees a good deal of Schlesinger; and not O'Donnell, who is often with O'Brien.

But that is about as far as cliquism goes in the Kennedy White House. For one thing, staff men tend to be too busy to develop alliances or feuds. "I've done hundreds of pieces of business with everyone in this office," one member says, "at lunch in the mess, over the telephones, in their office or in mine. But I have yet to have a long conversation with anybody." For another thing, Kennedy, unlike Roosevelt, does not cultivate opposing staff positions or play off one member against the other. Generally, the President will deal with one man at a time on one issue at a time. When he consults more than one, he tends to keep his own counsel as to what they say. Party lines, in consequence, do not have a chance to build up. There is probably no one on the staff who knew—or knows now—how the others stood on the matter of a tax cut when that issue was hot last summer.

Insofar as policy positions are established, moreover, they tend to reflect operational responsibilities more than personal philosophy and background. O'Brien, for example, led the fight to push the Trade Bill this year rather than next because he was convinced that to wait a year was to lose the initiative with the Congress. O'Donnell is known as the White House liberal—not because of an ideological bent that way, but because of his regular contacts with the urban Democratic leaders. Sorensen, though strongly averse to the "hard line," was called on to write the Berlin speech of July 25, 1961, and in producing what the situation demanded turned out an exceedingly tough expression on foreign policy. He also played a part in shaping the policy and in writing the Presidential speech when the Cuba quarantine was declared.

Probably the most convincing demonstration of the absence of friction is the story of what has happened to the staff since Inauguration. Or rather what has not happened. The basic nucleus of Kennedy's White House staff comprises men who have worked with him for years before he became President. Only one outsider has really penetrated the circle—McGeorge Bundy, who started with stature of his own and an assignment in foreign affairs that none of the veteran staff members had competence to fill. Four new boys never did get into the inner workings of the system and have left the White House: Harris Wofford, who went to the Peace Corps, and Fred Dutton, Richard Goodwin, and Walt Rostow, who were dispatched, in the "Thanksgiving Massacre" of 1961, to State Department jobs that badly needed filling. "Whatever else you want to say about the White House staff," one former member of the Truman staff says, "they stick together. They respect each other's competence and they don't get in each other's way. It's like a tacit treaty arrangement, marking spheres of influence."

Which, of course, is not to say that the White House staff—as some have claimed—is like a great big Irish family. A truer measure is perhaps provided by a personal feature common to the three most important figures on the White House staff. O'Donnell, Sorensen, and Bundy differ in outlook and background about as much as any three highly intelligent people can differ. But there is one thing they share—a certain stiffness. Bundy has a distinct New England reserve; O'Donnell is so given to silence that he has been called The Arab; Sorensen is so loath to talk about himself that one White House associate declares, "No one knows what Ted thinks." All three are at home with pragmatic day-to-day dealings that do not sink into friction or rise into friendship. They are at home, that is to say, in the Kennedy White House.

"IN THE THICK OF THINGS"

Nine months before he entered the White House, John F. Kennedy said that as President he would want to be "in the thick of things." It is the supreme achievement of the White House staff that it has helped keep the President—perhaps more than any of his recent predecessors—right there. From the Cuban invasion to the Cuba quarantine, from the steel case to the refusal to go for a tax cut last July, every major decision has been made by the President. At times, as in the case of James Meredith and the University of Mississippi, the White House has been transformed into a command post, issuing detailed orders direct to the field. When the Medicare proposal was up before the Senate, the President personally—and unsuccessfully, as it turned out—was in touch with the key Senator, Jennings Randolph of West Virginia. When the Tax Bill was before the House, the President personally—and as it turned out, successfully—was in touch with Representative Wilbur Mills. When newspaper stories satisfy or displease the Administration, it is often the President himself who lets reporters know his views.

Wide as the range of criticism may be, moreover, it does not include the charge that the President does not know what goes on in his Administration. If nothing else, the press conferences testify abundantly to the contrary. On April 21, 1961, for example, a reporter, pointing out that the Republicans in Congress had set up groups to study the effect of automation on employment, asked the President if he hoped the Democrats would follow suit. The President replied: "The subcommittee on, labor, a subcommittee headed by Congressman Holland of Pennsylvania, has been conducting studies on the effect of automation for some months." When a reporter asked the President about a surplus Air Force metal extrusion plant in Adrian, Michigan, Mr. Kennedy not only knew the case, but had personally talked to the man in charge—an official probably not one person in a million could name, that is, the man in charge of Emergency Operations in the Business and Defense Services Administration of the Department of Commerce.

Most serious complaints about the White House system spring precisely from the condition which makes it possible for the President to be so much in the thick of things—namely, the lack of insulation between Mr. Kennedy and the operating personnel of the government. In particular, it is argued that because he deals so directly, not enough collateral "input" goes into his decisions. One case in point concerns the announcement last spring that the White House had ceased to take the New York *Herald Tribune*; it is hardly believable that the announcement would have been made had the matter been talked over with even two or three members of the White House staff.

Neither does the bang, bang style always lend itself to a full consideration of alternatives. It may be that Wiesner and Heller are long-winded. But it may also be that the positions they take—that there should be a lid on the arms race, for instance; or that the tax system should be radically altered—do not lend themselves to concise expression. "The system now," one close student of White House affairs says, "favors people who know exactly what they want to do. It is tough on people who have dim misgivings—even if those misgivings happen to be very important."

A related complaint argues that because the President deals bilaterally with his aides, there is insufficient co-ordination between White House offices. In particular, it is asserted that O'Brien's men lack substantive knowledge of the legislation they are backing, and that, unable to argue the case on its merits, they fall back very rapidly on coaxing by favors and patronage. "In Roosevelt's day," says a White House assistant of that era, "Cohen and Corcoran used to draft the legislation and then take it up on the Hill and see it through. Now the functions are split." There is no indication that O'Brien's men, through lack of knowledge, have ever traded away vital clauses of proposed measures. Neither does the statistical record support the contention that O'Brien's office has been a bust. On the contrary, of some 99 Southern Democrats in the House, the number voting against the Administration has been cut from an average of over sixty during the Roosevelt and Truman years to an average of 45 in 1961, and 35 in 1962. And the Administration claims that 73 per cent of its program went through the last Congress—not a bad batting average, considering the strength of the conservative coalition.

Still, it does seem to be true that O'Brien has hinged legislation to patronage more closely than ever before. Some very respectable Congressmen have no doubt been offended when they were offered a postmastership in return for the right vote on a matter about which they happened to feel very deeply. More importantly, the widespread use of services and favors has tended to debase the currency, making it difficult to win support on high-priority measures. At least one Congressman who might have cast a decisive committee vote in favor of the aid program refused—not on principle, but because the Administration could not get the ante high enough to meet his demands.

Taken singly, these complaints may not amount to a great deal. But together they say something important. The staff operation, like many other aspects of the Administration, works to put all matters on a pragmatic, case-by-case basis. It does not contribute to the systematic elaboration of coherent programs expressing broad and easily identified public policies. A sense of inner purpose may—no doubt does—exist in the White House. But in part because the operation is so casual, so laconic, so frictionless, the purpose and direction of the Administration, its intrinsic character, so to speak, have not made themselves felt outside the White House. To that extent at least, the work of the White House staff, excellent as it may be on an *ad hoc* basis, does not yet serve the President's desire that his Administration achieve historic stature.

How Mr. Kennedy Gets the Answers
SIDNEY HYMAN

President Kennedy lives intimately with three questions. What am I looking at? How do I know what I know about it? What am I going to do about it?

He has faced these questions in the past over everything from the turmoil in the Congo to Soviet missile bases in Cuba and from the Berlin Wall to the Chinese Communist attack on India. He faces them today on everything from the revolt of the American Negro to the vetoes of Charles de Gaulle, and from the attacks on the Buddhists in South Vietnam to the loss of U.S. gold reserves.

In all such matters, Mr. Kennedy's problem of knowledge would be eased if he could find all the relevant facts in one place—like the books just picked for the newly formed White House "working library." But neither this nor even the Congressional Library contains a small part of what he needs to know in an hour of decision. How, then, does he become the master of the information he displays on occasions such as his press conferences? Who keeps him informed about men and events on the move at home and abroad?

Ideally, he is in a position to know everything, since the fact-finders and reporters at his command circle the wide world. His personal aides on the White House staff keep watch on the common frontiers of public opinion, politics, policies, programs

From *The New York Times Magazine* (October 20, 1963), p. 17. © 1963 by The New York Times Company. Reprinted by permission.

and personnel. The Budget Bureau, manned by the elite corps of the career civil service, serves as the President's "business agent" and "efficiency expert" throughout the whole frame of Government. He has his Council of Economic Advisers, the National Security Council, the Joint Chiefs of Staff, the Central Intelligence Agency and the Scientific Adviser—all covering the world of power and diplomacy.

The President also has at his command the fact-finding and reporting resources of 10 Government departments employing most of the 2,500,000 civil servants in the executive branch. The State Department alone daily sends out more cables, asking for and giving information, than the total wordage filed from Washington each day by the two major newspaper wire services combined. Yet even so, State is a deaf-mute compared to departments like Defense, Treasury and Agriculture.

And on top of all this, the President has at his direct or indirect command the resources of knowledge spread through some 55 independent agencies from the Commission of Fine Arts to the Atomic Energy Commission and the Veterans Administration.

But the President is not superhuman. His mortal senses could not possibly absorb the whole sea of information around him. He cannot remember everything or assign each fact its precise place and value. Nor can the experts at his command. In this atomic and space age, three Nobel laureates—a physicist, a chemist and a biologist—can each look at the same facts and interpret their meaning in three different ways. And the President, though an "amateur," must decide what the experts themselves bring into dispute.

Such is the complexity of modern life that some say a President is doing well if at any one time he is aware of 20 per cent of all the important factors affecting his Administration. And he is doing exceptionally well if he firmly grasps all the ins and outs of half the issues making up that 20 per cent. How Mr. Kennedy's own performance in this respect compares with such traditional estimates cannot be expressed arithmetically. But veteran observers in Washington generally agree that whatever can be said about the nature of his decisions, there have been few Presidents in modern times to equal his mastery of detailed facts. How does he do it?

He does not rely merely on the information that reaches his desk through official channels. The President has many auxiliary lines of communication within the Government, so that he can get different views on the same subject and allow subsecretaries to reach the ear of the White House by outflanking their departmental chiefs. And he still seeks information from many independent sources outside the Government—personal friends, elder statesmen, newspapers, books, polls, radio and TV, White House mail, professors and spokesmen for private organizations.

President Kennedy has never had regular morning White House staff meetings or a fixed schedule of Cabinet meetings or weekly National Security Council meetings with all the trappings of "position papers." He prefers the device of small "task forces" formed *ad hoc* (in contrast to standing interagency committees) to get at the facts of a major problem, to isolate the issues, to examine possible solutions and consequences, and to make recommendations. And the door to his office is always open to his aides who break in on him when they must.

Yet these apparently free-wheeling methods are reinforced by many routine measures. There are, for example, certain days of a working week when special reports on important issues reach him as a matter of course. At the start of each week, he also meets at breakfast with the Democratic leadership of the Congress and with his chief aide for Congressional liaison, Lawrence O'Brien. Any and all things are discussed here—the state of his program in the Congress, whose nose is out of joint, the strategy and tactics suited to pending legislation, the content and timing of new Presidential measures. And whenever his schedule permits, the President tries to meet with small groups of rank-and-file Democratic Senators and Congressmen for intimate, late afternoon gatherings where they can unburden themselves of their views and sorrows—and listen to a few of his.

Then again, one out of every 50 letters received in the White House mail room from private citizens is put into a special reading file for the President. (Letters from worthies whose opinions are known to carry weight with the President, or from unknown people who have something exceptional to say, are specially earmarked for his attention.) The ratio of one out of every 50 may be widened substantially if a Presidential speech or a crisis swells the volume of incoming mail above the average of 30,000 letters a week. But whatever the flow, at the end of every week the President is provided with a breakdown of all this mail and of the views expressed in it on a variety of topics. This analysis serves as a cross check on the public-opinion polls the White House hears about via the press, the National Democratic Committee and enterprising politicians around the country.

On Friday of every week, he receives from every department represented in the Cabinet and from the great independent agencies, a report on activities in the preceding six days. These give the President an overall view of the major decisions reached during the working week, the unfinished business in hand, and the emergent problems that may need Presidential attention.

The President's military aide reports to him every morning on the intelligence reports that have come in during the preceding night. Whenever anything exceptional comes in, it will be taken to the President by Special Assistant for National Security Affairs McGeorge Bundy and may be followed by an encounter with Secretary of State Dean Rusk or Secretary of Defense Robert McNamara. At intervals during the day, staff aides working in assigned fields will also visit the President's office with short oral reports or with a check list of items briefly outlining a development and suggesting a course of action. The President is said to average around 15 "spot decisions" of this sort in a 10-minute meeting.

Special efforts are called for whenever a press conference is scheduled. On the day before, Special Counsel Theodore Sorensen receives from the major departments and agencies of the Government a "briefing book" listing the questions the President is likely to be asked about their respective affairs, and giving the answers to them. This material is then cross-checked by Sorensen, by Press Secretary Pierre Salinger and, in some matters, by Bundy. Each may add his own questions to the briefing book or demand more information from the respective agencies.

Next morning, a few hours before the press conference, Sorensen, Salinger and such other persons as may be brought in for particular purposes meet with President Kennedy. The material in hand is reviewed and the President approves or criticizes the answers prepared by the departments and agencies. He will also have his own list of likely questions and answers and he will often insist on more precise information. With the small margin of time available, his demands are often hard to meet—especially, when they touch on conjectural subjects like economics—but a mighty effort is made to provide him with what he wants to know.

It all makes for a nerve-racking experience and, in one sense, a frustrating one. Only a very few of the important questions the President is prepared to answer are ever asked at the conference itself. But in a larger sense, it is invaluable. The President is compelled by the pressures of the occasion to make certain he is informed about all the significant events that touch upon his Administration.

The self-education involved in preparing for a press conference is comparable to the great stirring of facts, arguments and decisions that precedes a major Presidential speech or the preparation of the four great landmarks of a Presidential year: the Economic Report, the Budget, the State of the Union Address and the Tax Message.

Three individuals stand on a special plane of importance in keeping the President informed. They are his brother, Attorney General Robert Kennedy, Appointments Secretary Kenneth O'Donnell, and Special Counsel Sorensen.

Men in and out of the Government will entrust information to Robert Kennedy if they wish it to get to the President without telling him directly. And O'Donnell, for his part, is infinitely more than just the traffic manager for the flow of humanity in and out of the President's office. He is one of the President's most immediate channels of contact with politicians in the Congress and around the country, and his troubleshooter in emergencies involving many branches of the executive. In an ordinary work day, he will make up to 100 phone calls and receive up to another 100, seeking and communicating information in the President's name. As for Sorensen, he is infinitely more than just a speech writer or a draftsman of bills. He is involved in virtually everything—from budget-making, to high partisan politics and to the most fateful issues of war and peace.

But it is the driving curiosity of the President himself that is the mainspring of the fact-gathering and reporting process. The evolution of his daily appointment book graphically makes this plain.

As set in advance by O'Donnell, the appointment book contains very few names at the start of the day. But then the President arrives in his office. The night before, he may have read a batch of cables or other reports. That night, and at breakfast, too, he certainly read the newspapers he wallows in. He has marked one thing and another, and the orders begin to crackle. "This seems like a good idea—get some more information. . . . Check this out. . . . See if there is anything in the news report. . . . This is garbled. . . . See what's behind it."

It is not long before it becomes plain that some of the items are going to need a White House meeting between the President, his chief lieutenants in the Government or in the Congress. So the appointment book fills up as the day wears on; and as each participant in a White House meeting comes and goes, he can generate many other meetings at other levels of the Government, all to the purpose of finding out and reporting back what the President wants to know.

Without his driving curiosity, the President would be the "captive at the end of the paper chain," seeing and reacting only to what others want him to see or think he wants to see. With his driving curiosity, he is a force that is felt throughout the Government.

Sorensen puts the case succinctly in his forthcoming book on how decisions are made in the White House:

> It is commonly said that our Presidents need more time set aside to do nothing but think. Yet presumably we elect a man who is thinking all the time, who is thinking when reading or listening or conferring. Our real concern should be that the President has all the facts he needs to make certain he is thinking with profit. The "lonely isolation" of the Presidency refers to the solitude of his responsibility—not to insulating him from all the pressures, paper work and discussions which are essential to his perspective. . . . For the essence of decision is choice; and, to choose, it is first necessary to know.

5
LYNDON B. JOHNSON

1963-1968

Lyndon Johnson assumed the Presidency under the most tragic circumstances, following the senseless shooting of his predecessor. Many believe he was driven from office by a rising tide of dissatisfaction over the prolongation of the war in Vietnam during his Administration. Between these points in time, barely five years apart, he was reelected to office in a landslide and spent an arduous, triumphal two years redeeming the pledges of two decades of Democratic platforms by putting a wide-ranging program through Congress.

It is not hard to understand why there are many opinions about the Johnson Presidency, most of them firmly held. The Johnson years put President-watchers on an emotional roller coaster. Lyndon Johnson himself was regarded as one of Washington's most complex and colorful figures long before he became President, and the fishbowl of the Presidency did nothing to diminish either his eccentricity or his fascination.

Johnson brought many advantages to the Presidency, notably long and thorough knowledge of the legislative process, a wide acquaintance throughout official and semiofficial Washington stretching back to the days of the New Deal, phenomenal energy and ambition to succeed, and a keen and forceful intelligence. He also possessed traits that were less useful to him as President. Newsmen complained of an almost compulsive secretiveness, extending to the most trivial matters, interspersed with episodes of excessive bonhomie. Aides were showered with abuse when they were not showered with kindness. Johnson's private language by all accounts is expressive, earthy, anecdotal, and revealing; the face he insists on turning to the public is saccharine and formal. Such a presidential style could scarcely prevent the growth of a credibility gap. Indeed, as the Johnson Presidency wore on, such a gap developed, and Johnson became quite unpopular with many of those who earlier felt comfortable relying upon his word.

It was characteristic of the Johnson Presidency that Johnson took great pains to see that ample publicity and full credit for all the successes of his entire Administration were beamed his way. But in spite of this policy, many able people worked in his Administration. It was only at the end, when blame flooded in on many of the channels that had been established to focus credit, that the Johnson Administration began to lose its attractiveness to many of Johnson's most gifted recruits.

The selections that follow attempt to capture the Johnson Presidency in some of its many moods—at its beginning and at its end, in its relations with Congress, and in its organizational structure.

What's He Like? And How Will He Do?
JAMES RESTON

The inauguration of a President of the United States starts with a prayer and ends with a dance. This is not a bad combination. Most of the great occasions in life involve a little intermittent laughing and crying, and the installation of a new President is clearly a great occasion. It is a kind of birth or wedding in the nation's family life.

By some curious combination of intuition and caprice, it lifts one fallible mortal from among the millions and says: Go guide half the human race. No wonder the people pray. It asks the man in the Big White House to govern a vast, almost ungovernable continental nation, to "preserve, protect and defend" a Constitution which his fellow countrymen interpret in different ways, to lead a world-wide coalition of proud, independent and competitive nations, and to preserve the peace in a rebellious and revolutionary world. In the face of such a preposterous challenge, the people naturally look around for whatever heavenly help or earthly escape they can find. They kick up their heels and they pray—some for the President, some for the country and many for both.

Who, then, are we praying and dancing for? Who is this Lyndon Baines Johnson of Texas who will be installed on Wednesday as the 36th President of the United States? What is the explanation of this extraordinary man?

Lyndon Baines Johnson is to the politics of America what his State of Texas is to the other states. He is a gargantuan figure; he is a whopper. Measuring him for history is like measuring an active volcano with an inch-tape. He barbecues people who try and eats them for breakfast.

When you interview him, he ends up with your life story. He does not want to be analyzed or classified; he wants to be loved. Anything you say he said, he can usually neutralize with something else he said on the other side. If you say he's liberal, he can prove he's conservative, or vice versa. If you suggest he's from the South, he will insist he's from the West, or the other way around. If you don't tell the precise truth about him, which is almost inevitable, he thinks you are dishonest, and if you do, he feels you are disloyal.

This, however, is the caricature of Mr. Johnson and, like all caricatures, it magnifies one feature and minimizes all the rest. It is amusing, but it is unfair. The big slouching Texas Ranger on the ranch, the master politician on the telephone, the restless, sleepless "arm-twister," trading favors for votes in the smoky back room—all so dear to the cartoonists—are all true, but misleading.

He is more than that—far more. It is too early to say that he is a leader of men in the classic sense of being "quick to know and to do the things that the hour and his nation need," particularly in the foreign field. He has not yet proved that he can get and keep and inspire the best men in the nation to serve him, or even that he has mastered the art of using his staff and his time effectively. But he is a shrewd and

From *The New York Times Magazine* (January 17, 1965), p. 8. © 1965 by The New York Times Company. Reprinted by permission.

knowledgeable man, an elemental force of nature who commands respect and even a certain amount of fear.

"When you come into the presence of a leader of men," Woodrow Wilson observed, "you know you have come into the presence of fire—that it is best not incautiously to touch that man—that there is something that makes it dangerous to cross him."

Johnson conveys this feeling and it is both his strength and weakness. His technique works but it hurts. He can make men do what he wants them to do but he does not make them like it or him in the process. There is a kind of intimidating shamelessness about him that makes men feel that if they don't go along there may be the most frightful and embarrassing row. But he is a highly intelligent man who is not to be dismissed as just another brilliant political operator.

He is far more complex than the boys in the back room. The master politician on Capitol Hill and in the White House is not the same as the "Last Hurrah" types out of Tammany, Boston or Chicago, though Johnson has been hurt by the popular confusion of the two. The political leader in the capital has to deal not only with the masses of men but with a highly intelligent Cabinet, an expert civil service, and a staggering catalogue of problems and ideas.

This is not, by any fair test, an unintellectual process. It involves a great deal more than physical strength, tactical skill, personal acquaintance and a telephone. It requires immense concentration on the facts of a great many issues at the same time, a quick knack of identifying and absorbing the essence of complicated and critical questions, and a limitless memory for those intimate personal and political facts that will move men to compromise.

There is much confusion on this point. Lyndon Johnson is not Dean Acheson, with a clear vision of the world and a carefully worked-out plan of the role America might play in the human story. But he clearly did not get where he is on a bag of tricks alone.

He does not concentrate on thinking programs through but on getting them through. He does not believe in "inevitable conflicts," or think in terms of tidy programs imposed or manipulated from the top. He is one of those old-fashioned, small "d" democrats who think that The People and their representatives, if presented with the facts, will find reasonable solutions. He sees politics as an exercise in adapting oneself to all sorts of people and situations, of discussing and bargaining with legitimate groups in search of a consensus.

His university really has been Capitol Hill, his classroom the committee hearings. He retains the memory of his experiences in Texas and in the Congress, but it would never occur to him to try to organize them into a system. Life to him is full of surprises, more so as the tempo of change increases, and he would no doubt support H. G. Wells's dictum that "to be honest, one must be inconsistent."

This, of course, only adds to the caricature of Johnson the manipulator. But there is another side to it. He is an incorrigible believer. He believes in everything that works. He shares all the popular ideals, assumptions and illusions of the nation. Kennedy was troubled by what he called the "myths" of the American past. Johnson loves them. Kennedy came to the White House wondering out loud whether a country governed such as ours could endure. Johnson could no more think or say that than he could denounce Lady Bird or the flag. He believes in the American system. He accepts it as he accepts the weather in his hill country of Texas: a little irritating and even cruel at times, but inevitable.

Similarly, he accepts the Congressional system the way it is—warts and all. Kennedy was in the Congress, Johnson is of it. He struggled to the top through the system and therefore thinks it's all right. He is not a critic of the elders of the Congress but their companion. He has lived with them for 30 years, spoken for them in their elections, stood up with them at their family weddings and christenings and funerals; drunk whisky with them in Mr. Sam Rayburn's "board of education" hideaway in the House.

The pessimism and complexity of the modern world, accordingly, do not bother him. Unlike many of his intellectual critics, he is not paralyzed by excessive contemplation or doubt. He is all for the businessman making a pile, having made one himself. He believes in Horatio Alger's triumphant ragamuffin (who, after all, is Johnson). He believes in the hard doctrines of John Calvin and individual responsibility, and now that the planned deficit and the tax cut have increased prosperity, he even believes a little in John Maynard Keynes. He is fiercely patriotic. He genuinely believes that God looks out for Uncle Sam. He has no doubt that this nation was set apart to achieve good and noble purposes; that America is indeed the New Arcadia, or will be if he has his way.

This highly political, highly pragmatic and ceaselessly industrious approach, however, irritates a lot of people. Mr. Johnson is a hard, inconsiderate man, especially with his personal staff. He thinks of his staff as members of his family. At his ranch they eat all their meals with him, including his colored secretary. He showers them with presents, but he dominates their lives. He works night and day himself and he expects them to do the same. His personal considerations are not permitted to take precedence over the job; theirs are not expected to either.

It is interesting that the men of his own generation, who were his associates in the New Deal days, and whom he respects and consults on many of the most intimate questions of policy and personnel—Abe Fortas, Clark Clifford, James Rowe, and other friends such as former Secretary of the Treasury Robert Anderson and Donald Cook, the utilities expert in New York—have not joined his Administration. There are no doubt many reasons for this—maybe he wants it that way—but even some of these men prefer to work with him as outside advisers rather than under him as Government servants.

This is not surprising. He is blunt and intolerant of mistakes, like his father whom he strongly resembles. Sometimes he is in a rush and will not take time to listen. Sometimes he will give hours to people who are embarrassed to use up so much of his time. On one occasion he may listen attentively and say very little. On another he may carry on a monologue which stuns rather than persuades the visitor.

This torrent of activity is deceptive. It gives the impression that he is impulsive, but nothing could be more misleading. All the talking, all the telephoning, all the expenditure of energy are generally part of an elaborate system of checking and double checking to be sure he knows all sides of the question before he moves. He has a catalogue of persons with whom he talks on each subject, some in and some out of Government.

He knows these people extremely well and has them catalogued precisely in his mind. Each of them fits into a kind of Johnsonian political spectrum. "I know he regards me," explains one of his intimates, "as pessimistic and a little left of center and he judges what I say on this basis." If the answer given by the "pessimistic and left-of-center" friend conforms to that pattern, the President will probably not spend much time talking to him. But if, for whatever reason, the answer comes back "optimistic" or a little conservative, the President will pay attention and start rechecking. He may go back over the list entirely to clarify this one point. But one way or another, he will pay attention to that surprising answer, like a scientist exploring some odd chemical reaction.

He has a horror of making mistakes. He is highly conscious even now of Franklin Roosevelt's Court-packing blunder after the election of 1936. President Kennedy's fiasco at the Bay of Pigs in Cuba is a nightmare to him. "Never move up your artillery," he says, "until you move up your ammunition." Like a majority leader who does not like to call up a bill until he is sure he has the votes, he does not easily make decisions as President without being reasonably sure of victory. This is why he has been so restrained in responding to the Communist pressures in Vietnam, and this, of course, is why he is under attack from those who think a President must sometimes move without being sure of victory and without being certain of popular acclaim.

Lyndon Johnson is not to be explained in the newspaper clippings of today but in the writings of the past. He came to the Presidency with more Government experience than any man in this century, but personally, he is a throwback. He is a link between the Old Frontier of the days of William Jennings Bryan and the New Frontier days of John F. Kennedy.

When Frederick Jackson Turner came to the end of his long study of the influence of the American frontier on American character, he put himself to the task of defining the dominant human characteristics produced by frontier living, and in the process drew a word portrait of Lyndon Johnson. He defined the frontier characteristics this way:

That coarseness and strength combined with acuteness and inquisitiveness; that practical, inventive turn of mind, quick to find expedients; that masterful grasp of material things, lacking in the artistic but powerful to affect great ends; that restless, nervous energy; that dominant individualism, working for good or evil, and withal that buoyancy and exuberance which comes from freedom—these are the traits of the frontier or traits called out elsewhere because of the existence of the frontier.

In his attitudes toward his Government, likewise, Johnson retains a faith that was once more popular than it is today. The political critics of the present time wonder whether a man so preoccupied with political tactics can conceive of the programs essential to the well-being of a complicated modern society. They see the leader, or so it seems to me, in Churchillian or even in Gaullist terms as a man with a sharp vision of the world and his place in it, and with a precise plan for leading the nation toward his goals. This is not Johnson's way.

He retains the old faith that the *total society* will find the answers to its problems, not the President alone. "A President does not shape a new and personal vision of America," he said in his first State of the Union message after his election. "He collects it from the scattered hopes of the American past." Lord Bryce, in his monumental work, "The American Commonwealth," summed up this attitude 77 years ago.

The American people, Bryce wrote, "have unbounded faith in what they call The People and in a democratic system of government . . . hence a further confidence that the people are sure to decide right in the long run. . . . If you ask an intelligent citizen why he so holds, he will answer that truth and justice are sure to make their way into the minds and consciences of the majority. This is deemed an axiom, and the more readily so deemed, because truth is identified with common sense, the quality which the average citizen is most confidently proud of possessing."

President Johnson believes in this today. He was brought up on it. He loves to tell of the days when his grandfather and uncle campaigned together in the same horse and buggy for a seat in the Texas State Legislature, one on the Populist ticket and the other on the Democratic ticket. His mother, who was a great influence on his life, gave him a scrapbook in 1954 four years before she died. On a scrap of lined paper inside, she wrote:

May he find in the lives that have gone into the making of his life fuller understanding of his traits of mind and heart, deep appreciation of his ancestry, and continuing stimulation and incentive to a rich and rewarding life.

From this background has come that deep sense of home and country, which Tocqueville noticed in so many Americans when he came to this country in the eighteen-thirties. "There is," he remarked, in "Democracy in America," "one sort of patriotic attachment which principally arises from that instinctive, disinterested, and undefinable feeling which connects the affections of a man with his birthplace. This natural fondness is united with a taste for ancient customs and a reverence for traditions of the past; those who cherish it love their country as they love the mansion of their fathers."

President Johnson approached his first full term in much the same mood of nostalgia. The Presidency, he said, in his State of the Union message, brings no gift of prophecy or foresight and the President's hardest task is not to do what's right but to know what's right.

"The answer was waiting for me in the land where I was born," he said. "It was once a barren land . . . but men came and worked and endured and built. . . . There was a dream . . . a dream of a continent to be conquered, a world to be won, a nation to be made. . . . Remembering this I knew the answer. . . ."

This connection between Johnson and the concepts of the frontier is startling, but is it relevant to the present time? The young intellectuals do not seem to think it is. The university and diplomatic worlds are dubious. Who, they ask, is to lead and articulate the new American Idea, so casually called the Great Society? Where will we get the synthesizing intelligence that will rally the Government and the nation and reduce diversity to identity? The President represents the popular characteristics of the ordinary people, but paradoxically, is not wildly popular, maybe because the people want to be represented by qualities better than their own.

This hurts Mr. Johnson but it does not change his mind, and it clearly cannot change his character. He thinks the concepts of the past are relevant to the present day. He believes we are still on the hard frontier of a wicked world, where men are bound to get hurt and sensitivities overrun. He does not feel that it can be won without faith, and the faith he sees and hopes to nourish is the faith of our fathers. He does not think it can be done without a vast collective effort and without unity. And this is not feeling and sentiment alone.

He believes in an apparent paradox—namely, that the very complexity, mobility and menace of the world today, which are causing so many problems, are also affecting all regions, and classes and nations, and therefore making it a little easier to bring about reconciliations between North and South, labor and management, rich and poor, the Congress and the White House, and even between the squabbling nations of the world. Accordingly, he feels that he is not trying to impose the past on the present, but merely trying to use the symbols of the past to create popular support for the essential innovations of the future.

Since his spectacular victory in November he has seemed more calm, as if he had tamed his inner demons at last. He is not a deeply religious man, and his attitude toward life was little changed by his heart attack in 1955, but it would be surprising if he were not now affected by the startling change in his fortunes.

At 45, he was convinced that he was as well prepared for the Presidency as any man in his party. At 52, he was denied the nomination because of what he regarded, with some bitterness, as prejudice against his Southern background. At 55, all was changed by the assassination of President Kennedy, precisely when Mr. Johnson had finally concluded he would never reach the White House.

This is the central paradox of his story. The things he planned and manipulated in pursuit of the Presidency failed, and the thing he did not plan—he took the Vice Presidency for the sake of the party and against the opposition of his wife—carried him in the end to the top.

He does not talk about the election now; he doesn't even analyze the results, as he analyzed the polls before the vote. He merely talks unity, and who is to say at this moment that he is wrong? "The art of free society," wrote Alfred North Whitehead, "consists first in the maintenance of the symbolic code, and secondly, in the fearlessness of revision. . . . Those societies which cannot combine reverence to their symbols with freedom of revision must ultimately decay."

This is Johnson's theme and method. He does not study these things; they are in his bones. Kennedy's purpose was to make men think; Johnson's is to make men act. Both were reformers but went about it in different ways. Kennedy demanded reforms by challenging the conformists; Johnson got Kennedy's reforms by seeming to be a conformist himself.

So let us pray. He may back into the future but he will do so consciously, for he believes there is a spirit and wisdom in America's past that will guide her wherever she goes.

Johnson's Men: "Valuable Hunks of Humanity"
TOM WICKER

One sunny spring afternoon not long ago, a procession of three cars bounced across a lonely cattle range near Johnson City, Texas. Deadwood, silvering in the sun, littered the rolling, grass-covered hills; a few cattle, goats and sheep scattered before the automobiles, in the first of which rode the President of the United States.

Abruptly, his car halted. Behind him, a car carrying Secret Service agents and another carrying the White House physician and some communications technicians also stopped. A small dark man wearing a golfer's cap and white buck shoes got out of the President's car and trotted up the road ahead of it.

"Now, there," said Lyndon B. Johnson to friends who remained in the car with him, "goes a valuable hunk of humanity. He can do anything for you and do it fast."

A few yards ahead John A. Valenti, Harvard School of Business, '51, picked up a soft-drink bottle from the road—scarcely more than two tracks across the grassland—and threw it aside.

"That could have cut somebody's tire," the President of the United States remarked, with as much satisfaction as if he had just solved the unemployment question.

Jack Valenti returned to the car and got into the back seat.

"I see you're still wearing those Harvard shoes," Mr. Johnson said, winking and characteristically putting his hand over his mouth to hide a smile.

"Couldn't do without 'em, Mr. President," Jack Valenti replied, in the tone of a man making the expected response to a familiar joke.

Mr. Johnson gestured toward Mr. Valenti and said to another passenger:

"He's a Harvard man. He's got more Harvard degrees than Mac Bundy." (Mr. Bundy, a former Harvard dean, has only a Yale undergraduate degree.)

Without too much stretching of casual events and remarks, that scene and those exchanges can be made to illustrate a good deal about President Johnson's staff, his manner of using it, the people who serve on it and the President's attitude toward them.

From *The New York Times Magazine* (May 3, 1964), p. 11. © 1964 by The New York Times Company. Reprinted by permission.

Mr. Johnson's ideal staff man, for instance, is not a specialist in law or foreign policy or science but "a valuable hunk of humanity" who can "do anything for you and do it fast."

As an administrator, Mr. Johnson's eye is on the sparrow, and he is likely to ask of such a staff man virtually anything—from writing a speech to throwing a bottle out of the road—and sometimes it is hard to know which he considers the more important. The people who work with him are prepared for and unsurprised at whatever is demanded of them, and seem to respond willingly.

There is nothing aloof or formal in their relationship to the President. ("That girl out there working late at the typewriter," Mr. Johnson said to an evening visitor in the White House, "she's coming over to the mansion to have dinner with us. She'll sit right between the First Lady and the President and we'll be glad to have her.")

These days, moreover, Mr. Johnson is somewhat sensitive about the inevitable comparison of his men with those who served John Kennedy. He likes to point to Jack Valenti's Harvard degree and once declared that Mr. Valenti, a Texan, was not regarded as an intellectual only because he was "from the wrong side of the line"— the Mason-Dixon line—and he insists with some heat that Mr. Valenti and Bill D. Moyers, another high-level White House assistant, "can write speeches as well as anyone." For if one single charge has been made most often by Johnson's critics, it is that his speeches have not been as well written as those that Theodore C. Sorensen wrote for Mr. Kennedy. (A national magazine recently criticized a speech Mr. Johnson made on the 15th anniversary of NATO, attributing the offending lines to Jack Valenti. "Bundy wrote that," Mr. Johnson remarked, a day or so later. "It was a damn good speech, too." The President has since used a line from it—"Our guard is up, but our hand is out"—a number of times, once to describe his attitude toward the Republican party.)

All of these factors influence Mr. Johnson's manner of organizing his staff. Since a President's staff in modern times can hardly be separated from the President himself, from the totality of his performance, it also will influence, ultimately, the success or indifference of his efforts. After six hectic months in the White House, Mr. Johnson now seems to have created a staff situation stable enough for description, if not for the drawing of lasting conclusions.

There are two ways of looking at the Johnson staff, however—the way Mr. Johnson conceives of it, and the way a less involved but attentive spectator might view its activities.

Mr. Johnson concedes little difference—except in personalities—from the staff organization maintained by Mr. Kennedy. All the branches of the Kennedy staff, he points out, still exist and all except the press office are headed by a "Kennedy man."

Thus, in what he calls "the big item"—foreign policy and national security—Mr. Johnson is served by precisely the same small staff of experts, headed by McGeorge Bundy. In Congressional relations, the President leans heavily—as did Mr. Kennedy—on Lawrence F. O'Brien and his assistants, Henry Wilson, Mike Manatos and Charles Day. The office of the Special Counsel, once filled by Mr. Sorensen, now is handled by Myer C. Feldman, who was Mr. Sorensen's first assistant. Mr. Feldman's own assistants are Lee White, who was also on the Sorensen staff, and

Hobart Taylor Jr., a "Johnson man" new to the White House. The function of the counsel's office is changed mainly in that it no longer produces Presidential speeches.

The office of the Appointments Secretary, as Mr. Johnson describes it, still is headed by P. Kenneth O'Donnell of the old Kennedy staff, now aided by Bill Moyers. The President concedes, however, that Mr. O'Donnell ("my political antennae") is spending much more time these days arranging political appointments and appearances, while Mr. Moyers ("he knows my relations with people—he knows who I know and who knows me") is handling more and more of the general White House routine.

Mr. Kennedy had Arthur Schlesinger Jr. on the White House staff for what Mr. Johnson calls "special projects"—reports and research of various kinds, unusual statements and documents, occasional speeches. "And that's exactly what Horace Busby is going to be doing for me," Mr. Johnson says. Mr. Busby is the latest Johnson appointment to the White House staff.

Richard N. Goodwin, who held a variety of posts in the White House, State Department and Peace Corps under Mr. Kennedy, also is on the White House staff for "special projects." It is widely believed here that his duties, like Mr. Busby's, will include the writing of speeches and statements.

George Reedy has replaced Pierre Salinger as the news secretary, but the work of his office goes on about the same as before. Jack Valenti now does some of the press-office work—for instance, some of the arrangements for various speeches and appearances Mr. Johnson makes in the White House.

As for Walter Jenkins, the aide who has been with Mr. Johnson longest, the President describes him as dividing his time between a wealth of administrative tasks ("he can look after 100,000 letters a week and see that the right ones get to me") and assistance to the O'Brien Congressional-relations staff, based on his many years' experience on Capitol Hill with Mr. Johnson.

None of those statements are particularly disputable—and, in fact, Mr. Johnson's precise description of what the men around him are supposed to be doing and of what the lines of authority are would surprise those who think of his administrative technique as deliberately chaotic, governed by impulse and generally hit-or-miss.

It is true, moreover, that the functions of the Bundy national security staff, the Special Counsel's office and the O'Brien Congressional-relations staff go on about as before—although Myer Feldman is by no means as personally influential with Mr. Johnson as Ted Sorensen was with Mr. Kennedy, and the relations of Mr. Bundy and Mr. O'Brien to the President also are somewhat different. That was inevitable, since all these were Kennedy men first.

Thus, the President's view that he has scarcely altered the White House staff operation is largely justified, in an organization-chart sense. But to describe Jack Valenti as an associate press secretary strikes most of those familiar with the Johnson Administration as about like describing Mr. Johnson himself as, say, a man who presides over Cabinet meetings. Both are obviously more than that. And to cram Bill Moyers into an organization chart as a kind of co-appointments secretary is akin to pouring 10 gallons of Pedernales River water into a five-gallon L.B.J. hat.

One astute observer of White House activities has likened "Johnson men"— Valenti, Moyers, Reedy, Busby, Jenkins—to soldiers standing at attention. As tasks come up for action, Mr. Johnson beckons one or another. The man steps forward and does the job, and it may or may not be in some field already staked out for him—or in some field previously staked out for someone else.

Mr. Johnson's eye does not always alight on someone with an office in the White House. On the President's hectic, last-minute tour of poverty-stricken areas in four states, one of those most heavily involved in the logistics and planning was O. B. (Bill) Lloyd, a Johnson man who has been an official of the National Aeronautics and Space Administration since the beginning of the Kennedy Administration.

Sometimes confusion results from the seeming formlessness of the Johnson administrative system. One old Kennedy hand recalls that on a single day he was called by Mr. Valenti, Mr. Moyers and Gen. Chester V. Clifton, the military aide; all gave him exactly the same instructions from the President.

In some ways, however, lines of authority appear to be more rigidly observed than they were under Mr. Kennedy. A reporter, for instance, making an inquiry of Mr. Valenti or Mr. Moyers, is much more likely to be referred back to the press secretary, Mr. Reedy, than he was in the old days of Pierre Salinger.

Nevertheless, it is more difficult now to find out—even to surmise—who among the Johnson men may be handling, or knowledgeable about, a particular problem. With the exception of Mr. Reedy, none of them is a specialist. None is identifiably more expert in foreign than domestic affairs, or vice versa. None of them seems cast specifically in the role of "thinker" or "intellectual bank" that once was played by Ted Sorensen—unless it will be the newcomer, Mr. Busby.

The Kennedy staff, at its full development, was rather well-balanced between old Government hands, political professionals and academics. None of the Johnson men fall comfortably into any of these categories; Walter Jenkins and George Reedy may be old Government hands, but they are of the Capitol Hill variety, a different breed of cat from the "downtown" bureaucrat.

Here is a brief description, going beyond the President's organization-charter approach, of what can be learned about the functions of the primary "Johnson men" now on the White House staff:

Walter Jenkins—At 45, he has worked for Lyndon Johnson since 1939, serving both the Senator and the Vice President as administrative assistant. He now handles a number of administrative functions—hiring the clerical staff, setting salaries, making office assignments, overseeing correspondence. Sometimes he settles jurisdictional questions as to who should do what; often he serves the President as a follow-up man, checking on why some expected event didn't occur, or why an unexpected one did.

Mr. Jenkins, like Mr. Valenti, also has a certain power of "clearance" for the President; that is, he can approve certain letters and statements, usually not of the first importance, for Mr. Johnson's signature. He channels the weekly reports from Cabinet officers to the President, and is the notetaker and chronicler of Cabinet and other high Administration meetings. Other Johnson men are unanimous in their tribute to Mr. Jenkins as the senior staff man and as one who has "total rapport" with Lyndon Johnson.

Bill D. Moyers—A former Baptist minister and still officially the deputy director of the Peace Corps, Bill Moyers is—in Lyndon Johnson's phrase—"about the most unusual 29-year-old I ever saw." His duties are concentrated on, but not confined to, appointments and scheduling of trips and appearances. His past experience in Government has made him useful to the President on a number of substantive matters—foreign aid, for instance.

Mr. Moyers has done some speech-writing, too, and was responsible for most of the President's hard-hitting civil-rights remarks to a seminar of the Southern Baptist Convention—an organization Mr. Moyers knows from the inside. More than almost any other "Johnson man" he seems able to speak in the President's name, and he has one vitally important, if unofficial, function: as both an authentic Johnson man and an authentic New Frontiersman, he has the confidence of everybody on the White House staff and is a useful linchpin holding Kennedy and Johnson men together. His ability is conceded and his devotion to Mr. Johnson's interests remarkable.

"When other people go home at 6," the President said recently, "Bill stays until 9 because I stay until 9."

George Reedy—The only non-Texan among the Johnson men, Mr. Reedy is 46 years old, a 12-year veteran of the Johnson staff. His duties need little description since they are at least superficially those of any news secretary. Mr. Reedy, a large, rumpled man whose ponderous approach sometimes obscures a well-stocked and active mind, probably will be far less a personality in his own right than either of his predecessors, Pierre Salinger or James Hagerty. Probably, too, he will have less direct influence on the public-information activities of his boss. Like the other Johnson men, he seems devoted to the President's interests above anything else.

Mr. Reedy's briefings are not as much fun as Mr. Salinger's used to be ("You ask him what that tree is over there," L.B.J. once said, "and he'll tell you who first brought it to this country and talk half an hour before he tells you what you wanted to know in the first place. But he knows what he's talking about").

Horace Busby—A 40-year-old Texan and a talented writer who has been with the President in a variety of capacities since 1948. He has just joined the White House staff although he has been helping out since Nov. 22 in an ex-officio capacity. He probably will be a big help with the President's speech-writing chores, although Mr. Reedy insists that will not be his primary function. Having served on Mr. Johnson's old Senate payroll, Mr. Busby has considerable knowledge of national security and space affairs. He wrote the notable civil-rights speech the Vice President delivered at Gettysburg last July 4, and made all the Johnson foreign trips of the past few years.

He is still too new to the White House staff for his function to be clear—beyond the "special projects" Mr. Johnson says he will handle. But Mr. Busby has long been a trusted associate of the President, and his advice is listened to with respect.

Jack Valenti—At 47, a former Houston advertising and public-relations man with no experience in Government, Mr. Valenti is at once the most enigmatic and the most omnipresent of the Johnson men; he is also a complete newcomer to Washington, his official service to the President having really started only last Nov. 22 in Dallas. Since then he has been described as everything from a glorified valet to "the new Sherman Adams"; by now there is not much doubt that he is far more nearly the latter than the former.

Mr. Valenti usually sees Mr. Johnson first in the morning and last at night, and nobody in Washington underestimates that privilege. So far as is known, he has not missed a day's work in the White House (including Sunday), a Presidential trip or a Presidential speech since Mr. Johnson took office. He can be seen passing notes to the President at a news conference or alighting at his side from a helicopter. He writes many of Mr. Johnson's most important utterances—for instance, the concluding passage on world affairs in the speech to the building-trades unions (it was also Jack Valenti who tipped off reporters that those remarks would be added to the prepared text).

"He's the choreographer," a White House aide says of one facet of the Valenti activities. "He's the arranger of events as to the degree of the President's participation—whether he'll make a speech, whether it will be on television or whether he'll maybe just drop in and shake hands."

Less familiar with the substance of affairs than the Johnson men who have spent many years in Washington, Mr. Valenti is a quick study, a hard worker and a brain-picker. He seems almost constantly at Mr. Johnson's side, and the President, in private conversation, is plainly proud of his "Harvard man."

"That fellow gave up a $100,000-a-year income and came up here to Washington without asking a question or without even a clean shirt in his bag," Mr. Johnson once remarked. "He just moved right in like he'd been here all his life."

The President, who puts high value on the practical virtues, once offered this description of Jack Valenti: "He's wonderful with his energy, easy to get along with and he knows every TV program that's on."

For a President who avidly watches every news and special-events program the networks offer, that is no small assistance.

Another who belongs in the "staff" lineup, although he is not a White House employee, is Cliff Carter, the President's personal representative at the Democratic National Committee. Mr. Carter's function is almost purely political. He has traveled extensively on political missions, keeps an eye on the Byzantine politics of the President's home base in Texas, and helps coordinate Presidential and party activities and planning.

All these Johnson aides seem to fall into the "valuable hunk of humanity" category, rather than specifically into any one of the Kennedy staff types—Government veteran, political pro or academic.

It seems clear, six months after Mr. Johnson began making his first Presidential moves last Nov. 22 on the flight here from Dallas, with Jack Valenti and Bill Moyers at his side, that the staff he has assembled is primarily an operational one; there is little evidence that the "Johnson men" in the White House constitute a brain trust. It is not even likely that these men are, in the true sense, Mr. Johnson's closest advisers.

For one thing, particularly on the politics of a given situation, Mr. Johnson obviously does much of his own thinking—as well as his own reacting. The most visceral and instinctive of politicians, he seems to move too quickly and too naturally for long deliberation or wide consultation. This is less true, of course, in the field of foreign affairs—and here, as for Mr. Kennedy, the small Bundy staff does serve as something of a brain trust.

For another thing, when Mr. Johnson does seek advice—as distinct from "touching base" with people importantly affected by a move or a decision—he often does so outside his immediate staff circle, either within the Administration or among long acquaintances and trusted friends outside the Government. White House circles insist, however, that the stories of frequent phone calls to and constant conferring with such men—the Washington attorney, Abe Fortas, is most frequently cited—are greatly exaggerated.

But the President also has the services of those who remain from the Kennedy staff—Ralph A. Dungan, Feldman, O'Donnell, O'Brien and Bundy. The "valuable hunks," at least for the moment, are not substitutes for the others but an added category of their own.

The most obvious criticism of the Johnson staff arrangement is that there is not among these "valuable hunks" a reflective intellectual of wide experience and attainment, a man more concerned with the substance of policy than the implementation of policy, the far-away goals of an administration rather than its day-to-day problems. But such men are hard to find and harder still to heed in the tumble and rush of events; and it is not entirely accurate to picture the busy Ted Sorensen—as some nostalgic New Frontiersmen do—as having played such a role in the Kennedy Administration.

Moreover, it was late in the term of Mr. Kennedy when Mr. Johnson took over, and the tasks left him to complete were massive enough—the tax and civil-rights bills, for instance, the approaching crisis of the foreign-aid program, unemployment, the leveling off of the defense program, the continuing search for means of easing tensions with the Soviet Union. These matters largely occupied the President in his first six months, and his dramatization and sharpening of the "war against poverty" have been virtually his only contributions to long-range policy.

What his re-election and the construction of a complete Johnson Administration might bring—either in the substance of programs, or in the personnel to put them together—cannot yet be stated with any certainty. That remains, perhaps, the major question raised by Lyndon Johnson's pell-mell half-year in the White House: Where, in the long run, will this fervent believer of free enterprise and social welfare, this unabashed patriot and sentimentalist, this astonishing political cyclone, seek to take us?

A study of the Johnson staff does not offer an answer. It more nearly discloses a reflection of the man himself—constantly in motion, serving with remarkable dedication and energy, frequently entangled in detail and procedure, but getting results.

One veteran of the Kennedy days, a man of long experience in Government administration, has developed a somewhat reluctant respect for the Johnson system in the past six months.

"It isn't chaotic at all," he says. "Amorphous may be a better word because you really can't reduce the White House to an organization chart any more. But the thing works because it suits the President. There isn't any point in comparing it to a system that suited some other President. It isn't a staff system that I would have set up, but it's the kind of staff system Johnson is accustomed to and knows how to use. And that's what matters."

The "Inner, Inner Circle" Around Johnson
BEN H. BAGDIKIAN

WASHINGTON. Twenty-four hours after the assassination, Lyndon Johnson was, typically, on the telephone, running the United States Government from the sun room of his suburban Washington home. Typically, he had beside him two old friends who held no positions in government, Abe Fortas, a lawyer, and William S. White, a newspaper columnist. And typically for friends of the new President, one of them was an old New Dealer from the early days of Johnson's career, and the other was a Texan.

In the loneliness of Presidential responsibility, most Chief Executives have felt the need for trusted companions to provide simple human warmth. President Johnson seems to need friends even more than his predecessors. In the first hours after he became President he kept close to him Fortas and White, members of the "inner-inner circle." He made contact, telephonically or in person, with other friends of the "outer-inner circle": the first night he talked on the phone for almost an hour with Georgia's Senator Richard Russell, the companion and mentor who more than anyone else made Johnson Majority Leader of the Senate; he called Edwin L. Weisl Sr., New York National Committeeman, who first met the President through Harry Hopkins and F.D.R. in 1938 and became investment adviser to Mrs. Johnson, and told Weisl as he told many others, "I need you more than ever"; for the first nights of his Presidency he had another friend, Texas publicist Horace Busby, sit by his bed and talk until Mr. Johnson fell asleep.

Who are the men in the "inner-inner circle" of the President's friends? Where did they come from? What do they do when they get together?

From *The New York Times Magazine* (February 28, 1965), p. 21. © 1965 by The New York Times Company. Reprinted by permission.

The "Inner, Inner Circle"

There is no fixed solar system of friends, each with an established proximity to the President. Intimacy varies with time, problems and geography. Some intimates from years past are now mixed with newer stars in orbits around the White House. Most friend-consultants see Johnson according to what's bothering him. Some are in Texas, firm in his affections but necessarily seeing him less and less. Still others cannot be available at every moment, while a few have the time and money to devote all their energies to the needs of the man in the White House.

The President's volcanic activity makes even his best friends unsure of who is how close to him. When a number of friends were asked to compile a list of the President's intimates, no two lists were the same. However, such lists generally have seven names in common—at or near the top—and these seven may thus be considered the "inner-inner circle": Fortas and White, Thomas G. Corcoran, James H. Rowe Jr., Clark M. Clifford, Gov. John B. Connally of Texas and, not least, the President's wife, Lady Bird.

Like all men, Mr. Johnson looks to friends for solace, advice, conversation and, like most Presidents, he also uses friends for delicate political errands. Yet in many ways the inner Johnsonian circle differs in style, occupation and age from those who earlier kicked off their shoes in the private quarters of the White House.

John Kennedy was 43 when he entered the White House, a stage in life when it is easier to make new friends. An Easterner, he tended toward young Ivy League journalists and urbane academicians.

President Johnson is now 56, not an age when men experiment with friendships. He inclines toward Texans and aging New Deal politician-lawyers (though these include an accomplished amateur chamber-music violinist and a former Yale professor). A remarkable number of his present friends entered his life in the years 1937-41 when he was establishing his political foothold in Washington and in Texas. In 1937 he was 29 years old, and friends, especially helpful ones, were quickly entwined in his career and his personal life. Young Congressman Johnson attracted the attention of Franklin Roosevelt, who ordered his Young Turks to "take care of this boy." These Young Turks are now in their fifties and sixties and are the President's pals, his contemporaries and his fellow veterans of the political wars.

Johnson's habits also condition his friendships. Franklin Roosevelt and Harry Truman relaxed by playing cards, so their intimates included men who were fun at the poker table. Dwight Eisenhower was devoted to golf; his friends tended to shoot in the 80's. John Kennedy liked to sail and play touch football and this eliminated the high-cholesterol types that have clustered around earlier Presidents.

Johnson's taste in relaxation is hard to describe. Some say he never relaxes. He has no hobbies. When he was Vice President he conceded that "I love a little Scotch whisky, a little sun and a little sleep." But the fact is that Johnson's job is politics, his hobby is politics and his relaxation is politics. He does some hunting, cattle-counting and fence-checking when he is in Texas but his chief activity with friends is talking. And the only subject he stays on for any length of time is politics and politicians.

Not surprisingly, most of his friendships arose out of an amalgam of Texas and Washington politics. A thread of political evolution ties together most of these companions, typified by Thomas Gardiner Corcoran of the inner-inner circle. Called "Tommy the Cork" by F.D.R. when he was a brilliant operator for the New Deal, Corcoran now is in private law practice, devoted, he says, to raising "another Kennedy family." He is not particularly visible in the private White House social rounds of today, but his relationship to the President is one of the oldest and deepest Johnson has in Washington. Corcoran is an Irishman from Pawtucket, Rhode Island, but he knows more about Texas politics than most Texans. His association tells much of all Johnsonian friendships.

"I first met Lyndon Johnson in 1937 when I was assigned the job of keeping him from getting elected to Congress," Corcoran says. "Aubrey Williams ran the National Youth Administration, and Aubrey used to tell me he had two guys in N.Y.A. who were wonderful. One was Bill Campbell, who is now a Federal judge in Illinois, the man who sent Al Capone to jail. The other was a guy named Lyndon Johnson, who was running Williams's youth program down in Texas.

"One day Williams got hold of me at the White House and said, 'Tommy, you've got to get the President to make this guy Johnson lay off running for the Congressional seat down in Austin. He's my whole youth program in Texas and if he quits I have no program down there.' "

Corcoran went to President Roosevelt. "I told the Old Man and he gave me my orders to get this guy Johnson to lay off that House seat. I tried to find Johnson but before I could he had quit his N.Y.A. job and filed for Congress. So you see, I struck out on the first job that ever had to do with Lyndon Johnson."

Johnson ran in early 1937 to fill a House seat vacated by death. At the time, Roosevelt's Court-packing plan was creating serious desertions from Democratic ranks, none worse than the Texas delegation's. In Texas it was thought political suicide to be for the Court plan. But Lyndon Johnson ran on a platform of total support for F.D.R., Court plan and all. (Like much of Johnson's behavior, this was courage mixed with prudence and profit: he has always had an instinct to get close to power and F.D.R.'s was the ultimate power in 1937. Against a field of nine, where the others were against the Court plan, the minority of one could carry the election, as Johnson did.)

Roosevelt happened to be fishing off the Texas coast at the time. Corcoran recalled recently, "The Old Man had heard of this kid carrying the flag out there in Texas so he said he wanted to see this boy. Lyndon was invited to the boat at Galveston. When he got back to Washington, the Old Man issued orders to me, to Ben Cohen, Harold Ickes and Fred Vinson: 'Take care of this boy.' "

Ickes, then Secretary of the Interior, and Fred Vinson, a powerful member of the House and later Chief Justice, were to be friends of Johnson until their deaths.

Benjamin V. Cohen, now retired in Washington, is a friend of President Johnson's, though his quiet and withdrawn nature keeps him from the frenetic round at the White House. Because of this he is now consulted less than he used to be.

When he first met Mr. Johnson, Cohen was a member of F.D.R.'s legendary trouble-shooting team of Corcoran and Cohen. At that time they were in the power business—electrical as well as political. They combined both for the benefit of Lyndon Johnson. They helped him get Federal funds to build one of the country's largest rural power systems in his Congressional district, and they made available to him some of the most valuable manpower in Washington.

Cohen was general counsel for the National Power Policy Committee and Corcoran for the Reconstruction Finance Corporation, bases from which they ranged all through government. Working with them was William O. Douglas, another contemporary friend of Johnson's. Douglas, a former professor of law at Yale, ran the Securities and Exchange Commission in its early days, before F.D.R. elevated him to the Supreme Court in 1939.

Douglas and Corcoran used their agency payrolls as holding companies for bright young men they had tapped for Federal service but not yet placed in the right jobs. This talent pool, plus the personal influence of Corcoran, Cohen and Douglas, became a kind of lending library of brains to which Congressman Johnson had stack privileges. It gave him the talent to get things done in Washington and it also resulted in some lasting friendships.

For example, in 1948 Johnson ran for the Senate and became embroiled in a complicated legal battle to keep his name on the ballot, a fight that carried all the way to the Supreme Court. He needed a first-rate Washington lawyer. Justice Douglas remembered one of his best students at Yale Law School, a man from Memphis named Abe Fortas. Fortas had once worked for Douglas at the S.E.C., and had been Under Secretary of the Interior.

After World War II Fortas put together the formidable Washington law firm of Arnold, Fortas & Porter, in which Fortas was the expert on perfecting appeals to higher courts. Through Douglas's recommendation, Fortas took the case of Lyndon Johnson, won it, and established a fast friendship with the new Senator.

Today Fortas is the most intimate and omnipresent of the President's friends and advisers. He is a slight, quiet, meticulously groomed man who forms his words with surgical precision. He has won important cases, including that of Clarence Earl Gideon which revolutionized the rights of impoverished defendants to be represented by court-appointed lawyers. Fortas's hobbies include playing violin in a chamber-music group. It is widely believed in Washington that he was offered the Attorney Generalship and declined it but that he is the leading candidate for the first Supreme Court vacancy the President has to fill.

Fortas's involvement in the President's life seems total. He is personally present at crucial times. When the President's former protege, Bobby Baker, was sued, it was Fortas who took the case. When former Presidential aide Walter Jenkins (an exception to the rule that the President picks his family friends from outside government) became an issue in the election campaign, it was Fortas whom Jenkins called for advice. Fortas's wife, also a lawyer, is tax counsel for the Johnson family.

The Fortas connection is one of several personal ones to leading Washington law firms. In Corcoran's firm of Corcoran, Foley, Youngman & Rowe, both Corcoran and his partner, James H. Rowe Jr., are "inner-inner" friends, and partner Edward Foley is an "outer-inner" man. Another Presidential friend, former Secretary of State Dean Acheson, is elder statesman of the prestigious Washington law factory of Covington & Burling. The predominance of law firms in Presidential affections reflects not so much the President's predilection for law as lawyers' predilection for politics.

182 Lyndon B. Johnson

Rowe, for example—like Corcoran a former clerk to Justice Holmes—is an urbane Montanan who first met Lyndon Johnson while Rowe was one of F.D.R.'s White House assistants "with a passion for anonymity." One of his jobs was to help people Roosevelt wanted helped and this brought about the early friendship of Johnson and Rowe. Later, as Assistant Attorney General, Rowe helped guide Johnson in Congressional investigations, appointments and legislation.

Rowe has met the Johnson test of unflinching loyalty in time of trouble, or what the President likes to call, "a man you can go to the well with" (after the brave men who went for water outside the stockades during Indian sieges). By 1964 practically all Democrats were Johnson men, but Rowe was a Johnson man in 1956 and 1960 when the Kennedy men were in the ascendancy, and in the President's silent Legion of Honor this permits Rowe to wear the important though invisible *Croix de Guerre* in his political lapel.

Another lawyer-confidant of the inner-inner circle is Clark M. Clifford, a 58-year-old Missourian who is in private practice in Washington but has been indispensable to all postwar Democratic Presidents in finding talent, giving advice and planning strategy. It was Clifford, with Fortas, who visited Washington newspapers and asked them to delay publication of the Jenkins case.

Not all the President's close friends are lawyers. One of his most trusted companions is the author and syndicated columnist William S. White, former New York Times and Associated Press correspondent. White, 57, is a Texan who first met Johnson in 1933. He was an A.P. correspondent covering the Texas Congressional delegation, and Johnson was secretary to Representative Richard M. Kleberg of Texas. This makes the Johnson-White friendship one of the longest standing of the inner circle. Perhaps White's best-known book is a work on the Senate ("Citadel: The Story of the U.S. Senate"), whose qualities are personified by its former Majority Leader Lyndon Johnson. Last year before the Presidential campaign, White issued an admiring biography of the President called "The Professional."

A President wants his friends most during the heat of battle and since most of his battles are conducted from 1600 Pennsylvania Avenue it is the men who live in Washington who draw closest to a busy Chief Executive. Yet there are friendships back in Texas which are important and which the President maintains by telephone and by the visits he makes to his ranch whenever he can get away from the White House.

Closest of these, by far, is Gov. John B. Connally Jr. of Texas. This friendship goes back, as do so many of Lyndon Johnson's, to the power build-up along the Pedernales. When Johnson was first in the House of Representatives his district was arid and poor, the scene of incomplete fragments of the bankrupt Insull utility empire. A lawyer friend, Alvin Wirtz (no relation to Secretary of Labor Wirtz), was appointed receiver for the old Insull works, which included the beginnings of a hydroelectric dam.

With Corcoran and Cohen running interference, Johnson got masses of Federal funds to help build the largest rural electrification project at that time, all along the Pedernales River and in Johnson's district. A junior member of Wirtz's law firm at the time was a young man named John Connally. It was through Wirtz and the hydroelectric project that Connally and Johnson first met.

Connally, eight years younger than the President, has the reputation of being quite conservative and extremely influential with Johnson. He was for a time Johnson's administrative assistant. Later he took time off from private practice (including executorship of the billion-dollar estate of Sid W. Richardson) to run Johnson's political campaigns.

Another Texas-based friend is George Brown, of the construction firm of Brown and Root, which built much of the public works Johnson obtained for his district. It was in Brown's Middleburg, Virginia, home that Johnson suffered his heart attack over the Fourth of July weekend in 1955.

When he was Vice President, Johnson used to talk over each day's events with the late Sam Rayburn and with Homer Thornberry, the Representative from Johnson's old Texas district. Last year the President appointed Thornberry a Federal judge in Texas, elevating—but making more remote—a Washington friend.

A newer friend, also Texas-based, is Albert Wadel Moursund 3d, a 44-year-old county judge, rancher and lawyer who has practiced law in Johnson City since 1946 and is a neighbor of the LBJ Ranch. He is joint owner of a ranch with the Johnsons and a trustee of the extensive Johnson family holdings. When Johnson went to the LBJ Ranch in 1955 to recover from his heart attack, he was forced into the uncharacteristic playing of games and almost daily he played dominoes with Judge Moursund. Today, when he goes to Texas, the President goes by helicopter to neighbor Moursund's place and hunts deer and counts cattle with him.

Any list of the closest of friend-advisers to the President is incomplete without Mrs. Johnson's name. The President might respond, "That's no friend, that's my wife," but the President's wife plays a pervasive role in their political, business and personal decisions. She strikes the President's friends as a perceptive, knowledgeable and selfless woman, a judgment not always visited upon the wives of famous men.

Johnson has leaned on her advice in matters personal, financial and political. She used to manage their multimillion-dollar business enterprises. She sits in on many of the political bull sessions and decisions. One family friend says of her, "If Lady Bird is against something, you better look at it pretty damn carefully."

What does a President do when he gathers his friends about him? This one follows the observation of Ralph Waldo Emerson: "A friend is a person with whom I may be sincere. Before him I may think out loud." The principal activity of Lyndon Johnson with his friends is to think out loud.

Johnson thinks out loud with friends chiefly by telephone, and at all hours of the day and night. But some friends, like Fortas, Clifford, White and Justice Douglas, go to the White House more or less regularly for private dinners. On occasion the President will drop in on them in their homes.

Do these friends influence the President and therefore national policy? Men differ in how they separate business and pleasure, but it is doubtful that a man like Johnson is capable of rigid compartmentalization of his life. For one thing, politics is the air he breathes and it is from political life that he has drawn his friends. It is known that he asks his friends for advice on men, programs and policy. But it is also known that the President's decision-making is an arcane process; he absorbs the opinion all around him, lets it percolate inside him in some mysterious, instinctual way and then issues a decision "when it is ready." This makes it difficult for any one person to be sure what part he played in the President's decisions.

Since the President's friends come from the areas of his own successes—business and politics in Texas and Washington—it is natural that few of them are experts in the field now most vexatious to the White House, foreign policy. Dean Acheson, a hard-liner, is one of the few. So is Ben Cohen, who has done much work with the United Nations—but foreign relations is one subject on which Cohen and the President disagree.

In whatever field the President's friends may be knowledgeable, he uses them as a sort of screening device. One of them describes the process:

I've watched him for years and he does this an awful lot. Let's say Problem X comes up. He does a lot of telephoning and he calls, let's say, Jim Rowe, Tommy Corcoran, Clark Clifford, Abe Fortas and Dean Acheson. Now he has a picture in his mind of each man—the picture may not necessarily be correct in all its details, but he has one. He may think to himself, "OK, there's Rowe, a Northern liberal, a pessimist, and so forth. There's Corcoran, more conservative, an optimist, a little cynical." And he goes right down the line.

He has a pretty good idea of what each of these men will say on Problem X. I don't think he pays a great deal of attention unless one of them says something unexpected. Then he sees a signal he hadn't seen before. I've seen him do it over and over. He's looking for those warning lights.

Another close friend said:

I don't think he really expects answers from his friends most of the time. He uses his friends as sounding boards, letting his thoughts come out and bounce off them. He doesn't put things down on paper, pro and con, like a lawyer. He talks things out. This is how he formulates decisions. The chief function of his friends is to let him talk.

All Presidents have lived in the split world of the official man who needs his unofficial hours, of the public servant who requires the blessings of privacy and relaxation. For most Presidents, friends have provided this unofficial privacy and an escape from the working world. But for Lyndon Johnson friends seem not an escape but a joyful vehicle for deeper excursions into politics after everyone else has gone home.

LBJs Way: Tears, Not Arm-Twists
WILLIAM CHAPMAN

The Democratic Congressman, paged away from a Washington cocktail party, was surprised to find the President of the United States waiting on the other end of the telephone line.

"The ox is in the ditch," was President Johnson's opener. "I need your help."

It was the President's way of saying that a "must" bill was in trouble and that friendly help was needed, just as neighbors were summoned in frontier days when real oxen slipped into ditches.

In tone and substance, the appeal typified the President's method of rounding up the votes that have produced a legislative session of bewildering accomplishment. It was an appeal to get on the team, to help one's friend, and it fits in not at all with the legend of a Congressman's arm bent painfully behind his back by a demanding President.

TEARS COME THROUGH

That picture of an overbearing taskmaster is badly overdrawn, in the opinion of members of Congress who have been reached by the presidential hand or telephone this year. Cajolery, emotional pleading and sensitive personal attention—all these come through, but not the pressure or threat of retaliation that Republicans and other observers describe.

"You get the impression from reading all these stories that he's always twisting arms," says Rep. James A. Mackay (D-Georgia), who was enlisted to sign the District home rule discharge petition, "but what he really twists is your heart. He says he's got to have your help, and the tears are practically coming out of the telephone receiver.

"And he always seems to remember later. Six days after he called me, I went to a White House reception and was in line with 150 people. He gripped my arm and said, 'I really thank you.'"

Such casual personal touches and informal social lobbying at White House parties are far more common than the telephonic barrages assumed to be Mr. Johnson's forte. Actually, the President launches intensive telephone campaigns only when his congressional liaison chief, Lawrence F. O'Brien, reports that he can't win without presidential intervention.

This has happened only twice this year: on the rent supplement section of the Housing Act and in discharging the Washington home rule bill from the House District Committee.

From *The Washington Post* (October 17, 1965), p. E-1. © The Washington Post. Reprinted by permission.

BLUNTING THE POINT

As a 30-year veteran of congressional politics, Mr. Johnson believes that too many direct entreaties from the White House would be self-defeating, one aide said recently.

"Look at it this way," he explained. "A Congressman is standing at the rear of the floor and says to another, 'Guess who called me up last night.' But what if he can only say, 'Well, guess who called me up *again* last night.'"

Probably no amount of presidential pleading alone could have assured so agreeable and productive a Congress as the 89th, which came up with medicare, a housing act, voting rights insurance for Negroes and practically everything else that Mr. Johnson wanted except home rule for Washington and repeal of 14(b). O'Brien and his staff seemed to be at least as effective as their boss in soliciting votes.

How the personal "Johnson treatment" works was illustrated in closeup last March in a rare television performance starring him and Sen. Harry F. Byrd (D-Virginia). While the cameras ground in the Cabinet Room, Byrd was gently but insistently wheedled into promising early Senate Finance Committee hearings on the medicare bill.

Three times Byrd reluctantly agreed to hold hearings, but the President, not quite satisfied, drilled in again: "So when the House acts and it is referred to the Senate Finance Committee, you will arrange prompt hearings and thorough hearings?" "Yes," replied the proud but hard-pressed Byrd.

HIGH-LEVEL ASSISTANCE

Republicans who cry "arm-twisting" generally refer to instances in which Mr. Johnson's aides or Executive Department officials have closed in to make the Administration's interest clear.

Rep. John J. Rhodes (R-Arizona), who attributes pressures to a "congressional conformity corps," disclosed last month that John W. Macy, chairman of the supposedly nonpolitical Civil Service Commission, called him twice long-distance to solicit support for Administration positions.

Also, a minority on the House Public Works Committee reacted wrathfully when Special Presidential Assistant Bill D. Moyers and other White House officials sat in the anteroom while the Committee, in executive session, marked up Mrs. Johnson's highway beautification bill.

Is the acquiescent Congressman rewarded for casting his lot with the White House? There is scant evidence that an Administration vote earns a specific return favor, but one Southern Democrat says: "There's a sort of derived inference on the part of the Congressman who gets called by the President—a feeling that if you go along, things will be better for you over there at the White House."

There are scores of minor favors a President can offer—an invitation to the White House or the ranch; presidential attendance at a Senator's wife's funeral—to win the legislator's good will and support. Many of the 71 freshmen Democrats are indebted to him anyway, having ridden to Washington on his coattails a year ago. Their record of Administration support is good.

But let one of them stray, and his wandering is quickly noted. A Midwestern freshman who was not quick to sign the home rule discharge petition recalls:

> The White House liaison people came and talked to me. Then some contributors to my campaign back home called me up. Then my party chairman back home called to remind me that home rule for Washington was part of our Democratic platform.
>
> No one said the White House had enlisted them, but it was obviously a very carefully coordinated process. That's it: they're so damned well coordinated. It wasn't any accident. They've got a file on me over there a mile long.

THE O'BRIEN SYSTEM

That "coordination" is chiefly a product of five years of experience in vote-hustling by voluble, chain-smoking Larry O'Brien, congressional liaison chief under Presidents Kennedy and Johnson and soon to be Postmaster General.

Before O'Brien, executive-legislative liaison was a blend of begging and wire-pulling. Under him, it has become a systematic operation that followed 50 pieces of legislation into every Democratic legislator's office this year. O'Brien's liaison network is practically a new agency of government.

"When I was on the Hill as administrative assistant to a freshman Congressman, it never entered my mind to call the White House," recalls O'Brien. "It was just unheard of. Now we see the members on a continuing schedule and calls are going from here to the Hill and vice versa all day long."

O'Brien's office holds periodic skull sessions with some 40 congressional liaison men in the Cabinet departments and gets each Monday noon a rundown on problems their bills face. A digest goes to President Johnson Monday night so that he is prepared for his Tuesday breakfast with the congressional leadership.

O'Brien, whose baptism of fire came in President Kennedy's successful drive to diminish the House Rules Committee's power, insists that logrolling, patronage and favor-exchanging are of little importance in garnering votes on specific bills. The most he can offer, he says, are petty favors: arranging special White House tours for a Congressman's constituents; putting in a word for a supporter when an appointment is pending.

He and four assistants, who divide up the House and Senate, concentrate on providing technical information to answer legislators' questions, stressing the Administration's position, and making the vital head-counts on passage of a bill. Arm-twisting would be useless, O'Brien believes.

"We have to remember that every one of those fellows up there has been elected to office in his own right," he says. "All of them have their problems of political survival and we're not going to ask them to endanger themselves. We want them to know that they're dealing with people here who have political judgment, too."

O'Brien is respected on Capitol Hill because his head-counts are reliable and because he rarely asks for the unnecessary. "When Larry says so many votes are needed, they really are," one Democrat says. "Sometimes he will tell me that he has a little 'padding'—maybe three or four votes to spare—and just wants me to be ready if it slips away."

O'Brien also sees that broken fences get mended. When the President vetoed the military construction bill because one provision intruded on the Executive's domain, O'Brien's office called every member of the Armed Services Committees to explain the veto.

Backing up the President and O'Brien is an expanding network of politicians, bureaucrats, pressure groups and lobbyists whose aim is to help the pro-Administration Congressman stay on Capitol Hill where his vote can count. Few realize the extent of aid available to the Representative who votes regularly with the Administration.

A freshman Congressman wonders how he can get that sewage treatment plant for a town in his district. Confused by departmental red tape, he can call the Democratic National Committee, whose specialists on his region tackle the job through liaison officers in the appropriate agency. If the plant is built, the Congressman is a little stronger in his district and a little fonder of the Administration.

In the National Committee, the freshman also finds a ready-made publicity network. A new corps of Committee aides is handy for writing press releases, or the Congressman can pick up his office phone, read a statement into the Committee's tape recorders and know that it will be available to every radio station in his district by nightfall.

Even more sophisticated and less publicized is the congressional servicing program being developed slowly by the National Committee and lobbying groups. To make the fledgling Congressman better known in his district, the Committee works through the Washington offices of major pressure groups: labor, rural electric cooperatives, education associations and the like.

The Washington lobbyists are urged to get their local agents behind the Congressman, to help him arrange speaking engagements for his trips home. This system may now have reached its ultimate in a few districts where citizens and special interest groups have formed "coordinating committees" to keep the Great Society Congressman where he and President Johnson want him to be.

By Courting Congress Assiduously, Johnson Furthers His Program
ALAN L. OTTEN

WASHINGTON. A new picture is being prominently displayed in Congressional offices all over Capitol Hill.

A handsomely mounted eight-by-ten-inch color shot, it shows the particular Senator or Representative and his wife impressively posed with the President and First Lady in the White House Green Room. Handwritten across the bottom is the legend: "To the blanks, with best wishes," and the signatures, "Lyndon B. Johnson—Lady Bird Johnson."

The photos, snapped on an assembly-line basis as the lawmakers dropped by the White House recently for evening briefings and buffet dining with the President, are hardly likely in themselves to change any votes in Congress. But they're symptomatic of the special attention President Johnson is paying to Congressional relations, even in the midst of Vietnam and racial crises.

The pride with which the pictures are displayed by Republican as well as Democrat shows the President's shrewd judgment of what can win friends and neutralize enemies in Congress. Together with dozens of other similar touches, this personal consideration can on occasion make a vital difference in the progress of the President's legislative program.

"FLATTERED AND IMPRESSED"

"No matter how sophisticated a guy is, he's flattered and impressed by attention from the President of the United States," says a very sophisticated Senate Democrat. "There's no politician in either party who doesn't like to tell his friends and his constituents what the President said to him the other night and what he said to the President. As a man who was on the Hill over 30 years, Johnson knows that and is shrewd enough to take advantage of it."

From *The Wall Street Journal* (April 9, 1965), p. 1. Reprinted by permission.

Consider a few other random examples. LBJ drops by unexpectedly to josh with House members dedicating a new gymnasium. Top Democrats and Republicans on the Senate Finance and House Ways and Means committees are asked to the White House to comment on possible choices for Treasury Secretary; though the President has almost surely made up his mind already, the lawmakers feel their views truly matter.

Florida Democratic Rep. Bennett breaks his leg and receives a Presidential bouquet. Democratic Sen. Randolph of West Virginia and Rep. Jones of Alabama manage the Appalachia bill to successful passage and receive Presidential thank-you phone calls within minutes afterward. New Jersey Republican Sen. Case gets a thank-you call for his nice comments about the President's voting rights plan, and GOP Sen. Scott of Pennsylvania is asked up to the Johnson living quarters for a night-cap and talkfest after a White House briefing.

Freshman Rep. Hungate of Missouri worries that if he stays late on Friday to vote on the Administration's school bill, he won't be able to keep a long-standing commitment to address a Democratic breakfast session in Springfield Saturday morning; to keep Mr. Hungate on hand for the vote without angering the folks back home, the President wires the breakfasters his regrets for holding "this outstanding young Congressman" in Washington, plus assurances that Mr. Hungate is showing his "patriotic commitment to the great goals in the pathbreaking education bill now on the floor."

IMPROVING ON KENNEDY

There's no question Mr. Johnson pays more heed to Congressional relations than any President in recent history, though predecessor John Kennedy also worked hard at the task. Mr. Kennedy upgraded White House Congressional liaison with a six-man staff headed by his long-time political lieutenant Lawrence O'Brien. He and Mr. O'Brien strove to get outside groups such as the AFL-CIO or Farmers Union to team up with Administration lobbyists on individual bills. He sent congratulatory birthday notes to Senators and Congressmen, included them in prestigious state dinners, invited large groups to witness bill-signing ceremonies and receive pens used in the signing, and asked legislators to ride with him on the Presidential jet.

But Mr. Johnson goes at it harder, day and night, weekday and weekend. He wants to pass his "Great Society" bills for what they can accomplish for the country and for his own image in the history books. Not as eloquent as Mr. Kennedy in outlining his point of view, he is a master manipulator who almost intuitively knows how to advance his aims best, detecting where legislative roadblocks may develop, who can be pressured or flattered, and how best to do it.

Characteristically LBJ takes pains to clear his proposals in advance with private interest groups, as well as influential lawmakers, to minimize the opposition; he met once publicly and twice privately with groups from the National Education Association to put down rebellions in that important organization against the school bill provisions permitting aid to parochial schools.

BRIEFINGS AND BUFFETS

Not only has Mr. Johnson refined and expanded the Kennedy techniques but he's added some of his own. The groups he invites to the White House bill-signing ceremonies are larger. He sends out birthday notes and, on occasion, also phones congratulations.

Mr. Kennedy used to ask members in for informal coffee hours; Mr. Johnson has invited all 535 Senators and Congressmen and their wives this year to evening briefings and buffets. Over 500 actually came, in groups of about 50 couples, twice a week, on Tuesday and Thursday evenings for five weeks in February and March.

They would arrive at the White House around 6:30 p.m., have a drink, then stroll into the Green Room for the picture-taking. Next, Mrs. Johnson would take the ladies on a tour of the family living quarters and a film on the White House, while Mr. Johnson would take the lawmakers into the Blue Room for a briefing of two hours or more on Vietnam, the budget and other national and international topics.

Secretary of State Rusk, Defense Chief McNamara, Budget Director Gordon and Vice President Humphrey were the official briefers. But always, at some point, the President himself would jump in for 30 to 45 minutes, ending with the reminder that if any member ever wanted to talk to him, "I'm just as close as your telephone." The lawmakers could, and did, question the President and other officials at any point. With the briefing over, they rejoined the ladies for a buffet supper that lasted until 10:30 or 11 p.m.

Even the most conservative Republicans give grudging good marks to the meetings, and most Democrats are ecstatic about them. The President talks of the sessions as the nearest thing to the questioning of Britain's Prime Minister and Cabinet in the House of Commons, and plans to stage more from time to time. Even lawmakers who doubt they found out much that couldn't be learned in a close reading of the daily papers did welcome the intimate, first-hand impressions of the President's mood and goals.

"He neutralized in those briefings a lot of the resentment from his plans to close the veterans' hospitals and the agriculture research stations," a Senator asserts.

THIRTY-EIGHT EXTRA DEMOCRATS HELP

Of course, it's easy to overstate the importance of Lyndon's personal lobbying. Actually, many key lawmakers argue, Mr. Kennedy had his program pretty well on the track when he was assassinated and would have wound up the 1964 session with a record not very different from Mr. Johnson's. This year, the main secret of LBJ's legislative success is simply the extra 38 House Democrats elected last fall.

"The reason we're passing bills that were stalled last year is that we've got the horses now," says a House Democratic leader. Adds an Administration lobbyist: "I'd rather have those 38 votes than all the Presidential telephoning in the world."

Mr. Johnson's public support helps his legislative record, anyway, quite apart from any specific pressures he applies. Members want to be sure of Presidential aid in their re-election campaigns in 1966 and 1968. The goodwill LBJ has won in the business community has minimized the pressures felt in Congress against new welfare schemes and made it easier for many legislators to go along.

It must be noted, too, that reports of Mr. Johnson's lobbying activities, prodigious as they are, tend to be exaggerated. He does less phoning now than in his first lonely days in the White House; nowadays the calls go chiefly to Senate and House leaders, committee chairmen and old friends, or to someone who's done a particularly good job for the Administration. On a crucial vote, he may call 10 or 12 members seeking support, but there are lots of lawmakers who have never had a Presidential call.

FAR FROM INFALLIBLE

Moreover, White House liaison with Congress, despite Mr. Johnson's reputation for legislative legerdemain, is far from infallible. The Administration decision to close a number of veterans' hospitals produced such an explosive capitol reaction that it has prompted Presidential reconsiderations.

Another apparent failure: Some weeks ago, the White House heard rumblings that fiery Rep. Edith Green of Oregon, a key Democrat on school legislation, would probably fight important sections of the Administration's education bill. Presidential aide Douglass Cater invited her to a White House lunch, then took her in for a chat with Mr. Johnson. Mrs. Johnson invited her to a domestic Peace Corps ceremony in Florida. But the Congresswoman still fought two key provisions of the bill, forcing a major outpouring of Administration effort to defeat her on the House floor.

There's no question that from time to time the President and his lieutenants do twist Congressional arms with threats of retribution (Administration opposition to a pet bill or project or loss of patronage) or promises of reward (a better committee assignment or extra re-election help). But such instances, Mr. O'Brien insists, are far rarer than rumor has it.

The great bulk of White House legislative liaison work is far more routine. It consists largely of offering smaller favors, to create a generally friendly attitude on the part of lawmakers—"where he'll want to go your way unless there's some compelling reason back home against it," Mr. O'Brien puts it. Among the favors are invitations to the White House, advance news on awards of Government contracts and assurances that agency bureaucrats will carefully consider a member's suggestion. A large part of the job, too, is making sure the legislators have the facts and arguments for any pending bill, keeping the pressure on committee chairmen to push ahead with hearings, mobilizing outside support, and making sure Administration supporters are actually on hand for the voting.

In many ways, Mr. Johnson has tried to underline his belief in good Congressional relations. For example, he's set Mr. O'Brien's pay $1,500 a year above that of any other White House assistant. (Mr. O'Brien hopes to leave within a few months, but insists this is because four years on a job is enough and not because the President's wide-ranging role diminishes Mr. O'Brien's.)

HUMPHREY USED MORE

Mr. Johnson gets almost everyone on his team into the lobbying act. He is using Vice President Humphrey far more for legislative aid than Mr. Kennedy used Vice President Johnson—to take soundings, suggest Congressional strategy and influence individual members, particularly Democratic liberals. Mr. Humphrey asked a number of House liberals to his office to quiet doubts they had on the parochial school aid made possible by the Administration's education bill.

Everyone on the White House staff is expected to help the O'Brien shop. "What are you doing down here when my bill's up on the floor up there?" LBJ may demand of staff members. Among others, Special Presidential Assistant Jack Valenti is spending more and more time talking with Senators and Congressmen. At one point during House consideration of the school bill, there were two members of Mr. O'Brien's liaison staff outside the House chamber, plus White House aides Marvin Watson, Douglass Cater and Bill Moyers, an official of the Democratic National Committee and three representatives of the Department of Health, Education and Welfare—in addition to Administration-coordinated lobbyists from the National Education Association and other private groups.

Criticism of President's Style, Methods Mounts Among Small but Important Group
ALAN L. OTTEN

WASHINGTON. The white Lincoln Continental flashes down the Texas highway at 90 miles an hour. A motorcycle cop overtakes the car, waves it to the side of the road, parks his machine and walks back ticket book in hand. He looks in and gulps, "Oh my God."

"Yes," growls the voice from inside, "and don't you forget it again."

This rather unkind little Johnson-joke, swiftly making the Capital cocktail party rounds, is evidence of a fascinating phenomenon: While the President apparently retains overwhelming popular support across the nation, a small but influential group of people who see him up close are increasingly uneasy, unhappy, and uncharitable about him.

From *The Wall Street Journal* (July 6, 1965), p. 1. Reprinted by permission.

The undercurrent of criticism is as yet directed more at Mr. Johnson personally—his style and methods of operation—than at his policies. Thus far, too, most of the criticism has been private word of mouth rather than public speech or article. But the unhappy people are important—some of the top policy-makers in the Government, individual Senators and Congressmen, members of the press corps, lawyers and other men about town—and they seem to be becoming far more numerous and vocal in recent weeks.

The critical chorus voices many complaints: That the President drives people too hard, is too high-handed and arrogant, doesn't really want argument and independent point of view. That he is too preoccupied with his popular image, is too sensitive to criticism, spends too much of his time answering attacks he should ignore. That he tends to whine over his troubles and blame others for his mistakes. That when things go truly wrong, he frequently turns nasty.

THE VALENTI SPEECH

One incident, perhaps, best illustrates the current climate. Last week, in a speech in Boston, one of the President's closest aides discussed the burden of the Presidency. Special Presidential assistant Jack Valenti described the long hours Mr. Johnson works, the intelligence and experience he brings to the job, his sure command of the office. If Mr. Valenti had let it go at that, all would have been well and good.

But he also went on, in the richest and most purple of phrases, to picture the President as a sensitive and cultivated man, a great visionary, one who "homes in on the nerve-edges of the issue," a man who welcomes dissent. "I sleep each night a little better, a little more confidently, because Lyndon Johnson is my President," Mr. Valenti concluded.

The whole town exploded in a hilarious howl of disbelief. And it chortled further when the Washington Post's Herblock cartooned a slashing rebuttal view, titled "Happy Days on the Old Plantation." He drew three cringing White House staffers, bare to the waist and with their backs deeply slashed. Walking away is the President, bullwhip in hand. Below the picture, in irony, are quoted several of Mr. Valenti's most opulent observations.

The reaction to the Valenti speech, the rash of anti-Johnson jokes, the increasingly hostile tenor of conversation at Washington lunches and cocktail parties and dinners provide illuminating evidence. Everyone seems to have his favorite anti-Johnson anecdote, and perhaps even more interestingly, ones that have long circulated are even beginning to find their way into print. Example: The Washington Post recently told how Mr. Johnson had wandered into the office of then assistant press secretary Malcolm Kilduff, spotted a piled-high desk, and barked, "Kilduff, I hope your mind isn't as cluttered as your desk." A few days later he wandered in again, saw a spotlessly clean surface, and snapped, "Kilduff, I hope your brain isn't as empty as your desk."

Democratic Senators and Congressmen seem increasingly restive under White House pressure. They have not and will not rebel on major legislation; their own desire and need to enact Great Society bills prevents that. Instead they take their frustration out in minor revolts, such as the refusal to cut duty-free tourist imports as much as the President wanted, or the fierceness of the ultimately unsuccessful fight against permitting a retired military man to head the Federal Aviation Agency. Or they join the snickerers with remarks like this one by a usually pro-Johnson Democrat: "Lincoln went down in history as the Great Emancipator and Johnson will go down in history as the Great Emasculator."

Bureaucratic disenchantment also seems to grow, and top-level morale seems low, despite pay increases and record promotions for career men. Holdover Kennedy appointees snipe most openly, but more and more career men, particularly in the State Department, join them, and even some Johnson men show occasional embarrassment. Bureaus that should be bursting with enthusiasm as they put into operation programs they have sought for years—medicare, aid to education, new health programs—go about their work with an almost lackadaisical indifference. Only the anti-poverty warriors seem truly gung-ho about their current assignments.

The explanations for this current outcropping of criticism are many. For one thing, there's an early summer lull in Washington, no bold new domestic move, no fresh foreign crisis to absorb the town. So the people look more closely at the man who dominates the town as no recent President has. When the Emperor moves quickly, smoothly fielding foreign flaps and passing domestic legislative miracles, everyone concentrates on performance. When the action slows down, everyone has time to examine more carefully the Emperor's clothes.

For another thing, much of the criticism currently being leveled against Mr. Johnson personally is undoubtedly being made by people who would like to speak out against his policies but are reluctant or afraid to do so. This is particularly true of Democratic lawmakers and Government officials unhappy over Mr. Johnson's recent Dominican course and the steadily growing U.S. involvement in Vietnam. Many would like to attack these policies frontally, but believe Mr. Johnson has boxed them in with his repeated complaints, public and private, that foreign policy critics give comfort to Peking and Hanoi.

Finally, the fact is that Mr. Johnson does provide ample ammunition for those who want to censure. He obviously lacks the straightforward warmth of an Eisenhower or the wit and grace that won hearts for John F. Kennedy. Along with admirable qualities of intelligence, experience and dedication, Mr. Johnson possesses some less attractive attributes.

He does drive his people. Himself supercharged with energy, he expects everyone around him to match his prodigious pace. The White House atmosphere frequently seems grim and humorless. Some top officials, perhaps most notably Secretary of Defense McNamara, have been showing signs of near-exhaustion in recent months. In crises particularly, the President tends to summon aides into endless rounds of talks and meetings that eventually seem as much designed to bolster his own sense of security as to produce any thoughtful discussion of new moves.

The President often seems to lack respect for the individual. As soon as any official indicates he's quitting Mr. Johnson's team, the President is likely to tell callers that so-and-so "was really terribly overrated." Cabinet members are plainly uncomfortable at the way Mr. Johnson uses them as public relations flacks—inviting the press after Cabinet meetings to hear the Secretaries recite in turn, like so many kindergarten children, the glowing reports they've just handed teacher.

HE CAN TURN ROUGH

He asks and even wheedles Senators and Congressmen for support—but can turn rough. Much resentment on Capitol Hill goes back to his request for an extra $700 million for Vietnam. Many lawmakers suspected the Pentagon did not really need the money—a suspicion they thought confirmed when the Defense Department could not quickly present a detailed justification for the request—and that Mr. Johnson was merely using the vote as a device to extort support from critical Congressmen. Said one Democratic Senator: "He was pointing his six-guns at our feet, peppering the floor around us, and saying, 'Dance, damn you, dance.' "

He is accessible and talkative with at least some newsmen—until they question him closely. Then he can turn snappish. On one walk around the White House grounds during the Dominican crisis, several reporters pressed him to make public the then still-secret list of Communists in the rebel camp. He sharply accused them of advocating a course that would aid the enemy—yet next day the State Department made the list public.

Not even the President's closest aides would deny that he is tender about criticism. Much of his talking with correspondents is aimed at "setting the record straight" on something another correspondent said or wrote. His favorite subject remains the opinion polls showing his high national rating.

LBJ freely employs the usual Presidential prerogative to proclaim as his own any promising plan around Washington. Research into high-speed transportation between Boston and Washington is now a Great Society venture, and Rhode Island Senator Claiborne Pell, who first pushed the plan and kept it alive for several years, is frozen out.

Mr. Johnson also tends to blame others when things go wrong. His own staff told reporters he was canvassing the Government for "action proposals" on the United Nations and would not address the San Francisco meeting unless he had something more to offer than a pep talk. Yet when he did go there with just a pep talk, he blamed the delegates' coolness on lower-down U.S. officials who, he says, planted their pet proposals in the press in hopes of forcing the President to adopt them, and thus built up excessive expectations.

Despite Mr. Valenti's assertion that the President "is not fond of those who continually say 'yes' to him," the feeling persists around Washington that officials had better argue with Mr. Johnson only in the earliest stages of decision-making and only when he asks for their opinion. To volunteer advice or try to dissuade the President when he is already tending in one direction is, most bureaucrats believe, a perilous course for any but Presidential aide Bill Moyers and perhaps one or two other favorites.

REAL IMAGE BETTER?

Some who've watched Mr. Johnson closely argue he would actually fare better in the eyes of those around him if he gave up his frequent attempts to paint himself as something he's not—a loveable, easy-to-work-with, gentle soul—and instead stuck to the line that the times require what he is—a smart, hard-driving, purposeful, ornery hombre. The tone of sanctimony and humility in which Mr. Johnson cloaks many of his tough actions makes these actions all the harder for many to take.

Even after the explanation is sought and furnished for the current wave of Capital criticism, the question still remains whether it all matters. Isn't the criticism confined to a small group of liberal-oriented intellectuals? Is it really important what kind of person the President is, or isn't the important thing the policies he advances and the results he gets? The chewing-up of some close aides, the ruffling of easy-going lawmakers, the challenging of tradition-bound bureaucrats, the discomfitting of too-soft White House correspondents—might not these be necessary to make the Government move?

Mr. Johnson certainly took the Government over under difficult circumstances and drove it steadily ahead. He has amassed a monumental legislative record already, and is sure to add to it substantially. His foreign policies, though coming in for increasing criticism, have not yet produced a dramatic reverse of the magnitude of Mr. Kennedy's Bay of Pigs. In a number of speeches—on civil rights, education, the quality of American life—he has been impressively eloquent.

Chances are that new dramatic successes in Congress will muffle some of the current undertone of disenchantment. The danger for the President, however, is that with the undertone already there, some sudden reverses at home or abroad will result in an explosion of criticism and a marked drop in popular support. In any event, the current capital climate is still an interesting phenomenon in itself, worthy of at least passing note in the ups and downs of Presidential popularity.

Often Moody, Defensive
CARROLL KILPATRICK

Lyndon B. Johnson was often a moody man and he suffered fits of depression. When he was down, he was way down and the entire world was against him. Even his closest friends were suspect. One day, when one of his oldest and most trusted supporters offered words of advice, LBJ retorted: "You're just trying to get me defeated."

The former President now says that on August 26, 1964, he drafted a statement

From *The Washington Post* (December 27, 1969), p. A-1. © The Washington Post. Reprinted by permission.

declaring that he would not be a candidate for re-election. That was after the Democratic National Convention had assembled in Atlantic City to nominate him by acclamation.

If he had said "no" at that time there would have been chaos. There was no chaos. The convention ran like clockwork under LBJ's masterful direction.

The only question to be decided at the convention was who would be the vice-presidential nominee. LBJ himself finally gave the convention the name in the early evening of August 26, the same day he says he wrote out a statement declining the nomination.

To keep the suspense to the last moment, he invited Sens. Hubert H. Humphrey (Minnesota) and Thomas J. Dodd (Connecticut) to leave Atlantic City on the afternoon of August 26 and confer with him at the White House. When they arrived at the White House both Dodd and Humphrey were kept waiting in a limousine while LBJ walked round and round the drive with perspiring reporters.

In California, his lead was two to one. In Indiana, he said, he had "only" 55 per cent and in Wisconsin "only" 60 per cent.

He did not sound like a man who had any doubts at all about his future. The world was waiting for him to be nominated and for him to name his running mate. His mood was euphoric the very day he said he drafted a memo saying he would not be a candidate. Everyone, including all the polsters, knew that he was a winner.

When I read the transcript of the former President's interview with Walter Cronkite I remembered that famous walk on the South Lawn and the exuberant President. Could he have entertained doubts on August 26 of all days? And I began to search my own notes.

They show, to my surprise, that in May 1964, three months before the convention, LBJ told a group of reporters that "maybe the country needs a new man as President, one who has fewer scars than I have." But he quickly added that "as long as I'm the only President you've got I'm going to call the shots as I see them."

No doubt he said to others that he might not run again, but no one paid any attention, any more than the old friend had taken seriously the jibe that he was trying to bring about LBJ's defeat. That was the way Mr. Johnson talked.

Despite the evidence the former President now produces to show that he considered bowing out, the recollection of nearly everyone who knew him is that few men in American political life ever wanted the high office more than LBJ.

Often as a senator he talked about what he would do if he were President; he complained about the hurdles that he, a Southerner, faced in seeking the office. As one of his closest friends in those days said at the time when asked if the senator wanted to be President: "He wants it so much he can taste it."

LBJ's depression was enormous when he failed to win the presidential nomination in 1960 and was offered instead second place. When be became President on November 22, 1963, he took immediate command. He was a natural leader. He had great confidence in himself. He knew what the presidency was, what it meant and how it should be used.

From the moment he became President, LBJ's aim was renomination and re-election in 1964, or so it seemed to all who watched him. One who was with him

Often Moody, Defensive

daily during that period said yesterday that there was never any doubt in the minds of any who worked with him that re-election was the big goal.

In the spring of 1964, he had a number of polls taken to determine whether Humphrey, Robert Kennedy, Eugene McCarthy, Edmund Muskie, John Pastore or some other Democrat would be a help as his running mate. He discovered from the polls, and proudly told visitors, that whomever he chose as a running mate hurt his own standing by two or three percentage points.

In May, 1964, when it seemed fairly clear that Barry Goldwater would be the Republican nominee, a visitor chided the President on his strong showing in the polls and asked him if he didn't feel sorry for the Republicans. "Don't you think you should let them have one state?" the visitor asked.

"Oh, no, no," President Johnson solemnly replied. "Gene Pulliam (a conservative Republican and publisher of the Arizona Republic) called me the other day from Arizona and said that if I would come there he would have the Republican Governor out to meet me, all the Republicans in the state and others and that they would put on a huge reception for me." LBJ was not even willing at that point to concede Barry Goldwater's home state.

The campaign of 1964 began early. Of course, LBJ did not call it a campaign, but it began and ended in a whirlwind. In early May 1964, The Washington Post began a story with these words: "In the last two weeks, President Johnson has made 30 speeches—and the campaign hasn't even begun."

He traveled to Appalachia twice in two weeks. He spoke in Atlanta. Then he flew to Ann Arbor, Michigan, to project the vision of a "great society," to outline his program for the future.

In June, he was in San Francisco and Los Angeles. The June 19 story in The Washington Post began: "Cheered by a huge crowd here, President Johnson today predicted a Democratic victory in November and declared that Sen. Barry Goldwater's ideas are as out of date as the dinosaur."

After his nomination, LBJ waged an exuberant campaign from one end of the country to another. He said that he never tired and afterwards he called it "the best-run campaign in history."

It was a breathtaking campaign with LBJ ahead all the way and finally winning by the biggest margin in history. He was in seventh heaven. "Y'awl come to the speakin';" he shouted until he was hoarse.

Sophisticates didn't like the way LBJ talked, but they admired his skill in skewering the hapless Republicans. LBJ knew that many persons were laughing at him behind his back, making fun of his corny mannerisms and speech. The jibes hurt him to the quick and helped produce the depression that caused him to tell his wife he might not run.

He took all the criticisms personally.

But he was too proud not to run. He was a professional politician; the highest goal in his reach was the presidency. He wanted it in 1960; he demanded it in 1964. The laughter at his expense was almost more than even a strong man like himself could bear. But he was proud, inordinately proud. The prize was his in 1964 and he sought ferociously to keep it.

6
RICHARD M. NIXON

1969–

Lyndon Johnson's mercurial personality produced sharply varying estimates not only of the gains and costs of his administrative style but of what to expect of that style at any given moment. Richard Nixon's administrative style is comparatively easy to describe, and as the selections that follow indicate, there is great consensus on its main ingredients. These are order, privacy, thorough staff work, and plenty of homework for the President himself. President Nixon's preferred method of learning appears to be through reading. This sets him apart from the great bulk of American politicians, who learn through their ears, and generates its own organizational design.

Under Richard Nixon the Cabinet has lost stature, while the White House staff has grown in importance. It goes without saying that the people who run most of the government have very little to say about the President's own initiatives, activities, and choices. In addition, it is President Nixon's staff men, not agency advocates, who have far and away the best access to the President at points of decision affecting agency budgets and options. As time has gone on, the White House staff has grown larger than at any time since the beginning of modern Presidency.

These are some of the findings and observations contained in the articles reprinted below.

A Passion for Order and Privacy
ROBERT B. SEMPLE, JR.

WASHINGTON. After four months in office, President Nixon has started running the United States Government in a style and manner that is very much his own.

"Running the Government" is, of course, a misleading term. No modern President has exercised complete executive control over the Federal bureaucracy, although Lyndon Johnson gave it a valiant, protean try. Mr. Nixon is no exception. There is no visible evidence that he takes a day-to-day interest in, say, George Romney's problems at the housing agency. Like all Presidents, he prefers to reserve his energies against the day when George Romney's problems become Presidential problems.

Even so, there is a Nixon style and a Nixon pattern to the way he conducts the public business. It is a style distinguished mainly by two characteristics: a passion for order, and a passion for privacy. Order, to insure that the President receives a regular flow of the best advice that Government is able to give him; privacy, to insure that when he gets all these options he can retreat and, in an atmosphere of studied detachment, reach the correct decision.

IMPOSING ORDER

Like most executives, President Nixon has tried to impose order on the decision-making process through machinery. His own peculiar machinery is rather simple on paper, although in practice it is frequently cumbersome and occasionally inept.

There are three major elements to it: the National Security Council, revitalized under Henry A. Kissinger, which churns up foreign policy options for Presidential decision; the Urban Affairs Council, under Daniel Patrick Moynihan, which churns up domestic options for Presidential decision; and an administrative apparatus, headed by former Nixon campaign official H. R. Haldeman, who monitors the flow of both people and paper in and out of the President's office and who zealously budgets the President's time.

There are other groups, such as the Cabinet and his economic advisers, to whom the President turns fairly regularly for advice. And this weekend he established yet another Cabinet-level advisory group, known as the Environmental Quality Council to serve as the "focal point" of the Administration's efforts to protect the nation's natural resources.

From *The New York Times* (June 1, 1969), p. IV-1. © 1969 by The New York Times Company. Reprinted by permission.

In the first hundred days (the ratios have changed little since then), Mr. Nixon met with his National Security Council 15 times, his Urban Affairs Council nine times, the Republican Congressional leaders nine times, the joint Congressional leadership three times, and the Cabinet four times. These figures, incidentally, give a pretty fair indication of his priorities and preoccupation during the last few months. He is clearly dominated by foreign policy, and so far he prefers to talk to Republicans.

PRESIDENTIAL METHODS

Mr. Nixon is reportedly a good moderator at these meetings. He enjoys watching Dr. Moynihan and the conservative Dr. Arthur Burns, his counselor, spar over an issue; and he does not indulge in either the long-winded harangues or the endless, heavy silences of Lyndon Johnson. He is, by all accounts, a good listener and a perceptive questioner, and when he is unsure of something raised in the meeting (e.g., whether malnutrition in fact causes brain damage in children), he will later ask Mr. Haldeman to dispatch a memo to an aide to find the answer (in this case, Dr. Moynihan, who sent a note back saying that the statistical evidence was inconclusive).

When the options are finally in, the President leaves the field of debate and retreats—sometimes to his oval office, more often to the Lincoln sitting room in the family quarters of the East Wing—to make up his mind. His aides are never sure what will emerge.

Mr. Nixon's decision to move ahead with the major assault on hunger, for instance, took most of his staff by surprise. His decision to name Warren Burger as Chief Justice was reportedly shielded from all of his closest advisers including the ubiquitous Mr. Haldeman. When the time came to make a decision on whether or not to alter the 7 per cent investment credit and the 10 per cent surtax, aides were so unsure of Mr. Nixon's mind after a 90-minute meeting on April 23 that they prepared one announcement justifying changes in the credit and surtax, and another announcement justifying no changes at all.

And just this weekend, Nixon retreated with a couple of thick notebooks to Key Biscayne, Florida, to examine the options on the welfare system and the supersonic transports. His associates insist they really don't know what he will do.

In short, Mr. Nixon's manner is distinguished by a kind of progressive isolation, beginning at the committee level, where the alternatives are reduced to manageable proportions, and ending with the President alone in the Lincoln sitting room. While there are obvious virtues to such a system, and obvious advantages to Presidential detachment, there are disadvantages as well.

For example, Mr. Nixon tends to concentrate on one issue at a time, and occasionally lets other issues slide. He was so preoccupied with the Burger appointment to the Supreme Court, according to aides, that he was not even aware until the next day of Senator Edward Kennedy's savage attack on his military policy in Vietnam.

CEDING AUTHORITY

Moreover, wide areas of authority are ceded to others. Mr. Haldeman, John Ehrlichman and Peter Flanigan (all friends, all close) make important decisions on who goes where in the White House hierarchy, with the result that some men who thought they were close to and respected by the President find themselves in far-off corners of the Executive Office Building or inexplicably on the skids.

Isolation also produces embarrassing episodes. Mr. Nixon has been forced to rescind unwise appointments (Willie Mae Rogers, Dr. Franklin A. Long) that a President more fully engaged in day-to-day business might never have made in the first place. Another President might have taken a more careful sounding of the political opposition on Capitol Hill to the antiballistic missile system.

But good or bad, this is the Nixon style—considerably less rigid than President Eisenhower's yet far more carefully structured than Lyndon Johnson's, and something must be right. Mr. Nixon has negotiated his first four months rather smoothly, given the narrowness of his election mandate, and beyond that he is visibly happier and more relaxed in the job than most of the men whose styles he has chosen not to emulate.

The Nixon Style: President Seeks Order in His Decision-Making, but Events Intrude
JOHN PIERSON

WASHINGTON. "We are going," President Nixon told his first press conference, "to devote the whole day on Saturday to the Mideast problem, just as we devoted the whole day this last Saturday on the problem of Vietnam."

A State of the Union Message? "I will make a determination within the next two weeks," he replied.

The nuclear nonproliferation treaty? "That matter," he assured his audience, "will be considered by the National Security Council by my direction, during a meeting this week."

Thus, at the outset, Mr. Nixon suggested the order, organization and utter rationality that he has tried to bring to every phase of decision-making—from idea to

From *The Wall Street Journal* (July 7, 1969), p. 1. Reprinted by permission.

study to final yes or no—during his first half-year in office. That he hasn't always succeeded or that orderliness may be carried too far has not deterred Mr. Nixon.

Currently, the orderly White House approach is being applied to such issues as welfare overhaul, reorganization of manpower training programs and sharing of Federal revenues with state and local governments.

STRENGTHS AND WEAKNESSES

If the system works on these issues as on others, it may well culminate in providing the President with a handily packaged summary, in one or more notebooks, of the problem up for decision—along with a brief outline of the proposed choices. Mr. Nixon can simply check the solution he favors or he can write in his own.

The results of the current studies are not yet predictable, but on the basis of the experience thus far, the strengths and weaknesses of the Nixon system are becoming clear.

When successful, it may yield a wise decision that will command maximum Congressional and public support. But the system hasn't always succeeded. Witness the disorderly search for an Assistant Health, Education and Welfare Secretary—the post for which Dr. John Knowles was rejected after months of controversy. Some skeptics, moreover, are concerned that Mr. Nixon may have overorganized things to a point where the White House staff gets between him and people he ought to be seeing, such as opponents of the antiballistic missile.

Like any President, this one begins his decision-making with an idea. And since ideas can pop up anywhere, any time, this is possibly the least orderly and most creative part of the Nixon process.

Henry Kissinger, Mr. Nixon's adviser on national security matters, sent his boss an unsolicited memo on the Nigerian-Biafran problem. A routine staff summary of a television program about "black lung" sparked a White House study before the dread disease that affects miners became a national issue. Republican Rep. William Mailliard of California sent the President some ideas for improving the U.S. merchant marine.

SCRIBBLING ON MENUS

Mr. Nixon's guests at White House dinners have also been filling the Presidential ear, to judge from the note-scribbled menus he often brings to his daily 8:30 a.m. meeting with chief of staff Bob Haldeman and White House Counsel John Ehrlichman. Certainly, too, ideas leap spontaneously from the mind of Richard Nixon.

But ideas must be carefully scrutinized before they can become policies or programs. As a rule, a Presidential memo, via Mr. Haldeman or Mr. Ehrlichman, to the appropriate Cabinet member or White House staff man ("Please look into this . . .") sparks the examination.

Not surprisingly, Mr. Nixon delegates most of this research to his aides, saving his time and energy for the big decisions. More unusual, perhaps, is the degree to which Mr. Nixon prefers to let the White House staff and top department men see concerned outsiders—to become, as one staffer put it, "his eyes and ears to the outside world."

While the President does meet a number of such visitors, he left it to Mr. Kissinger to speak to three noted scientists and four Republican Senators who had asked to see Mr. Nixon to express opposition to the Safeguard antiballistic missile system before he made up his mind. One of the Senators, John Cooper of Kentucky, was worried about the effects of ABM deployment on coming arms-control talks with Russia but was told the President had already considered that problem. Outsiders who want to express an opinion on welfare revision are directed to Urban Affairs Adviser Daniel P. Moynihan, HEW Secretary Robert Finch or White House Counselor Arthur Burns.

Mr. Nixon carried his arms-length style to its highest degree when he purposely avoided seeing Warren Burger, his choice for Chief Justice, until three minutes before he went on TV to announce the appointment. The job of interviewing Mr. Burger and other candidates was left to Attorney General John Mitchell.

Every President works differently, explained Mr. Nixon, but he, for one, likes to be detached and stand back and decide as coolly and objectively as possible. What's more, he wants every Supreme Court Justice to feel absolutely independent of both President and Congress.

White House Counsel Ehrlichman explains Mr. Nixon's reluctance to talk to many outsiders by saying that the President doesn't like to see anyone for only 15 minutes "on a complex subject"; since the staff has more time, it can conduct a more thorough interview. In addition, Mr. Nixon believes that encounters with advocates of one side have "a single dimension," says Mr. Ehrlichman. According to another insider, Mr. Nixon is simply "a very interior guy" who "doesn't want to be bombarded constantly with people."

Results of the interviewing and the study generally find their way into a fat looseleaf notebook—sometimes several—put together by Mr. Ehrlichman and his staff. Mr. Ehrlichman prepares a "cover" for the package, a single page outlining what's inside: "Here are three reports on the XYZ problem from Messrs. A, B and C. Mr. A proposes you do such-and-such. Mr. B says you're barred by statute from acting. Mr. C feels there should be more study."

From the start, Mr. Nixon has said he wanted his staff to bring him not bland consensus but "the conflicts," so that he himself would be making the important choices. "The President doesn't like anyone to force his decision," says a White House man. "You'd better not go in there with only one recommendation."

So far, the staff appears to be complying. In fact, some people both in and outside the White House feel the staff is sending Mr. Nixon too many conflicts, including minor ones that should be resolved at a lower level. One State Department man was surprised to see a memo he sent to Mr. Kissinger come back covered with penciled comments from Mr. Nixon.

Mr. Nixon seldom finds time to read the Ehrlichman volumes during daylight hours of weekdays, since he is, as Mrs. Nixon recently put it, "always at a meeting."

There's the National Security Council, the Urban Affairs Council, the Cabinet, the Cabinet Committee on Economic Policy, the Environmental Quality Council, the 8:30 a.m. meeting with Messrs. Haldeman and Ehrlichman, a 9 a.m. meeting with Mr. Kissinger, a weekly session with "the domestic group" of top White House aides and countless other sessions with staff members, individually or in groups.

WORKING AT NIGHT

Appointments Secretary Dwight Chapin keeps track of his boss's time in 15-minute intervals, a vestige perhaps from Mr. Nixon's lawyer days. His working day is, as another assistant puts it, "sliced into little segments."

Small wonder then that the President is in the habit of taking the notebooks back to the Lincoln sitting room in the White House living quarters to read between dinner and bed. The heftier volumes are saved for weekends at Camp David, Maryland, or Key Biscayne, Florida, where Mr. Nixon just spent a Fourth of July sojourn thinking about his trip to Asia and Rumania; at those retreats, the atmosphere is said to be "more conducive" to reading and reflection.

When a notebook comes back from the President, Mr. Ehrlichman and his staff not only look to see what solution he may have chosen but also comb every page for the notes and instructions he likes to pen in the margins.

On minor matters, Mr. Nixon simply indicates a course of action. But on important issues, he will call at least one meeting to refine his thinking before he makes a decision. The tax reform session was a cozy get-together in the President's Oval Office. Insiders also recall a meeting on the District of Columbia crime bill where Mr. Nixon sat on one side of the Cabinet table, his back to the windows, and shot questions at a dozen aides drawn up rather formally on the other side.

His approach can be direct or oblique, but either way, according to one Administration man, Mr. Nixon "asks the right questions." An aide compares him to a prosecutor "who examines you without your knowing just what he's trying to get."

SPARKING A DEBATE

Sometimes the President will try to draw people out by sparking a controversy. He wondered, for example, whether Vice President Hubert Humphrey's commitment to the mayors was reason enough for retaining the Johnson Administration's program of summer jobs and recreation for needy youth. So the point was argued in the Urban Affairs Council, and the supporters of the program won out; Mr. Nixon has made good on Mr. Humphrey's promises.

According to participants, Mr. Nixon "almost never" indicates at a meeting what his final decision will be. Budget Director Robert Mayo came away from a review with the President unsure where Mr. Nixon would cut and where he would add to the budget for the year that began July 1. Officials who met with the President on tax reform were so uncertain of his intentions that they prepared two statements, one calling for repeal of the 7 percent investment tax credit and the other calling for retention.

Some aides claim to have left such meetings with a "pretty good idea" of what Mr. Nixon was going to decide. The President opened one session of the Urban Affairs Council by saying he was "very skeptical" about the Model Cities program. But after much discussion, some staffers suspected Mr. Nixon had changed his mind; later he did back the program.

Those who talked with him about the ABM got the impression that the President leaned toward deployment of the Safeguard system. Encouraged perhaps by this impression, the Pentagon, which previously had presented a range of options, came down hard for Safeguard. That may explain why Mr. Nixon likes to keep his intentions to himself.

"If the bureaucracy thinks it knows what the President wants," explains an adviser, "they'll give it to him."

In some instances, many meetings may be needed before Mr. Nixon has all the information he wants. According to one White House man, the President has a way of "coming up to a solution, laying down a hypothesis and then going away and letting people think about it." As a result, decisions often take longer than anticipated; Mr. Nixon's plan for welfare reform, expected weeks ago, may not be ready until fall.

SEEKING SOLITUDE

When all the information is in, Mr. Nixon withdraws to decide. At moments like this, Lyndon Johnson liked to gather friends and aides about him in his office and get on the phone to others all over the country. But Mr. Nixon usually decides in solitude.

Again, he prefers the Lincoln sitting room, Key Biscayne or Camp David to his office. He used the sitting room to map a response when North Korea shot down a U.S. spy plane, Key Biscayne to decide about the ABM and Camp David to pick a Chief Justice. And while he's said to be growing more accustomed to the telephone, an aide describes Mr. Nixon as still "reticent . . . subdued . . . somewhat apologetic" when he calls.

Thus the President attempts to keep his decision-making orderly, rational, detached. But the world doesn't always cooperate. Willie Mae Rogers was persuaded to become his consumer consultant and then, when a furor arose in Congress and elsewhere, had to be persuaded she didn't want the job after all. Franklin Long accepted the job of director of the National Science Foundation, was ruled out and then restored to favor but finally declined to serve.

The antihunger program, which Mr. Nixon would like to have developed in his own good time, had to be cranked up overnight in the face of Congressional pressure. And Mr. Nixon, who preferred to let tax revision wait until next year, suddenly found it expedient to come forth with a reform package designed to corral liberal votes for extension of the surtax. Such changes in course may tend to erode his image as an effective leader or, rightly or wrongly, to suggest an absence of guiding principles.

There may be more important problems with the Nixon system. By holding himself aloof while delegating the job of listening to passionate advocates of controversial views, Mr. Nixon can maintain his own serenity. But this sort of detachment prevents the President from getting a first-hand feel for a situation, the kind of feel that comes from being face to face with a living, breathing person.

Then there's the ever-present danger that the staff may become more protective of the President and begin to censor ideas coming from the departments and elsewhere outside the White House. It would be only human nature for a staffer, sooner or later, to start supressing proposals he doesn't like or thinks the President may not like.

Mr. Nixon is aware of the danger and seems confident it can be licked. Mr. Kissinger, he says, will not act as a buffer between the President and the departments of State and Defense because Mr. Kissinger, too, recognizes the existence of this potential problem.

Which suggests yet another hazard: An over-reliance on reason. Mr Nixon justifies the Safeguard ABM partly on the ground that it's purely defensive and the Russians know it; thus, he reasons, Moscow won't respond by escalating the arms race. But there may be a question whether the Russians are that logical.

The Presidency: Still Very Private After First Year
DON OBERDORFER

The man rises from behind the polished desk in the Oval Office, his shoulders somewhat stooped, for one last moment fingering the scenario his staff has prepared to tell him who is coming to his office and why, to suggest small talk and specify how and when the meeting is to end. He is withdrawn unto himself, projecting so strong a sense of aloneness that aides are sure they would never break silence even if he were not President of the United States.

His visitors arrive, the scene begins. The shoulders go back. The face brightens. He welcomes them and proceeds with the articulateness which has carried him through two decades of public life. At the signal, the audience is over, and the visitors and aides depart. He is alone again.

Each one of us has, in the poet's phrase, "a face to meet the faces that you meet," but Richard M. Nixon has more faces for the world than most. There are, by popular report, the old Nixon, the new Nixon, the really new Presidential Nixon, the

From *The Washington Post* (January 18, 1970), p. A-1. © The Washington Post. Reprinted by permission.

political Nixon and the private Nixon. Behind them all somewhere is the 5-foot, 11-inch body and resilient, disciplined mind of the Nation's 37th President, who completes his first year in the White House on Tuesday.

The year has revealed a good deal about the policies, politics and tendencies of the Nixon Administration, and a fair amount about the workings of the organizational machinery which surrounds the President. It has revealed precious little about the man at the center of it all.

What is the product of Richard Nixon, and what the product of Nixon Inc., the apparatus which surrounds him? What does he do? What is his role? How does he decide? How has he changed or grown in this year in office?

Unlike most of his modern predecessors in the White House, he does not see journalists except in the conventional public setting of news conferences or other highly restrictive situations, and therefore it is not possible to find the answers directly from him. Few men beyond his inner circle of five or six close associates have detailed knowledge of his work and life habits, and even these men know only in part.

For all the supposedly pitiless publicity of the office and the fluoroscopic probings of the television eye, much about him remains unknown and some perhaps unknowable. He is "a very interior man," one is told. If Lyndon Johnson's was a very personal Presidency, as a student of chief executives has written, Richard Nixon's is in many respects a very private Presidency.

The official utterances of his public relations man, who claimed some time ago that he'd never seen the President upset, gives hardly a clue that the man is irritated to the point of mild profanity when little things go wrong. "What in hell is going on here?" he is reported to have demanded of aides on one occasion. Among the things which have irritated him are trouble with the heating system in the Oval Office, the months of delay in building a new press room over the White House swimming pool, and the persistant failure of White House mess stewards to follow his order to serve him last, not first, at meal and coffee time.

According to intimates, he likes to put his feet on his desk. He likes to chew on the tips of his eyeglasses (which are never seen in public), to chew on pencils, on peanuts, on anything he can find while mulling over difficult problems. They testify that beyond the innermost door of the innermost room, there is flesh and blood.

Those who have seen him at close range say the Presidency in this year has changed Richard Nixon far less than he has changed the Presidency.

Heeding his Inaugural injunction, he has lowered his own voice, literally, in his office. "He can whisper now, and everyone in the room will strain to hear him," said an aide. "He speaks softly."

SAVORING THE VICTORY

The unanimous judgment of friends and associates is that he is more at ease with himself and others than ever before. He worked and maneuvered and planned and ran during all those years to get where he is today, and now that he has arrived he savors the achievement. "The immensity of the fact that you are President of the United States affects you," says one close associate who has seen Presidents come and go. "Wherever you are, you are the centerpiece, and this carries you externally and internally."

By his own choice and on his own instruction, his life as President is programmed, managed and scheduled with meticulous care by a personal staff under Harry Robbins (Bob) Haldeman, the former Los Angeles manager of J. Walter Thompson Advertising Agency, who has been an aide and friend since 1956. Everyone has a tendency to deal with what is on his desk, and Mr. Nixon has instructed Haldeman to make sure that the matters of greatest urgency and importance are put before him in a manner conducive to decisions and management, and to see to it that he has time to consider well what to do.

Dwight Chapin, who was an aide to Haldeman at J. Walter Thompson and now is personal aide to the President, is working on the Presidential schedule four months ahead. The other day Mr. Nixon added some ideas of his own—for events to take place several months from now.

There is an agenda for every meeting and a scenario for every ceremonial occasion. When Mr. Nixon dropped in by helicopter to play golf with Bob Hope in North Hollywood, California, two weeks ago, he bantered before the cameras for a few moments with the comedian, thanking him for his recent Christmas USO tour. Across the continent in Washington, a government official was able to tell a newsman in advance that the President would speak on camera of the importance of GI educational benefits. He did.

Spontaneity is an appealing trait, but in the Presidency careful planning has its uses. Whatever the ultimate effectiveness of Mr. Nixon's foreign and domestic policies, it seems clear that they are more thoroughly planned and methodically processed than the corresponding policies of the previous three administrations.

Much has been said and written of the circle of committees, councils and counsellors that serve as the working parts of his policy-making machine, but most of these reports leave the role of the President unclear. Two recent cases, one in the national security field and one in the domestic field, give some indications of the timing and extent of Mr. Nixon's direct involvement. In each case, he was personally aware of the inception of the study which led to the ultimate decision. In each case, he was presented with written alternatives as the basis for his choice.

Last March, Prof. Matthew Meselson of Harvard University came to see Henry A. Kissinger, Assistant to the President for National Security Affairs, to discuss the issues of chemical and biological warfare. Kissinger knew little about them, but he was well acquainted with the Harvard biologist, and promised to look into the matter. About the same time, Joseph Slater, president of the Salk Institute of La Jolla, California, asked Kissinger about the same topic. A few days later, Secretary of Defense Melvin Laird raised the chemical biological issues with the security adviser.

Kissinger and Laird decided that a thorough review at the presidential level was warranted, and Mr. Nixon informally agreed. Kissinger drafted and the President signed on May 28 a document titled National Security Study Memorandum 59, directing a study of the nature and alternative approaches to chemical and biological warfare.

For the next 5 1/2 months the study went forward in five U.S. agencies—the State and Defense Departments, Central Intelligence and Disarmament Agencies—and in an interagency committee and the White House staff. The President was not involved until mid-November, when a 70-page paper presenting the pros and cons of alternative policies arrived at his office.

PRIVATE WORK AT CAMP DAVID

Mr. Nixon studied the paper and supporting documents in private—he often does such work on weekends at the presidential retreat at Camp David, Maryland—and discussed his questions with Kissinger on November 17, the night before a National Security Council meeting devoted entirely to the subject.

The President made copious notes at the meeting, but did not disclose his thinking. He took notes and documents away with him for further study in private. Three or four days later he informed Kissinger of his decision, which was then drafted into official form as a National Security Decision Memorandum and issued to the agencies involved.

The decision to recommend to Congress a new $3.8 billion merchant shipbuilding program began with a September, 1968, campaign promise to sharply increase the capacity and trade of the U.S. maritime industry. Last March 20, the White House ordered an interagency study of possible programs and approaches.

Six months later, in September of last year, the study group sent Mr. Nixon six pages of background information plus charts for his night reading. That was a sign to him that a final report was drawing near, and on October 17 the nine-page document reached his office.

The study group set out the pros and cons of three alternative policies—a new 30-ship, 10-year construction program with incentives and requirements for the industry; continuation of the present 10-ship program; or continuation of the present construction program with removal of the protective devices which keep U.S. ships in business in foreign trade.

STANDS BY CAMPAIGN PLEDGE

Mr. Nixon called in Peter Flanagan, the White House assistant who supervised the study, for a discussion of the alternatives. Not surprisingly, in view of his campaign commitment, he told aides four days thereafter that "I've decided to go for alternative one." Final polish was given a draft message to Congress, and it was dispatched to Capitol Hill.

Senior assistants in the foreign and domestic policy fields use the same words to describe Mr. Nixon's way of arriving at a difficult decision. "He worries a problem," they say. One of them explains: "He will come at it, back off, come at it from another angle, ask more questions, work it over, reach out for more information and somebody else's thinking."

MITCHELL A KEY ADVISER

In the final stages, he often discusses his thinking with Attorney General John N. Mitchell, his former law partner and 1968 campaign manager and a man in whom Mr. Nixon places unusual confidence and trust. Sometimes aides will get the drift of the President's thinking by his questions. Sometimes he will say which way he is leaning and ask, "What could be wrong with that?"

He expects the personal recommendations of the staff member principally involved before the final decision. According to Haldeman, Mr. Nixon modifies the recommendation of the staff aide about one-third of the time and overrules it completely in about 10 percent of the cases.

He does not "worry" a problem until he feels the time for decision is necessary. Some of the men in the higher reaches of crisis-prone Washington discovered this in dramatic fashion on Saturday, February 22, just a little more than a month after Inauguration Day.

In South Vietnam that day, Communist forces had fired mortars and high-explosive rockets into Saigon and more than 100 other populated areas in the kickoff of a new offensive. Pentagon officials, who received the news through the National Military Command Center, sent word to the White House that they were standing by to brief the President on the military action, in keeping with the standard practice in the Johnson Administration.

Mr. Nixon was in the Oval Office preparing for his first Presidential diplomatic voyage abroad which was to begin the following day. Briefing books for his European trip were spread out on his desk for study, and he was pouring over the handwritten notes he had made on one of his ubiquitous yellow legal pads.

Kissinger interrupted to say that there had been a widespread attack in Vietnam, and that the Secretary of Defense and Chairman of the Joint Chiefs of Staff were standing by to come to the White House.

"Do they want me to make a decision?" the President asked.

"No," Kissinger replied.

"Is there anything I can do about it right now?" asked the President.

Kissinger said not.

"Then I don't want to see them," Mr. Nixon said, returning to his solitary study of the personalities and problems he would meet in Europe.

An associate of Mr. Nixon who sees him often and who has known previous Presidents well says that this chief executive is the least gregarious man to hold the job in 35 years. "He is not cold, but there is a reserve, an introspection in him," says the aide. "He's more of an independent thinker than any of the others," he adds. Mr. Nixon wrote the November 3 speech on Vietnam virtually alone, and against the weight of the advice of most of his principal advisers. Some of them now feel this speech and its impact on public opinion is the President's most important accomplishment in his first year.

Mr. Nixon's penchant for privacy and his liking for working alone extends to his official quarters.

OFFICE ACROSS THE STREET

On his first day in the White House, a year ago this week, Mr. Nixon informed photographers and reporters who'd come for an official picture that he planned to establish a second office in the Executive Office Building across the way and spend considerable time there. The newsmen first thought he must be joking, because they could not conceive of a President leaving the magic and grandeur of the Oval Office for another place.

The second office was established, though, and Mr. Nixon decorated its anteroom with 92 framed cartoons from his vice presidential days, and 19 souvenir gavels. The inner office he decorated with 18 more gavels, 67 souvenir elephant statuettes and one miniature rhinoceros, and 18 photo panels on hinges from his former New York apartment on Fifth Avenue with early pictures of his wife and children and his political travels and a few from recent days. The President spends considerable time there, particularly when he is writing or studying. It is an unwritten but rigidly enforced rule that when he is in the Executive Office Building sanctuary, he is only to be disturbed in case of urgent necessity.

From someplace in the 1600 Pennsylvania Avenue complex—the bedroom, the Lincoln sitting room in the family quarters, the Oval Office, the Executive Office Building or perhaps from some other private place not yet discovered—emanates most nights a steady stream of ideas and directions, inscribed in large, clear script on yellow legal pads or in the margins of government memoranda.

Many are one-line items that can set in motion a train of study and consideration involving numerous aides. "Within three weeks, submit a proposal for strengthening the consumer efforts," said a recent one-liner. It was duly noted and assigned.

James Keogh, a former Time Inc. executive who heads the speech-writing staff, said some time ago that Mr. Nixon is extraordinarily work-oriented: "when he rests, he's resting to work; when he reads, he's reading to work; when he's relaxing, he's relaxing to prepare himself for work." Except during the trips to his vacation villas at Key Biscayne, Florida, and San Clemente, California, Mr. Nixon does an hour or two of work after 8 p.m. almost every night. Newsmen permitted to tour the new Nixon home at San Clemente noticed that there is a desk for work in the President's bedroom, in addition to a study upstairs and a full-blown Presidential office in the U.S. Coast Guard compound next door.

FAMILY AND SPORTS EVENTS

Mr. Nixon's main interests outside his job and politics are his family and sports events. Only a few people beyond his inner circle spend enough time with him to explore the turn of his mind, but one group which did so during this first year came away dismayed by what was thought to be a lack of broad interest. He was like a light-bulb computer, one of them said later, which would idle and hum until something of particular interest activated it. The bulb would go on and the computer would work, swallowing facts and spewing out answers, until it tired of the subject. The light would go out, and the computer would idle again.

His personal and official interest has often been piqued by problems he can relate to his own life. One such incident began one afternoon late last summer when Mr. Nixon looked down from a White House bound helicopter and saw the main Navy and Munitions Buildings on the Mall. "Why are those buildings still there? Why haven't they come down?" he asked John Ehrlichman, his chief assistant for domestic affairs. The structures were placed there as "temporary buildings" in World War I. Mr. Nixon worked there as a young Naval officer in World War II.

A study was begun on August 8, and an order was transmitted through Col. Don Hughes, the Presidential military aide, that the buildings must be removed. The Navy and General Services Administration worked out a plan under which the buildings are to be razed and the land seeded for use as a park by the end of 1970. The program was announced by the White House last month.

A YEAR OF PREPARATION

Beyond the scan of his eye and the orbit of the places that he knows, there are abundant indications that one year is a very limited time. This year has largely been spent in attempting to turn around unfavorable trends or situations, to propose governmental reforms and to lay foundation stones of future positive efforts.

Nixon Staff Had Central Role in Missile Decision
ROBERT B. SEMPLE, JR.

WASHINGTON, March 18. Despite the public furor that swirled about him, President Nixon relied largely on the private channels of government, particularly the machinery of his National Security Council, to reach his decision to deploy a limited antiballistic missile system.

Although he instructed his aides to seek out all sides of the argument, the President appears to have had little direct contact with opponents or advocates of the missile system outside his own circle.

He saw few Senators, and even fewer scientists. He appears not to have

From *The New York Times* (March 19, 1969), p. 22. © 1969 by The New York Times Company. Reprinted by permission.

consulted widely with old companions, as President Johnson had a habit of doing, or with friends in the universities, as President Kennedy did.

He substituted for the more informal and less systematic decision-making processes of his predecessors a controlled but intense dialogue limited to his own staff and principal foreign policy advisers.

INTERNALIZED DEBATE

So internalized was the debate that what the White House described as the "most brilliant" argument yet produced against deployment was written by a staff member on Henry A. Kissinger's National Security Council—as a Socratic exercise.

The way Mr. Nixon arrived at his decision to employ the "Safeguard" system—which may tell much about the way he is likely to arrive at other decisions in the future—emerged today in interviews with high-ranking Government officials who witnessed the process at close range.

These interviews also disclosed at least three other little known aspects of the decision:

1. There were two major decisions, not one. The first decision, described as the important "conceptual" decision, was reached over the weekend of March 7-8 in Key Biscayne, Florida, where the President made up his mind to move ahead with a modified Sentinel system concentrating on protection of the country's capacity to strike back after a nuclear attack.

SPEED OF CONSTRUCTION

The second decision, largely tactical occurred after the President's return to the capital March 10. This decision involved the speed with which the system would be constructed, which had not been resolved in Key Biscayne.

It was the complexity of this second decision that, in part, delayed the President's final announcement until Friday, March 14, several days later than he had promised.

2. David R. Packard, Deputy Secretary of Defense, played at least as prominent a role in the process as his chief, Defense Secretary Melvin R. Laird. Mr. Packard not only heavily influenced the decision to move ahead with the system, but also helped decide how quickly and in what manner deployment would proceed.

Other major participants were Mr. Kissinger, who organized and stabilized the process; Secretary of State William P. Rogers; Under Secretary of State Elliot Z. Richardson; and Gerard C. Smith, director of the Arms Control and Disarmament Agency. The final decision was Mr. Nixon's alone.

3. As portrayed in these interviews, Mr. Nixon, in the weeks leading up to a decision, was deeply preoccupied with the diplomatic consequences of deployment—its impact on the Russians, on East-West relations, on the arms race—and reviewed each option before him with these questions uppermost in his mind.

SOVIET THREAT WEIGHED

Military considerations, particularly his reading of the Soviet threat, dictated his final decision to deploy, but diplomatic considerations—his desire not to "provoke" a further arms race or destroy all chances of Soviet-American cooperation on international questions—did the most to determine the shape of that decision.

He was not, of course, unmindful of the fierce debate on Capitol Hill, and there are those here who argue that his final decision was tailored in large part to meet the objections of his critics.

But those who witnessed the process insist that this was at best a secondary influence, and that his judgment of Soviet intentions and possible Soviet reactions was far more compelling.

The process began shortly after Mr. Nixon's inauguration January 20, when Mr. Laird placed Mr. Packard in charge of two major studies: an over-all military budget review and a general assessment of the country's strategic posture.

ROLE OF PACKARD

The studies forced Mr. Packard to come to grips with the question of the antiballistic missile system: Should the Administration proceed with the $1.8-billion Sentinel system inherited from Mr. Johnson, should it adopt another approach, or should it junk the system?

Mr. Packard held conferences nearly every day for four weeks, usually with Dr. John Foster, the Pentagon's director of research and engineering, and Dr. Ivan Selin, acting Assistant Secretary of Defense for Systems Analysis.

One of Mr. Kissinger's band of bright young men at the National Security Council, Laurence Lynn, a former Defense Department official, joined the meetings on a regular basis. Mr. Lynn was later to play an even larger role.

PRESIDENT'S OPTIONS

On February 20, a few days before Mr. Nixon left for his European tour, Mr. Packard, representing the Defense Department, presented what he felt were the major options available to the President:

- A "thick" system, long advocated by the Joint Chiefs of Staff, which called for a combination of long- and short-range missiles to defend the 25 largest cities.
- The Sentinel, or "thin," system inherited from the Johnson Administration, under which a somewhat lighter shield would be provided for about 15 urban areas.
- A modified Sentinel system, later to be known at the Pentagon as Plan 1-69, which would use roughly the same weaponry as the Sentinel but would move it from the cities and deploy it around Minuteman bases and other segments of the country's second-strike retaliatory force.
- No system at all.

FURTHER STUDY ORDERED

Mr. Packard made no recommendations. Mr. Nixon asked for further studies on each of the four options from Mr. Packard and told him to seek advice on the diplomatic consequences of each from the State Department.

Mr. Kissinger, meanwhile, asked Mr. Lynn to embark on a special and unusual project. He was, with Mr. Packard, to help lay out the options; but he was also to begin writing papers containing the best possible arguments he could devise against each of the options, particularly the 1-69.

Although preoccupied with the forthcoming European tour, Mr. Kissinger, who some weeks earlier had started consulting with groups of scientists, asked some of his friends in Cambridge, Massachusetts, to provide him with several papers on the technical feasibility of the project and to give him a reading of the sentiment among the scientific community at Harvard University and the Massachusetts Institute of Technology.

Mr. Nixon left for Europe at dawn February 23. The antimissile decision was never far from his thoughts or those of Mr. Rogers and Mr. Kissinger, who accompanied him. The three men talked about it whenever they could take time from the ceremonial duties and substantive requirements of the trip. Nixon constantly questioned his companions for their assessment of how the Soviet Union would regard a decision to proceed with some sort of deployment, particularly the system known in the Pentagon as 1-69.

The President did not then seem close to a decision. Long impressed by what he regarded as the rapid build-up of the Soviet Union's offensive capacity, as well as Russia's deployment of more than 60 antiballistic missile sites of its own, he leaned toward deployment as a means of restoring balance to the system of mutual deterrence, which had served for years as a shield against unilateral attack.

The 1-69 system attracted him because it was designed in part to protect second-strike capacity and thus stood the best chance of being construed by the Soviet Union as a defensive, stabilizing move rather than an offensive, and potentially provocative, gesture. But his mind was far from certain.

NIXON PROMISES DECISION

Mr. Nixon returned the night of March 2. On March 4, at a news conference, he said he would announce a decision on the Sentinel at the "first" of the following week, which was taken to mean either the 10th or 11th.

The next day, the National Security Council convened. Mr. Packard again reviewed the options, but this time he came down firmly on the side of the 1-69—moving Lyndon Johnson's Sentinel defense from the cities to the bases.

His arguments reflected some of Mr. Nixon's own private thoughts: Such a system would protect the deterrent against the Soviet Union's known offensive capacity and defuse some of the opposition building up among citizens of the cities themselves.

At the same time, if properly interpreted by the Soviet Union, it would not be sufficiently provocative to trigger a new round of arms escalation or deter arms control agreements.

Mr. Packard and Mr. Kissinger agreed to draft the "rationale" for the 1-69—that is, to set forth on paper the arguments that, until then, had been best expressed orally.

The next day, having added his endorsement to Mr. Packard's for a redesigned Sentinel system, Mr. Laird left for Vietnam. Gerard Smith, the arms control director, who had attended the National Security Council meeting, testified on Capitol Hill that a "thin" system might in fact accelerate arms control by giving the United States something to bargain with. Mr. Nixon prepared to fly to Key Biscayne for the weekend.

On Friday morning, March 7, three prominent Republican Senators—Jacob K. Javits of New York, Charles H. Percy of Illinois and John Sherman Cooper of Kentucky—went to the White House to see Mr. Kissinger.

Synthesizing much of the opposition that had been boiling up all week on Capitol Hill, they argued vigorously against development pointing to what they regarded as a number of technological, political and diplomatic defects.

When they left, Mr. Kissinger wrote out a summary of their views, which he promptly incorporated into a 40-page briefing book, which he had prepared for the President's weekend reading in Key Biscayne.

The 40-page briefing book was a special product. For weeks, Mr. Kissinger had been furnishing the President on a daily basis with 8-page to 10-page summaries of arguments pro and con the antiballistic missile system.

The 40-page compendium, however, included not only a concise summary of the major arguments so far, but a review of the principal options originally presented by Mr. Packard, Mr. Lynn's paper opposing the modified Sentinel plan and the arguments of the three Republican senators.

Mr. Nixon took it to Key Biscayne and read it over the weekend. Sometime that weekend he made his decision to proceed with the modified Sentinel.

He summoned Mr. Kissinger to Key Biscayne on Monday, and the two men began to hammer out the specifics of the proposal the President would announce to the nation and eventually recommend to Congress.

SECOND STAGE BEGINS

These conversations represented the start of the second stage of the decision-making process. Mr. Nixon had intended to announce his decision shortly after his return, but it had become clear to both men that the implementation of the system would be as important as the theory behind it.

The theory—to defend the country's second strike capacity without unnecessarily provoking the Soviet Union—had been ratified by the President's decision. But the question was how those aims could be most efficiently and safely achieved.

When he returned to Washington with the President Monday night, Mr. Kissinger requested opinions from the Departments of Defense and State and the arms control agency. He then joined Mr. Foster, Mr. Packard and Mr. Richardson in yet another "review of the options."

There were, they agreed, four ways in which defense could be deployed at the bases:

First, the Johnson Sentinel system could be packaged and moved from the cities to the bases, at a cost of $1.8-billion in fiscal 1970.

Second, the Johnson system could be deployed at the bases starting next spring, which would reduce the fiscal year cost to $1.1-billion.

The major problem with both choices, they agreed, was that they required simultaneous starts on 12 to 15 sites—thereby "locking the Administration in" to a rather sizable expenditure of funds and reducing its flexibility to expand or reduce the system depending on other developments, such as progress in arms control talks with the Soviet Union.

A third option was to proceed with research and development for another year. This was, in the words of one participant, "the most politically attractive option."

It had been urged on Mr. Kissinger by some of his friends in the academic community and had been urged on Mr. Nixon by many in Congress.

This option was rejected for two reasons. Despite the unfavorable scientific testimony on Capitol Hill, the Administration had concluded that it "had come to the end of the R. & D. road," and that further technological improvements would be reached only if tests could be carried out at actual sites.

The President and his advisers were also persuaded that to delay decision by a year would delay actual deployment by more than two years, since most of the existing technical staff would scatter to other jobs.

So they chose option four—a phased system of deployment. The system would eventually call for 12 sites, but Mr. Nixon would ask only for $800-million to $900-million to begin work at two of them and to continue research and development, subjecting the other ten sites to annual review.

The idea for the phased system, agreed upon Wednesday, was largely Mr. Packard's invention.

STATEMENT DRAFTED

On Wednesday night, Mr. Kissinger and a few of the others began drafting the statement Mr. Nixon would deliver Friday.

Thursday, the President cleared his schedule. Every line of the statement was reviewed, and every decision made along the way was re-examined. Some insertions were made, most notably the pledge that every year the President's Foreign Intelligence Advisory Board would review the need—if any—for further deployment of the system.

This pledge had an interesting history. Two days earlier, on Tuesday night, three distinguished scientists, all opponents of deployment, had come to see Mr. Kissinger.

One of them, Dr. James Killian of M.I.T., urged the Administration to withhold deployment pending a review by an independent council of distinguished private citizens of the country's strategic requirements.

Mr. Kissinger transmitted their thoughts to the President later that night. Mr. Nixon was particularly struck by the Killian suggestion.

He felt that to turn over to a private group the function of reviewing the nation's strategic requirements would be an abdication of executive responsibility. However, he liked the idea of having such a group contribute an annual assessment of the country's requirements, including particularly the usefulness of the antimissile system itself, to supplement the Government's own intelligence resources.

Thus at least part of Dr. Killian's message crept into the final presentation.

Presidential Isolation Is Part of the Job
JOHN PIERSON

WASHINGTON. By now, thousands of words have been written about President Nixon's apparent isolation from Cabinet, Congress, the young, the black, the press and all but a few of the White House inner circle.

And by now, the official denials have been issued. White House Chief of Staff Bob Haldeman calls Mr. Nixon the "most unisolated" President in recent times and insists he's in "far closer touch than the little group (of journalists) who selected 'isolation of the President' as this week's password."

To clinch the point, Mr. Nixon has taken part in a spate of well-publicized meetings with some of the very people he has been accused of ignoring.

Many of the critics have focused on the personality of Richard Nixon. To them, he's a loner and an introvert, surrounded by a few trusty subordinates who have orders to guard the door to the Oval Office and keep people out.

COMPLEX CONDITIONS

Undoubtedly there's some truth to this. Mr. Nixon is, as an aide once put it, "a very interior guy." But in pointing the finger at the man in the Oval Office, the critics may be missing more basic causes of Presidential isolation nowadays. Perhaps it comes, in large measure, from the chaos and complexity of the modern world—wars, assassinations, wealth amid poverty, the birth rate, race, pollution—and from the ways in which the Presidency has had to evolve to deal with these conditions.

From *The Wall Street Journal* (June 5, 1970), p. 1. Reprinted by permission.

A simple example is the security of the President. The Secret Service and the White House police have more than doubled their manpower since Dallas and will more than triple their numbers by the time of the 1972 election. Protests have made it increasingly hard for the President and his family to move freely about the country. And now the Government is considering banning demonstrations within a block of the White House.

Perhaps these measures are needed to safeguard the life of the President. But they also deny him the kind of personal contact with the people that most politicians claim they need to maintain "a feel" for the public's mood.

Beyond a feel for things, a President needs good hard information. Any President who wants to tackle today's chaotic world must develop some orderly means of getting the facts essential for decision-making. People criticized President Johnson because he conducted his Presidency on the run. When did he ever have time to think?

Mr. Nixon is doing things differently, not only because he's a different personality and wants to draw a politically useful contrast between himself and LBJ, but also because he figures the times require well-ordered White House machinery. The elaborate staff system that distills the issues for Mr. Nixon and carries out his orders is frankly the envy of many a former White House staffer, including some Kennedy and Johnson liberals who believe in a strong executive.

The White House staff has been accused of shielding Mr. Nixon from reality. Critics argue that at least the President could hire men of different backgrounds and philosophies from his own, to provide him with fresh insights and responses to the world.

REALISM ON DISSENTERS

But how realistic is it to expect a President to surround himself with dissenters, particularly in embattled times like the present? Mr. Haldeman, John Ehrlichman and Henry Kissinger are sitting at the right hand of power today because Mr. Nixon feels comfortable with them. He feels comfortable with them because they see the world much as he does.

Daniel Moynihan, counselor to the President, is no longer so important in the White House scheme of things because he was a poor administrator and, one suspects, because the colorful, gabby Mr. Moynihan just isn't Richard Nixon's kind of guy.

The Cabinet is another group that could help Mr. Nixon see the world through different eyes. But the Cabinet represents a dozen interests, each competing for the President's ear and for the Federal budget pie.

Since the President himself can't possibly umpire every dispute, he has to have umpires around him who see the world the way he does. Interior Secretary Hickel resents having seen Mr. Nixon alone only twice since the inauguration. But Mr. Nixon wants staff members to sit in—to take notes and follow up on decisions and then to indicate when his Cabinet man is throwing him a curve.

Like Cabinet men, students who would prefer to see the President himself usually end up seeing an underling. It's hard to argue with the White House view that most students either don't know what it is they want, or if they do, are incapable of articulating it. So rather than waste hours in probably fruitless bull sessions, Mr. Nixon asks his staff to meet with the young people and then draft a memo for him.

The trouble with a memo is that it fails to convey either the passion of the young or the depth of their disenchantment with "the system." As for their program, if it's "Get out of Vietnam," the President agrees on the goal but not on the means. If it's "Love one another," the President is at a loss about how to apply it.

Presidential consultation with Congress is fine in theory, but in foreign policy the need for secrecy often makes it difficult or impossible for the Chief Executive to consult. President Kennedy couldn't go gabbing about the Russian missiles in Cuba before he was ready to act. Had Mr. Nixon asked Sen. Fulbright whether he should invade Cambodia, the chairman of the Foreign Relations Committee probably would have said "no." Had the President stayed to debate the point, even the rice and the bombs would have been gone by the time the GIs got to the sanctuaries.

And Congressmen, like Cabinet secretaries, have their own competing and parochial interests that make it hard for them to look at the big picture. Often when Mr. Nixon has had a group in for a talk, White House staffers complain, the men from Capitol Hill just want to talk about their pet projects—dams or post offices.

Further, when the President consults with one Senator, another may get jealous. And when a group comes in, the large number makes it difficult to have any real give-and-take.

Frequent contact with the press can provide a President with a window on the world, but here again the needs of a modern Presidency get in the way. Mr. Nixon has cut his press conferences, interviews and other contacts with reporters to a bare minimum, preferring to take important matters directly to the people on TV.

In defense of Mr. Nixon's downgrading of press encounters, the White House points to the extensive news summary that goes to him each morning. Pat Buchanan, a highly conservative aide, prepares it, and while everyone swears to its fairness, there's no way of telling, since the summary is "for the President's eyes only."

Anyway, it would be asking a lot of Mr. Nixon to spend much time with a press corps that he regards as basically hostile, particularly when he has another means of getting to the people. And in this day, even a President who gets along well with reporters is likely to emphasize TV.

IT WOULD BE NICE, BUT . . .

It would be nice if the world were such a quiet place that Presidents could spend their days in leisurely conversation with Cabinet, Congress, students and the press— and particularly with dissenters from national policies. But the world isn't that way. Despite attempts at long-range planning, contemporary government seems more like crisis management, which leaves little time for leisurely conversation with anyone.

Some people would try to prevent isolation of the President by changing Richard Nixon or by making the Presidency a sort of philosopher kingship. Perhaps it would make more sense first to try to reform Congress and organize the students and other groups to provide more effective opposition to the White House. If they were strong and effective, the President would have to consult with them more seriously.

Meanwhile, a little progress on some of the world's most dreadful problems, particularly the arms race, could lessen the need for a powerful and secretive Presidency. And it might give the President and everyone else a little more time to talk to each other.

The Scorecard: President's Cabinet Gets Mixed Reviews for Efforts to Date
ALAN L. OTTEN

WASHINGTON. Independent and creative thinkers. Generalists and broad-gauge advisers. Outstanding men to supply that extra dimension of leadership. Good team players.

Thus Richard Nixon described his ideal Cabinet in speeches during the 1968 campaign and the actual choices he presented to the U.S. television audience in December of 1968. Now, more than two and a half years later and with a few new faces in the lineup, how does Mr. Nixon's Cabinet measure up to his ideals?

A dozen reporters in The Wall Street Journal's Washington bureau put this question to scores of people who deal intimately with members of the Cabinet—to White House officials, bureaucrats, Senators, Congressmen and spokesmen for private interest groups. Their clear consensus:

- Mr. Nixon does indeed have loyal team players. Again and again, each Cabinet man is described as a "good soldier" who faithfully lobbies for the President's program even when it goes against his grain. The one nonteam player, former Interior Secretary Walter Hickel, got cut from the squad.
- The Nixon choices, for the most part, are doing a pretty fair job of congressional relations and of running their own departments.
- But almost all the Cabinet members fall far short of being broadly influential presidential counselors. "If I want to find out policy," says one outsider, "I go to the White House. That's where policy is made. The men who count are the Ehrlichmans and Kissingers—not the Cabinet."
- Within the Cabinet, Treasury Secretary John Connally and Attorney General John Mitchell stand out as the strong men, though Mr. Mitchell is increasingly preoccupied with the 1972 campaign rather than current government policy. On a

From *The Wall Street Journal* (September 8, 1971), p. 1. Reprinted by permission.

second level of importance come Defense Secretary Melvin Laird, Health, Education and Welfare Secretary Elliot Richardson, and Secretary of State William Rogers, with the other Cabinet members strung out well behind.

PRESIDENTIAL NEGLECT

A few specific judgments: Mr. Richardson and Interior Secretary Rogers Morton are doing a good job of repairing the departmental damage and disarray left by their predecessors—Robert Finch and Mr. Hickel—though Mr. Richardson's image is being tarnished by the controversy over whether he does or doesn't agree with the President's school-busing policy. Mr. Rogers is highly effective when he zeroes in on a subject, but he doesn't do that often enough. Labor Secretary James Hodgson has to fight to get out from under the shadow of predecessor George Shultz. Agriculture Secretary Clifford Hardin is no great shakes, but, as one GOP lawmaker asks, "Who could they get better to take that lousy job?"

Despite his campaign talk, Mr. Nixon continues the traditional neglect of the Cabinet as any sort of broad, policy-making or advisory group. Cabinet meetings not only are infrequent but also when they do occur they are usually briefing sessions or pep rallies rather than decision-shaping sessions. Significantly, at last month's Camp David planning session for the President's new economic policy, Mr. Connally was the only departmental chief present: the other decision-shapers were presidential assistants, budget chiefs and members of the Council of Economic Advisers.

"It's a very sad Cabinet," says one relatively objective House Democrat. "The whole executive apparatus is organized around key advisers in the White House."

The downgrading of the Cabinet springs from many factors: the shortcomings of some members; the expansion in the size of the Cabinet that has made it an unwieldy discussion group; the departmental demands that leave Cabinet officers little time to stay abreast of policy problems outside their own areas; the physical proximity, ideological identity and close personal ties between the President and most of his White House crew.

MANY CRITERIA

Like his most recent predecessors, Mr. Nixon has given Cabinet rank to a number of people in addition to the secretaries of the 11 departments—to men including presidential counselors Robert Finch and Donald Rumsfeld and Budget and Management Chief George Shultz. The Journal survey, however, centers on the 11 department heads, seven of whom are the original Nixon nominees.

Any appraisal of a Cabinet member must be made from several, often clashing, perspectives—how much influence he has with the President and how much impact on administration policy; how well he carries out that policy; whether he's an effective spokesman for the administration; whether he runs his department well; how good his relations with Congress are. There's also the fundamental question of how well he serves the public, which may or may not be the same as how well he serves the President.

From these various viewpoints, here are the capital's thumbnail verdicts, inevitably oversimplified, on the performance of each Cabinet member:

CONNALLY

The newest member, Treasury Secretary Connally has rapidly emerged as the Cabinet superstar. The speculation that he may be the President's running-mate in 1972 results from this stellar stature and simultaneously enhances it further.

The Secretary's preeminence is due only in part to his role in helping persuade the President to change economic course and in administering the new policy. Even before that, he had established himself as fast to learn, incisive, self-confident—able to put overweening White House aides promptly in their place; able to sell key Congressmen on administration proposals with strong public testimony and persuasive follow-up calls and visits; able to excite his own bureaucrats by snapping up their ideas and pushing them at the White House. The staff, says one Treasury man, "regards him with a mixture of admiration and fear."

If the new economic policy works well, Mr. Connally's stock will soar higher, though there are some onlookers who think he's almost bound to suffer reverses in coming months, and a few around town (not all of them Democrats) who even hope he will.

MITCHELL

Despite Mr. Connally's surge, the taciturn, pipe-smoking Attorney General is still as powerful and close to the President as ever—and that's very close and very powerful. He remains a key adviser and confidant on many issues. Though he insists he would prefer to remain at the Justice Department, Mr. Mitchell will probably leave there later this year to manage Mr. Nixon's election campaign, as he did in 1968.

As Attorney General, Mr. Mitchell has diligently promoted Nixon law-and-order policies. He has maintained close ties with Chief Justice Warren Burger and FBI Chief J. Edgar Hoover, and he has been careful to confine his congressional appearances mostly to friendly forums.

Some lawmakers—members of the House Judiciary Committee, for example—complain that Mr. Mitchell ignores them. "We just don't hear from Mr. Mitchell or his top people," a key House Democrat charges. "There's a vacuum. They send up bills, but they don't push them. I don't think they're very interested in legislation."

Mr. Mitchell is not liked by civil-rights and other liberal groups, but he doesn't appear upset by this. From time to time, he has clamped down on activists in his department's antitrust and civil-rights divisions, and this has occasionally given an image of departmental dissension. The Attorney General's close relationship with the President has enabled him to survive setbacks, notably the Senate's rejection of two Mitchell-researched Supreme Court nominees, that probably would have cost another man his job.

ROGERS

The Secretary of State doesn't set foreign policy. More than most Presidents, Mr. Nixon does this himself. But surprisingly often, Mr. Rogers doesn't even play a major role in helping the President set policy, even in so critical an area as Vietnam. When the Secretary does get involved—on Mideast or China policy, for example—he usually comes off well; he is, after all, an old and close friend of the President. But aides still puzzle over how rarely he chooses to exert influence.

On most matters, he appears willing to leave the shaping of departmental positions to under secretaries, assistant secretaries and committees; these positions are forwarded to the White House rather routinely, permitting Nixon lieutenant Henry Kissinger to take it from there and emerge as the chief influence on the President on foreign-policy matters.

A courteous and friendly fellow, Mr. Rogers has been most adroit in dealing with foreign diplomats and Congress. Despite deep policy differences, he has managed to muffle the complaints of such prickly lawmakers as William Fulbright, chairman of the Senate Foreign Relations Committee. White House men fault Mr. Rogers for not doing more to shake up the State Department bureaucracy, but White House men always voice this complaint against Secretaries of State.

In the two policy areas he has concentrated on, Mr. Rogers has had considerable success. From the start, he pushed the President toward better relations with mainland China, though Mr. Nixon probably leaned that way already. Mr. Rogers' cool, common-sense lawyer's approach has kept the two sides in the Mideast talking longer than most people expected; at a minimum, he has delayed the start of a new war, and at the most he might achieve a permanent Arab-Israeli settlement.

LAIRD

The Defense Secretary is inevitably compared with his once widely admired predecessor, Robert McNamara, and in the eyes of many insiders Mr. Laird comes off well—perhaps not as glamorous but with a much shrewder sense of the political and institutional realities. A long-time congressional buddy of Mr. Nixon, he has the President's ear whenever he needs it; awareness of this association helps him in intra- and inter-departmental battles.

Mr. Laird has skillfully managed to walk a tightrope between military leaders and congressional hawks on one side and congressional doves and budget-cutters on the other. He has been a strong advocate of accelerated withdrawal from Vietnam. Despite long congressional advocacy of military strength, he moved early in his Pentagon tenure to cut military manpower and armaments, and he managed to avoid any violent backlash from military and conservative groups. Now he is moving to rebuild military strength, and he appears to have minimized liberal opposition in Congress.

The military chiefs applaud his willingness to listen to them and his downgrading of the McNamara "whiz kids" and their computerized cost-benefit analyses; "I think the military-civilian relationship has improved," declares Admiral Thomas Moorer, chairman of the Joint Chiefs of Staff. "I think the military input is given fair and serious consideration." Goodwill like this has enabled Mr. Laird to win the military over to some previously opposed projects, such as the all-volunteer Army.

RICHARDSON

Elliot Richardson took over at HEW when the department appeared foundering and demoralized, and until recently he seemed well on the way to rebuilding its influence and esprit. Brilliant and coolly competent, he has avoided predecessor Finch's mistakes of making large public promises and instead has concentrated on running the department and working with Congress.

He has improved department morale by being willing to listen to and adopt aides' ideas; this has, in turn, made some of them a little more willing to listen to the Secretary. He has impressed lawmakers with his availability, grasp of detail, and decisiveness. House Labor Committee Chairman Carl Perkins of Kentucky, no easy man to deal with, says, "He's the most outstanding administrator I've ever had any contact with in that department since I've been in Congress."

Though a liberal Republican, Mr. Richardson is respected by more conservative White House men as a political pragmatist able to compromise. He has persuaded the President, over budget officials' objections, to provide extra funds for health and education programs, but he is staunchly supporting the President on a school busing policy obviously designed to satisfy conservatives. Mr. Richardson's support of this policy inevitably seems to many Washingtonians to be a sellout of his liberal principles, and this could in time erode the respect and cooperation he has had from his own bureaucrats, liberal lawmakers and outside interest groups.

Education associations and other HEW constituent groups have until now generally taken the line that "he's doing the best job we can expect in this lousy administration." Weak points: He can easily appear arrogant or condescending; his speeches and press conferences tend to be pedantic; his record of legislative accomplishment isn't impressive and could be downright dismal if welfare reform is ditched.

STANS

If President Nixon wants a Commerce Secretary who espouses a conservative, business-oriented point of view, he has him in Maurice Stans. Mr. Stans has filled this role—fighting to relax proposed consumer legislation and pollution controls and auto-insurance regulation—with a determination often greater than that of businessmen themselves. This has estranged not only liberal public-interest groups and liberal lawmakers but even some administration colleagues. "He's bad news," growls one. "The only bright spot is that he doesn't win many of his fights."

And, in fact, despite long political association with the President and close ties with several White House aides, Mr. Stans is not one of the more influential Cabinet members. He doesn't play any substantial role in formulating economic policy. Fairly or unfairly, he's blamed for having botched negotiations with Japan some months ago for a new treaty to limit textile imports.

His White House entree and his willingness to speak out on tough issues have, nonetheless, given some small boost to morale in the Commerce Department, long one of the more placid backwaters of government. Though warned he would touch off angry controversy, for example, Mr. Stans boldly went ahead with far-reaching recommendations for U.S. conversion to the metric system.

HODGSON

A basic problem faced by Labor Secretary James Hodgson is that predecessor George Shultz remains in government as head of the Office of Management and Budget and remains one of the President's most trusted advisers. Almost inevitably, Mr. Shultz speaks out on labor policy from time to time as though he were still secretary, and the White House often tends to view him that way. "How come Mr. Hodgson wasn't at the Camp David meeting?" a reporter asked one White House man. "Why should he be there?" came the reply. "George Shultz was there."

And friendly, low-keyed Jim Hodgson seems content to let this impression persist and to exercise influence at the White House how and when he can.

His relations with organized labor have never been easy. Formerly a Lockheed labor relations executive, he was suspect to union chiefs from the start, and his White-House-ordered blast at AFL-CIO President George Meany last month didn't help matters. About all union officials will concede is that he has made good use of Assistant Secretary W. J. Usery Jr., a union man, to work with labor chiefs. Mr. Hodgson's congressional relations could be better, too; many lawmakers complain he ignores them. Rep. James O'Hara of Michigan, a senior House Labor Committee Democrat, sarcastically says, "I don't think I've really met the man. He's been around to testify a few times, but that's the extent of it."

ROMNEY

George Romney, the Housing and Urban Development Secretary, enjoys the strengths and suffers the weaknesses of the zealot he tends to be on many issues. He usually says what's on his mind, however impolitic, and if he loses a battle he finds it hard to make it appear that he won. He gets careless with details, and frequently he seems ill-informed. Occasionally he's naive; "he gets converted too easily by his own bureaucracy," a White House man complains. "He hurt himself and the administration by his zeal in pushing integrated housing in the suburbs."

But Mr. Romney's passion keeps in there pitching when a less-driven bureaucrat would give up. Partly because of his perseverance, production of subsidized housing is beginning to increase rapidly, and despite the administration's coolness, some of it is even going outside the city limits.

Members of Congress who deal with the HUD Secretary give him good marks. "He's very impressive," says liberal Democrat Henry Reuss of Wisconsin. "He fights hard for his programs, and while he may get overruled, he usually gets something out of it." Urban officials agree. "He gets along well with the mayors," one of their spokesmen reports. "He's open, and they're convinced he tries for them even when the odds are against him."

VOLPE

Though no presidential intimate, Transportation Secretary John Volpe is applauded at the White House as a team player. For example, after the White House watered down his department's bill for tough auto-insurance regulation, Mr. Volpe loyally urged Capitol Hill to enact the White House approach. Last fall he made speeches for the GOP Senate candidate in Indiana even though he knew that Democratic Sen. Vance Hartke, if reelected, would head the Senate Commerce subcommittee on surface transportation and would give him an extra-rough time.

Mr. Volpe has successfully backed creation of a new corporation to run passenger trains and a sizable expansion of federal funds for mass transit. He has been willing to take on hard fights, too—challenging supporters of highways by stopping road projects on environmental grounds and dipping into the highway trust fund for auto-safety work.

But some White House men complain that the department's projects are often late in emerging and sloppy in detail. More important, a few criticize Mr. Volpe for failing to do more than he has to cut back outmoded types of transportation and stimulate new ones.

HARDIN

"I don't know if you could put God in that job and have him look good after two and a half years," one White House man says, and that's a pretty typical reaction to Mr. Hardin's performance as Secretary of Agriculture. Most observers agree that he isn't as decisive as he might be, that he has had difficulty running his sprawling department, that he isn't a particularly forceful farm spokesman and that he hasn't developed any particular clout at the White House or with Congress.

They also say, however, that his low profile has kept him less controversial than Ezra Taft Benson and Orville Freeman were at comparable points in their careers. "When the farmers are as upset over prices and income as they have been recently, being noncontroversial is in itself quite an accomplishment," a colleague contends.

MORTON

Mr. Morton, a former Maryland congressman, is an unusually personable and knowledgeable politician. Since taking over as Interior Secretary in late January, he has set out to clear away some of the debris left by Walter Hickel's abrupt departure. He has restored traditional lines of communication within the department, and morale there seems to have lifted with the assurance that the agency has a boss in good standing at the White House. He has worked hard at cementing relations with his old congressional colleagues; Rep. Julia Hansen, the shrewd, tough lady from Washington who bosses the House Appropriations subcommittee on the Interior Department, says, "I'm tremendously pleased with the way he has taken hold of the department and the way he's working very closely with us."

What isn't clear yet is just where Mr. Morton will come out on the big issues. Though he has given the impression of strong leadership, he has straddled most of the industry-environmental conflicts that boobytrap his bailiwick.

He can't keep that up much longer, however, and environmentalists fear he'll come down most of the time on the side of economic development; that would almost certainly mean trouble for him on Capitol Hill.

"He may have the same difficulty at Interior that he had as National Republican

Chairman," worries one long-time acquaintance. "His nature is to want to be the good guy, the guy everybody likes, and he may have a very hard time making some of the tough decisions."

Nixon's Top Command: Expanding in Size and Power
U.S. NEWS & WORLD REPORT

When Richard Nixon became President in 1969, he made clear his belief that he could operate with a relatively small White House staff.

The theory then was that policy ideas would spring mostly from the Cabinet. As Mr. Nixon saw it, presidential assistants would serve as co-ordinators—rather than formulators—of national aims and actions.

Things have not worked out that way.

In a little more than three years, the White House staff has grown greatly in size and even more in cost . . . . It is now the largest in history and is increasing almost daily.

In policy making, the role of the Cabinet has declined, while the role of the White House staff has expanded.

More than ever before, the reins of power over the entire executive branch are now firmly held in the White House.

What caused the change in the President's operational plan?

One answer given is that it has been necessary to build a whole new layer of control in order for President Nixon to gain mastery over the sprawling federal bureaucracy.

SADDLING A BEHEMOTH

An insider spells it out this way:

> Nixon inherited a vast bureaucracy, which included some incompetents, some partisan political holdovers from previous Administrations, some with long-standing, built-in connections with congressional committees or key members of Congress, some with similar ties to outside pressure groups.

Reprinted from *U.S. News & World Report* (April 24, 1972), pp. 72-74. Copyright 1972 U.S. News & World Report, Inc.

The President found that some segments of the bureaucracy were unresponsive to presidential directives, slow moving, or unreliable. He decided to get around all this by building his own system of control, command, and policy making at the White House level.

The Nixon moves to centralize policy planning and decision making have led to complaints that Cabinet officers are being bypassed and the authority of some federal agencies is being usurped.

To such complaints, an Administration official makes this reply:

The White House is dealing with 60 or more old-line departments with agencies. Each one is its own advocate. Not one of them can turn out an objective program. Each one is thinking in terms of its own existence. The White House, we have found, is the only place where policy can be made objectively.

NEW PATTERN

One example of the control technique on which Mr. Nixon now relies is seen in the enlargement and enhanced importance of the machinery of the National Security Council, core of the policy-making process on both defense and diplomacy.

Under Henry A. Kissinger, Assistant to the President for National Security Affairs, manpower has tripled in three years. Mr. Kissinger's staff—officially set at 80, but nearly double that according to some reports—includes specialists drawn from nine other agencies of the Government.

Another example is the Chief Executive's creation of two new power centers in the White House—the Office of Management and Budget (OMB) and the Domestic Council.

The OMB, directed by former Secretary of Labor George P. Shultz, has a payroll of 660. It is in this office that most domestic policy evolves.

An illustration of how policy is made in the White House, as related by a well-informed source:

While the President was in China last February, Mr. Shultz began working out the Nixon stand on busing of schoolchildren to improve racial balance.

In meetings with the two Cabinet officers from whose departments busing policy might normally be expected to flow—John N. Mitchell, then Attorney General, and Elliot L. Richardson, Secretary of Health, Education and Welfare—Mr. Shultz acted as chairman. His views were dominant. He knew what the President would accept. Under his guidance, the position later enunciated by Mr. Nixon took shape.

The staff of the Domestic Council operates under the direction of John D. Ehrlichman, Assistant to the President for Domestic Affairs. The mission of this White House group of 27 specialists is to search out policy ideas and then work with OMB and traditional agencies to whip them into shape.

The Council's work cuts across every Government department and agency. To keep it rolling, Mr. Ehrlichman has a deputy and four senior aides, all with staffs of their own.

NIXON'S OWN STAFF

In a time of White House expansion, one area has been subjected to a cut. That is the President's immediate staff, which now has 510 full-time employes—a 6 per cent decrease from the 540 employed last August, when Mr. Nixon ordered a 5.5 per cent reduction in employment throughout the executive branch.

The chief of staff is H. R. Haldeman, Assistant to the President, whose duties include budgeting Mr. Nixon's time and channeling the flood of presidential paper work. Mr. Haldeman has a personal staff of six—plus dozens of people he can call upon as needed.

So complex has the White House operation become that Mr. Haldeman recently approved a directory—with circulation limited to the executive offices—designed to make it easier to find out who is doing what.

A sample listing shows Peter M. Flanigan, an Assistant to the President, as working on such matters as aerospace, defense-industry unemployment, business problems, civil aeronautics, communications, energy resources, the proposed Federal Financing Bank and the Federal Maritime Commission. He is also working on ideas for a volunteer Army. Mr. Flanigan has a staff of 12.

There are 153 White House officials who rate assistants or secretaries—and a special telephone code service. The code tells them when the President or one of his key aides is calling, and that only the official who is being called should pick up the phone.

Besides people carried on the White House payroll, a number of workers from other agencies are assigned more or less temporarily to executive offices. This is not a new practice. Other Presidents have done the same thing. Explaining why it is difficult to get an accurate count, an official remarked:

> People come and go. The National Security Council, for instance, pulls out aides from other agencies for six months or more, and nobody knows much about it except Henry Kissinger. The only thing I know for sure is that the whole White House staff has increased.

AREAS OF INCREASE

Among offices in which personnel increases are evident:

- Herbert G. Klein, Director of Communications for the Executive Branch, has a staff of 17. Mr. Klein's operation is something new in Government.
- Ronald L. Ziegler, Press Secretary to the President, has a deputy, four assistants, and a battery of secretaries. The press-office staff has nearly tripled since the Johnson Administration.
- Clark MacGregor, Counsel to the President for Congressional Relations, has a staff of 20, about one-third more than the number engaged in legislative liaison work under LBJ.

- Raymond K. Price, Jr., Special Assistant to the President, directs a team of five speech writers and three other aides—two more than previously.
- Charles W. Colson, Special Counsel to the President, deals with religious groups, veterans' organizations, the aging, trade associations and unionized Government workers. He has a staff of six. In the Johnson Administration, these duties were divided among a number of aides as additional duty.

PROLIFERATION OF AGENCIES

A major factor in expansion of the White House sphere is the array of task forces, councils, commissions, committees and such groups set up by Mr. Nixon. The President has created 39 organizations by executive order and 21 by directives to Cabinet officers and other officials. An additional 64 organizations have come into being through legislation. Of all these 124 organizations created during the Nixon Administration, 99 still exist.

The White House itself—which once contained virtually all the executive aides—is now the center of a whole complex of buildings housing offices under presidential control. . . .

Most impressive of the White House adjuncts is what is now called the Old Executive Office Building. This six-story structure once was headquarters for the State, War and Navy Departments. It has been used as presidential office space for many years. Among its new features is a dining room for high officials. It also has a large cafeteria. Mr. Nixon has a "hideaway" office in the building.

Across Pennsylvania Avenue, on Seventeenth Street, is the New Executive Office Building, finished during the Johnson Administration. It has 10 floors, almost entirely occupied by groups or individuals who serve the President.

Adjacent to Lafayette Park, across from the White House, are a number of restored "row houses"—almost all of which have important historical background. Five of these buildings have been assigned to groups created during the Nixon Administration. Two others are used by the State Department in conjunction with Blair House, the President's guest house for visiting dignitaries.

In the White House itself, the staff dining room has been expanded into two rooms—one for top-echelon officials, the other for those a notch lower.

Besides the White House garage, which has 51,336 square feet of space, there are more than 700 reserved parking spaces for staff officials.

CHANGING FUNCTIONS

One explanation of why the White House work force has mushroomed during the Nixon Presidency was given by a man who has served in several Administrations:

> In Eisenhower's day, a smaller staff was adequate because most of the policy input came from the Cabinet, rather than from the White House.

When an idea was developed in the White House, it was passed along to a Cabinet officer. He would work it up with his own team.

Today, when an idea develops, a White House team is appointed. These people do touch base with Cabinet officers or agency heads, but there are no formal Cabinet policy papers, as such.

Instead, policy papers—which incorporate Cabinet views—are written at the White House, with various options set forth. Senior staff members such as George Shultz and John Ehrlichman can reject proposals which they feel the President would disapprove.

As final policy is being evolved, there may be more input from senior White House officials, but seldom from the Cabinet. Finally, the policy making boils down to the President and his speech writers, headed by Ray Price. After maybe eight or nine drafts, a presidential message emerges.

Often, Cabinet members are not told about major policy decisions until just before public announcement is made.

POWER AND PEOPLE

A top-level official emphasized that, as individuals, some Cabinet members in the Nixon Administration exert strong influence over policy even though the President does not look upon the Cabinet itself as a policy-making body.

In comment on the dominant role of the White House staff, a presidential adviser said that it is part of the job of men close to the Chief Executive to know exactly what he wants, so that in meetings with Cabinet officers they can authoritatively accept or reject proposals.

Each of the 14 White House officials in the top bracket—such as Mr. Shultz, Mr. Kissinger, Mr. Ehrlichman and Mr. Haldeman—receives a salary of $42,500 a year. Down the line, White House pay is in accord with civil-service standards.

From staff members come these points of view on expansion of the Nixon White House:

A key official—

The pot has boiled over. There are problems everywhere and people want them solved. Look at all the attention the President must give, for instance, to social problems, minority groups, the environment. He has found that he must have a large staff.

Another top aide—

Everybody wants to do business at the top these days. The President receives more than a million letters a year. He has to have a lot of people to cope with that sort of thing.

And a Nixon insider sounds a note heard frequently—

Every President wants his own men—this President especially. Distrustful of bureaucracy, Mr. Nixon has built a kind of defense against it—and in doing so, he has built his own bureaucracy.

ABOUT THE AUTHOR

Nelson W. Polsby is Professor of Political Science at the University of California, Berkeley, and Managing Editor of *The American Political Science Review*. He was born in Norwich, Connecticut, in 1934 and received his B.A. degree from The Johns Hopkins University and his M.A. and Ph.D. from Yale. His earlier books include *Presidential Elections* (with Aaron Wildavsky), *Congress and the Presidency,* and *Congressional Behavior* (Random House, 1971).

MONTGOMERY COLLEGE LIBRARIES JK 511.P671973b
The modern Pr

0 0000 00015452 6

JK511 .P671973B

MODERN PRESIDENCY